Welcome

At *Cooking Light*, healthy eating means balance: Instead of banishing foods we love, we enjoy them in moderation. And when we go for what we crave, we want real cheese. Juicy meat. A decent slathering of mayo. Intense chocolate. Creamy, thick shakes. Buttery cookies. We want food that satisfies, not pale substitutes.

For the people who love food like we do, we present *Cooking Light Crave!* It's full of pizzas, burgers, and sandwiches—**craveworthy, handheld foods that give us comfort.** Snacks, sides, and desserts (can't ignore a sweet tooth!) round out the book. If you like to experiment in the kitchen, you'll find recipes to inspire such play, including pizza sauces, sandwich spreads, burger toppings, and dessert sauces.

All the recipes have been perfected in our Test Kitchen to make sure they hit all the right notes: **crispy pizza crusts, juicy burgers, oozy cheeses, irresistible fries, and desserts that make you want to sing a sweet aria.** Our staff's registered dietitians have made sure every recipe meets the same nutrition guidelines we use in *Cooking Light* magazine.

Bottom line: The next time a craving strikes, give in—with *Cooking Light Crave!*

The *Cooking Light* Editors

Contents

Welcome..3

Pizzas... 6

make your own pizza dough 66

resting dough 68

secret to a perfectly crispy crust 69

7 good crusts...70

8 good cheeses 71

5 good pizza sauces 72

200-calorie pizza slices 74

Burgers 76

secrets to a tasty, juicy, healthy burger 132

8 good breads..134

6 good cheeses 135

6 good burger toppings 136

100-calorie burger combos....................138

4

Sandwiches..........................140

6 good breads..................................220

7 good cheeses 221

5 good condiments...........................222

build a healthy sandwich.................224

Snacks & Sides......................226

Sweets...................................264

5 great dessert sauces 322

low-caloric fro-yo toppings 325

Nutritional Analysis 326

Metric Equivalents 327

Index...328

PIZZAS

STRETCH, SAUCE, TOP, SLICE.

(fold and eat, or fork and knife...
we won't judge.)

This meat-lover's pizza is equally pleasing as a family dinner or for a casual party. For the best flavor, shred and grate the cheeses yourself.

Beef and Bacon Pizza

Hands-on time: 20 min.   Total time: 45 min.

1   pound refrigerated fresh pizza dough
Cooking spray
½   pound ground sirloin
1¼   cups sliced onion
3   garlic cloves, minced
1   teaspoon chopped fresh rosemary
½   teaspoon freshly ground black pepper

1   tablespoon yellow cornmeal
½   cup marinara sauce
1   cup (4 ounces) part-skim mozzarella cheese, shredded and divided
½   cup (2 ounces) grated fresh Parmesan cheese
4   center-cut bacon slices, cooked and crumbled

1. Place dough in a bowl coated with cooking spray. Let stand, covered, 30 minutes or until dough comes to room temperature.

2. Preheat oven to 450°.

3. Cook beef in a large nonstick skillet over medium-high heat until browned; stir to crumble. Drain. Add onion to pan; sauté 6 minutes or until tender and beginning to brown. Add garlic; sauté 1 minute. Add beef, rosemary, and pepper to onion mixture.

4. Sprinkle cornmeal on a large baking sheet. Roll dough into a 12-inch circle; place on prepared baking sheet. Spread sauce over dough, leaving a ½-inch border. Sprinkle with ½ cup mozzarella cheese. Spread beef mixture over cheese. Top with remaining mozzarella and Parmesan cheeses. Sprinkle with bacon.

5. Bake at 450° for 15 minutes or until crust is golden. Cut pizza into 8 wedges. Serves 8 (serving size: 1 wedge)

CALORIES 268; FAT 7.2g (sat 3.1g, mono 2.3g, poly 0.6g); PROTEIN 17.5g; CARB 34.7g; FIBER 4.5g; CHOL 30mg; IRON 1.2mg; SODIUM 498mg; CALC 150mg

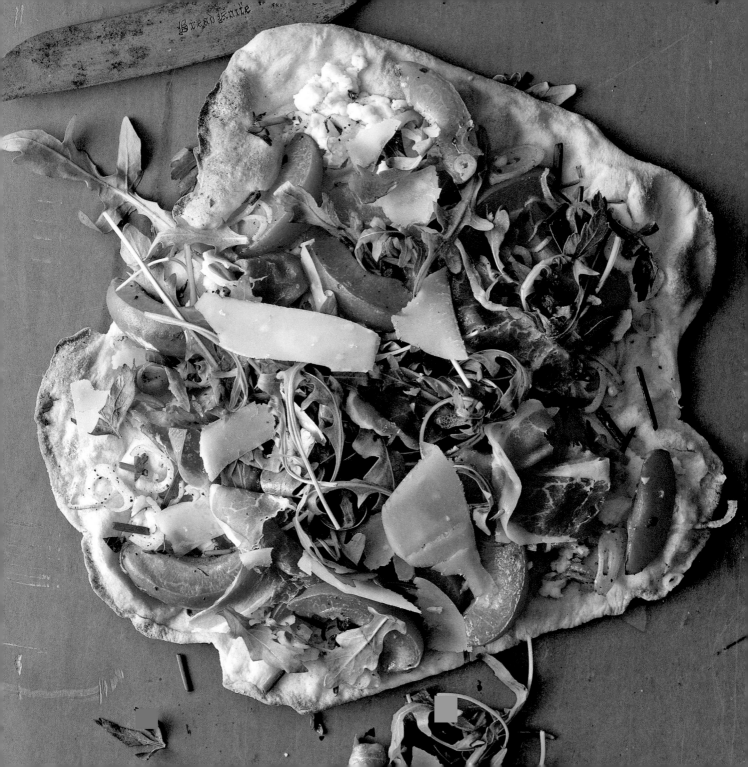

Apricot and Prosciutto Thin-Crust Pizza

Hands-on time: 31 min.   Total time: 26 hr. 1 min.

½ cup warm water (100° to 110°)
½ teaspoon dry yeast
8½ teaspoons olive oil, divided
½ teaspoon kosher salt, divided
6 ounces bread flour (about 1¼ cups)
Cooking spray
2 tablespoons yellow cornmeal
1 teaspoon chopped fresh thyme
¼ teaspoon freshly ground black pepper
3 apricots, each pitted and cut into 8 wedges

2 shallots, peeled and thinly sliced
¾ cup (3 ounces) crumbled goat cheese
1½ tablespoons finely chopped fresh flat-leaf parsley
1 tablespoon minced fresh chives
1 cup arugula
1 ounce thinly sliced prosciutto
¼ cup (1 ounce) shaved fresh Parmigiano-Reggiano cheese

1. Combine ½ cup warm water and yeast in the bowl of a stand mixer with dough hook attached; let stand 5 minutes or until bubbly. Add 4 teaspoons oil and ¼ teaspoon salt to yeast mixture. Weigh or lightly spoon flour into dry measuring cups; level with a knife. Sprinkle flour over yeast mixture; mix 2 minutes or until a soft dough forms. Place dough in a large bowl coated with cooking spray; cover surface of dough with plastic wrap lightly coated with cooking spray. Refrigerate 24 hours.

2. Remove dough from refrigerator. Let stand, covered, 1 hour or until dough comes to room temperature. Punch dough down. Sprinkle cornmeal on a lightly floured baking sheet without raised edges. Roll dough into a thin 12-inch circle on prepared baking sheet. Crimp edges to form a ½-inch border. Pierce dough several times with a fork. Cover dough loosely with plastic wrap.

3. Position oven rack in lowest setting. Place a pizza stone or heavy baking sheet on rack. Preheat oven to 550° (keep pizza stone or baking sheet in oven as it preheats). Preheat pizza stone or baking sheet 30 minutes before baking dough.

4. Combine 1 tablespoon oil, thyme, pepper, apricots, shallots, and ¼ teaspoon salt; toss gently. Remove plastic wrap from dough; slide dough onto preheated pizza stone or heavy baking sheet, using a spatula as a guide. Bake at 550° for 4 minutes. Top dough with goat cheese and apricot mixture. Bake an additional 5 minutes or until crust is golden. Cut pizza into 10 wedges; sprinkle with parsley and chives. Toss arugula with 1½ teaspoons oil; arrange arugula over apricot mixture. Top with prosciutto and Parmigiano-Reggiano cheese. Serves 5 (serving size: 2 wedges)

CALORIES 307; FAT 14.3g (sat 4.8g, mono 6.9g, poly 1.2g); PROTEIN 12.1g; CARB 32.7g; FIBER 2g; CHOL 17mg; IRON 2.9mg; SODIUM 459mg; CALC 120mg

With artichokes, arugula, pesto, prosciutto, and Parmesan, this pizza has intense, addictive flavor. Splurge and try it with homemade pesto.

Artichoke and Arugula Pizza with Prosciutto

Hands-on time: 13 min. Total time: 24 min.

Cooking spray
1 tablespoon yellow cornmeal
1 (13.8-ounce) can refrigerated pizza crust dough
2 tablespoons commercial pesto
½ cup (2 ounces) shredded part-skim mozzarella cheese

1 (9-ounce) package frozen artichoke hearts, thawed and drained
1 ounce thinly sliced prosciutto
2 tablespoons shredded Parmesan cheese
1½ cups arugula
1½ tablespoons fresh lemon juice

1. Position oven rack in lowest setting. Preheat oven to 500°.

2. Coat a baking sheet with cooking spray; sprinkle with cornmeal. Unroll dough onto prepared baking sheet, and pat into a 14 x 10–inch rectangle. Spread pesto evenly over dough, leaving a ½-inch border. Sprinkle mozzarella cheese over pesto. Place baking sheet on bottom rack in oven; bake at 500° for 5 minutes. Remove pizza from oven.

3. Coarsely chop artichokes. Arrange artichokes on pizza; top with sliced prosciutto. Sprinkle with Parmesan. Return pizza to bottom rack in oven; bake an additional 6 minutes or until crust is golden.

4. Place arugula in a bowl. Drizzle juice over arugula; toss gently. Top pizza with arugula mixture. Cut pizza into 6 (4 x 5–inch) rectangles; cut each rectangle diagonally into 2 wedges. Serves 6 (serving size: 2 wedges)

CALORIES 260; FAT 7.9g (sat 2.4g, mono 3.8g, poly 0.4g); PROTEIN 11.3g; CARB 37.5g; FIBER 3.8g; CHOL 12mg; IRON 2mg; SODIUM 762mg; CALC 131mg

The refrigerated French bread dough used as the crust is quick, but it's also delicate. To work with it, find the seam in the dough and carefully unroll.

Bacon, Onion, and Mushroom Pizza

Hands-on time: 23 min.   Total time: 38 min.

- 1 tablespoon olive oil, divided
- 2 cups vertically sliced onion (about 2 small)
- 1 (8-ounce) package presliced cremini mushrooms
- 2 teaspoons yellow cornmeal
- 1 (11-ounce) can refrigerated French bread dough

- ¾ cup (3 ounces) shredded white cheddar cheese
- 6 bacon slices, cooked and coarsely crumbled
- ¼ cup finely chopped fresh flat-leaf parsley

1. Position oven rack in lowest setting. Preheat oven to 425°.

2. Heat a large nonstick skillet over medium heat. Add 2 teaspoons oil to pan; swirl to coat. Add onion; cook, stirring frequently, 6 minutes or until tender and lightly browned. Place onion in a bowl. Add 1 teaspoon oil to pan; add mushrooms. Cook, stirring often, 6 minutes or until liquid almost evaporates. Add mushrooms to onion mixture; toss well.

3. Sprinkle cornmeal on a large baking sheet. Gently unroll dough onto a lightly floured surface. Roll dough into an 8 x 12–inch rectangle; transfer to prepared pan. Spread onion mixture over prepared dough to within ¼ inch of edge. Sprinkle onion mixture with cheese and bacon. Place pan on bottom rack in oven. Bake at 425° for 15 minutes or until crust is golden. Sprinkle with parsley. Cut pizza into 6 pieces. Serves 6 (serving size: 1 piece)

CALORIES 244; FAT 9.7g (sat 3.9g, mono 3.4g, poly 0.7g); PROTEIN 11.1g; CARB 30.8g; FIBER 1.7g; CHOL 20mg; IRON 2mg; SODIUM 488mg; CALC 120mg

Bacon, Tomato, and Arugula Pizza

Hands-on time: 29 min.   Total time: 1 hr. 47 min.

4 applewood-smoked bacon slices
2 cups grape tomatoes, halved lengthwise
½ teaspoon crushed red pepper
1 tablespoon yellow cornmeal
Whole-Wheat Pizza Dough (page 67)
½ cup lower-sodium marinara sauce
¾ cup (3 ounces) shredded part-skim
  mozzarella cheese
1 cup arugula
1 teaspoon extra-virgin olive oil
½ teaspoon white wine vinegar

1. Position oven rack in lowest setting. Preheat oven to 450°.

2. Cook bacon in a large nonstick skillet over medium heat until crisp. Remove bacon from pan, reserving 2 teaspoons drippings; crumble bacon and set aside. Add tomatoes and red pepper to drippings in pan; cook 2 minutes, stirring occasionally.

3. Sprinkle a large baking sheet with cornmeal; roll dough into a 12-inch circle on prepared baking sheet. Spread sauce over dough; top with tomato mixture. Sprinkle bacon and cheese over tomato mixture.

4. Bake at 450° on bottom rack in oven 17 minutes or until crust is golden. Combine arugula, oil, and vinegar; top pizza with arugula mixture. Cut pizza into 6 wedges. Serves 6 (serving size: 1 wedge)

CALORIES 357; FAT 10.9g (sat 3.4g, mono 5.2g, poly 1.2g); PROTEIN 13.3g; CARB 56.7g; FIBER 4.2g; CHOL 16mg; IRON 2.6mg; SODIUM 542mg; CALC 137mg

Use the convenience of a store-bought prebaked crust to make this pizza a quick weeknight meal with Spanish flavor.

Manchego and Chorizo Pizza

Hands-on time: 8 min.   Total time: 24 min.

½ pound broccoli rabe (rapini), trimmed
⅛ teaspoon salt
1 (12-ounce) prebaked pizza crust
½ cup (2 ounces) shredded Manchego cheese

⅔ cup chopped plum tomato
¼ cup vertically sliced red onion
1 link Spanish chorizo sausage (about
   2 ounces), thinly sliced

1. Preheat oven to 450°.

2. Cook broccoli rabe in boiling water 4 minutes or until tender. Drain and rinse with cold water. Drain; squeeze excess moisture from broccoli rabe, and pat dry with paper towels. Coarsely chop, and sprinkle with salt.

3. Place pizza crust on a baking sheet. Sprinkle evenly with Manchego cheese. Top with broccoli rabe, plum tomato, red onion, and chorizo. Bake at 450° for 12 minutes or until crust is golden. Cut pizza into 8 wedges. Serves 4 (serving size: 2 wedges)

CALORIES 382; FAT 15.4g (sat 4.7g, mono 3.7g, poly 5.6g); PROTEIN 15.1g; CARB 46.1g; FIBER 5.1g; CHOL 23mg; IRON 3.6mg; SODIUM 624mg; CALC 175mg

Pit peppery arugula against a base of creamy, sweet caramelized onions. Also appearing: prudent amounts of salty prosciutto, cheese, and walnuts.

Pear and Prosciutto Pizza

Hands-on time: 26 min.   Total time: 38 min.

2 teaspoons olive oil
2 cups vertically sliced sweet onion
1 (12-ounce) prebaked pizza crust
½ cup (2 ounces) shredded provolone cheese
1 medium pear, thinly sliced

2 ounces prosciutto, cut into thin strips
Dash of freshly ground black pepper
2 tablespoons chopped walnuts, toasted
1½ cups arugula
1 teaspoon sherry vinegar

1. Preheat oven to 450°.

2. Heat oil in a large nonstick skillet over medium-high heat. Add onion to pan; cover and cook 3 minutes. Uncover and cook 10 minutes or until golden brown, stirring frequently.

3. Place pizza crust on a baking sheet. Top evenly with onion mixture; sprinkle with cheese. Top evenly with pear and prosciutto. Sprinkle with pepper. Bake at 450° for 12 minutes or until cheese melts. Sprinkle with nuts. Place arugula in a medium bowl. Drizzle vinegar over greens; toss gently to coat. Top pizza evenly with arugula mixture. Cut pizza into 8 wedges. Serves 4 (serving size: 2 wedges)

CALORIES 446; FAT 18.8g (sat 4.9g, mono 5.1g, poly 7.3g); PROTEIN 16.6g; CARB 55.5g; FIBER 3.8g; CHOL 17mg; IRON 3.6mg; SODIUM 664mg; CALC 221mg

A bready crust, plenty of cheese, and America's favorite pizza topping: This pie satisfies several cravings at once.

Pepperoni Deep-Dish Pizza

Hands-on time: 21 min.   Total time: 26 hr. 11 min.

 1 cup warm water (100° to 110°), divided
12 ounces bread flour (about 2 ½ cups)
 1 package dry yeast (about 2 ¼ teaspoons)
 4 teaspoons olive oil
 ¼ teaspoon kosher salt
Cooking spray

 1 cup (4 ounces) shredded part-skim mozzarella cheese, divided
1½ cups Basic Pizza Sauce (page 73)
1½ ounces pepperoni slices
 2 tablespoons grated Parmigiano-Reggiano cheese

1. Pour ¾ cup warm water in the bowl of a stand mixer with dough hook attached. Weigh or lightly spoon flour into dry measuring cups; level with a knife. Add flour to ¾ cup warm water; mix until combined. Cover and let stand 20 minutes. Combine ¼ cup warm water and yeast in a small bowl; let stand 5 minutes or until bubbly. Add yeast mixture, oil, and salt to flour mixture; mix 5 minutes or until a soft dough forms. Place dough in a large bowl coated with cooking spray; cover surface of dough with plastic wrap lightly coated with cooking spray. Refrigerate 24 hours.

2. Remove dough from refrigerator. Let stand, covered, 1 hour or until dough comes to room temperature. Punch dough down. Roll dough into a 14 x 11–inch rectangle on a lightly floured surface. Press dough into bottom and partially up sides of a 13 x 9–inch metal baking pan coated with cooking spray. Cover dough loosely with plastic wrap.

3. Position oven rack in lowest setting; place a baking sheet on the rack. Preheat oven to 450° (keep baking sheet in oven as it preheats).

4. Remove plastic wrap from dough. Arrange ½ cup mozzarella evenly over dough; top with Basic Pizza Sauce, pepperoni, Parmigiano-Reggiano, and ½ cup mozzarella. Place pan on baking sheet in oven; bake at 450° for 25 minutes or until crust is golden. Cut pizza into 6 rectangles. Serves 6 (serving size: 1 rectangle)

CALORIES 381; FAT 14.7g (sat 4.5g, mono 6.8g, poly 1.5g); PROTEIN 15.4g; CARB 46.6g; FIBER 2.6g; CHOL 19mg; IRON 3.7mg; SODIUM 519mg; CALC 209mg

Jazz up a classic pizza by adding olives and thinly sliced sweet onion to the pepperoni. Try this combo on the Whole-Wheat Pizza Dough (page 67) for an earthy switch.

Pepperoni, Onion, and Olive Pizza

Hands-on time: 7 min.   Total time: 54 min.

1 pound refrigerated fresh pizza dough
Cooking spray
1 tablespoon yellow cornmeal
½ cup lower-sodium marinara sauce
½ cup thinly sliced sweet onion

1 ounce pepperoni slices (about 18 slices)
10 pitted niçoise olives, halved lengthwise
¾ cup (3 ounces) preshredded reduced-fat 4-cheese Italian-blend cheese

1. Position oven rack in lowest setting. Preheat oven to 450°.

2. Place dough in a bowl coated with cooking spray; let stand, covered, 30 minutes or until dough comes to room temperature.

3. Sprinkle a baking sheet with cornmeal; roll dough into a 12-inch circle on prepared baking sheet. Spread sauce evenly over dough, leaving a ½-inch border. Top with onion, pepperoni, and olives; sprinkle with cheese. Bake at 450° on bottom rack in oven 17 minutes or until crust is golden. Cut pizza into 6 wedges. Serves 6 (serving size: 1 wedge)

CALORIES 281; FAT 6.7g (sat 2.4g, mono 2.6g, poly 0.7g); PROTEIN 12.1g; CARB 44.2g; FIBER 5.8g; CHOL 13mg; IRON 1.3mg; SODIUM 584mg; CALC 109mg

Prosciutto Pizza with Tangy White Sauce

Hands-on time: 38 min.   Total time: 27 hr. 1 min.

2/3 cup warm water (100° to 110°)
1 teaspoon dry yeast
6.75 ounces bread flour (about 1½ cups)
4½ teaspoons olive oil, divided
½ teaspoon kosher salt
Cooking spray
1 tablespoon yellow cornmeal
¾ cup 2% reduced-fat milk
2 teaspoons Dijon mustard

½ teaspoon freshly ground black pepper
1 large egg yolk
1½ tablespoons butter
1½ teaspoons minced fresh garlic
2 teaspoons all-purpose flour
¾ cup (3 ounces) shredded Gruyère cheese
2 ounces thinly sliced prosciutto, torn
1 tablespoon chopped fresh chives

1. Combine ⅔ cup warm water and yeast in the bowl of a stand mixer with dough hook attached, and let stand 5 minutes or until bubbles form. Weigh or lightly spoon 6.75 ounces (about 1½ cups) flour into dry measuring cups; level with a knife. Sprinkle flour over yeast mixture. Add 1 tablespoon olive oil and salt. Mix at low speed 2 minutes or until dough forms a ball. Increase speed to medium, and mix 8 minutes or until smooth and elastic. Place dough in a medium bowl coated with cooking spray, turning to coat top. Cover and let rise in a warm place (85°), free from drafts, 1 hour or until doubled in size. Punch dough down.

2. Cover surface of dough with plastic wrap lightly coated with cooking spray. Refrigerate 24 hours. Remove dough from refrigerator. Let stand, covered, 1 hour or until dough comes to room temperature. Punch dough down. Sprinkle cornmeal on a lightly floured baking sheet without raised edges. Roll dough into an 11 x 16–inch rectangle on prepared baking sheet. Brush dough evenly with 1½ teaspoons olive oil. Cover dough loosely with plastic wrap.

3. Place a pizza stone or heavy baking sheet in oven. Preheat oven to 500° (keep pizza stone or baking sheet in oven as it preheats). Preheat pizza stone or baking sheet 30 minutes before baking pizza.

4. Combine milk and next 3 ingredients in a medium bowl, stirring with a whisk. Melt butter in a medium saucepan over low heat. Add garlic; cook 3 minutes or just until butter and garlic begin to brown, stirring frequently. Add 2 teaspoons all-purpose flour to pan; cook 30 seconds, stirring constantly with a whisk. Stir in milk mixture; bring to a boil. Cook 1 minute or until thick, stirring constantly. Remove plastic wrap from dough. Spread sauce over dough; sprinkle evenly with cheese. Slide pizza onto preheated pizza stone or heavy baking sheet, using a spatula as a guide. Bake at 500° for 18 minutes or until crust is golden. Arrange prosciutto on pizza; sprinkle with chives. Cut pizza into 12 pieces. Serves 6 (serving size: 2 pieces)

CALORIES 289; FAT 13.9g (sat 6.1g, mono 6g, poly 1.3g); PROTEIN 12.8g; CARB 28g; FIBER 1g; CHOL 68mg; IRON 1.9mg; SODIUM 536mg; CALC 191mg

For a kid-friendly pie, substitute fresh mozzarella for the blue cheese, and choose a sweeter barbecue sauce over a bold and spicy sauce.

BBQ Chicken and Blue Cheese Pizza

Hands-on time: 10 min.   Total time: 20 min.

1   (8-ounce) prebaked thin pizza crust
⅓   cup barbecue sauce
1½ cups shredded skinless, boneless rotisserie
    chicken breast

½   cup vertically sliced red onion
½   cup coarsely chopped yellow bell pepper
½   cup (2 ounces) crumbled blue cheese
2   plum tomatoes, thinly sliced (about ¼ pound)

1. Preheat oven to 500°.

2. Place pizza crust on a baking sheet. Spread sauce over crust, leaving a ½-inch border. Top with chicken and remaining ingredients. Bake at 500° for 10 minutes or until cheese melts and crust is crisp. Cut pizza into 12 pieces. Serves 6 (serving size: 2 pieces)

CALORIES 252; FAT 8.5g (sat 3.1g, mono 2.2g, poly 2.7g); PROTEIN 16.7g; CARB 27.4g; FIBER 1.8g; CHOL 38mg; IRON 1.6mg; SODIUM 494mg; CALC 92mg

Chicago Deep-Dish Pizza

Hands-on time: 45 min.   Total time: 1 hr. 42 min.

2 teaspoons sugar
1 package dry yeast (about 2¼ teaspoons)
1 cup warm water (100° to 110°)
4 teaspoons extra-virgin olive oil, divided
12.38 ounces all-purpose flour (about 2¾ cups), divided
¼ cup yellow cornmeal
½ teaspoon salt
Cooking spray
1½ cups (6 ounces) shredded part-skim mozzarella cheese, divided

2 precooked mild Italian chicken sausages (about 6 ounces), casings removed, chopped
1 (28-ounce) can whole tomatoes, drained
1½ teaspoons chopped fresh oregano
1½ teaspoons chopped fresh basil
2 cups thinly sliced mushrooms (about 6 ounces)
¾ cup chopped green bell pepper
¾ cup chopped red bell pepper

1. Dissolve sugar and yeast in 1 cup warm water in a large bowl; let stand 5 minutes. Stir in 1 tablespoon olive oil. Weigh or lightly spoon flour into dry measuring cups; level with a knife. Combine 11.25 ounces (about 2½ cups) flour, cornmeal, and salt in a bowl. Stir flour mixture into yeast mixture until dough forms a ball. Turn dough out onto a lightly floured surface. Knead until smooth and elastic (about 5 minutes); add enough of remaining flour, 1 tablespoon at a time, to prevent dough from sticking to hands (dough will feel sticky).

2. Place dough in a large bowl coated with cooking spray, turning to coat top. Cover and let rise in a warm place (85°), free from drafts, 45 minutes or until doubled in size. Punch dough down; cover and let rest 5 minutes. Roll dough into a 15 x 11–inch rectangle on a lightly floured surface. Place dough in a 13 x 9–inch glass or ceramic baking dish coated with cooking spray; press dough up sides of dish. Sprinkle 1 cup cheese evenly over dough. Arrange chopped sausage evenly over cheese.

3. Preheat oven to 400°.

4. Chop tomatoes; place in a sieve. Stir in oregano and basil; drain tomato mixture 10 minutes.

5. Heat 1 teaspoon olive oil in a large nonstick skillet over medium heat. Add mushrooms; cook 5 minutes, stirring occasionally. Stir in bell peppers; cook 8 minutes or until tender, stirring occasionally. Arrange vegetables over sausage; spoon tomato mixture evenly over vegetables and sausage. Sprinkle evenly with ½ cup cheese. Bake at 400° for 25 minutes or until crust is golden and cheese bubbles. Cool 5 minutes. Cut pizza into 8 rectangles. Serves 8 (serving size: 1 rectangle)

CALORIES 321; FAT 8.3g (sat 3.1g, mono 4g, poly 0.7g); PROTEIN 15.7g; CARB 44.9g; FIBER 3g; CHOL 30mg; IRON 3.1mg; SODIUM 543mg; CALC 188mg

Béchamel is often used in lasagna or as the base for a mac-and-cheese sauce. Here, it's flavored with garlic and cheese, and replaces tomato sauce to make a delicious pizza.

Chicken and Herb White Pizza

Hands-on time: 20 min. Total time: 52 min.

1 pound refrigerated fresh pizza dough
Cooking spray
1 tablespoon butter
2 garlic cloves, minced
2 tablespoons all-purpose flour
½ teaspoon freshly ground black pepper
¾ cup 2% reduced-fat milk
½ cup (2 ounces) grated fresh pecorino Romano cheese

1 tablespoon yellow cornmeal
1½ cups shredded boneless, skinless roasted chicken breast
¼ cup diced red onion
1 tablespoon chopped fresh oregano
1 tablespoon chopped fresh chives
1 tablespoon chopped fresh parsley

1. Position oven rack in lowest setting. Preheat oven to 450°.

2. Place dough in a bowl coated with cooking spray; let dough stand, covered, 30 minutes or until dough comes to room temperature.

3. Melt butter in a medium saucepan over medium heat. Add garlic; cook 30 seconds, stirring constantly. Add flour and pepper; cook 1 minute, stirring constantly with a whisk. Gradually add milk, stirring constantly with a whisk. Cook 3 minutes or until thick and bubbly, stirring constantly with a whisk. Remove from heat; add cheese, stirring until cheese melts.

4. Sprinkle a baking sheet with cornmeal; roll dough into a 12-inch circle on prepared baking sheet. Spread white sauce over dough, leaving a ½-inch border. Top with chicken and onion. Bake at 450° on bottom rack in oven 17 minutes or until crust is golden. Sprinkle with herbs. Cut pizza into 6 wedges. Serves 6 (serving size: 1 wedge)

CALORIES 328; FAT 7.3g (sat 3.3g, mono 2.4g, poly 0.8g); PROTEIN 20.6g; CARB 41.1g; FIBER 5.7g; CHOL 44mg; IRON 1.6mg; SODIUM 502mg; CALC 115mg

Add quick-cooking chicken cutlets and refrigerated pizza dough to a mix of fresh vegetables for a light and lovely superfast meal.

Cobb Salad Pizza

Hands-on time: 26 min. Total time: 26 min.

1 (11-ounce) can refrigerated thin-crust pizza dough
Cooking spray
3 tablespoons crumbled blue cheese, divided
4 teaspoons extra-virgin olive oil, divided
1 tablespoon white wine vinegar
½ teaspoon Dijon mustard
¼ teaspoon black pepper, divided

2 applewood-smoked bacon slices
8 ounces skinless, boneless chicken breast cutlets
½ cup quartered cherry tomatoes
2 tablespoons chopped red onion
2 cups lightly packed mixed baby greens
½ cup diced peeled avocado

1. Preheat oven to 425°.

2. Unroll dough on a baking sheet coated with cooking spray; pat dough into a 14 x 12–inch rectangle. Lightly coat dough with cooking spray. Bake at 425° for 8 minutes or until golden. Remove from oven; sprinkle evenly with 1½ tablespoons cheese. Set aside.

3. Combine 1 tablespoon oil, vinegar, mustard, and ⅛ teaspoon pepper in a large bowl; stir with a whisk.

4. Cook bacon in a large nonstick skillet over medium heat until crisp. Remove bacon from pan; crumble bacon into oil mixture. Wipe pan clean with paper towels. Heat 1 teaspoon oil in pan over medium-high heat. Sprinkle chicken with ⅛ teaspoon pepper. Add chicken to pan; cook 4 minutes on each side or until done. Remove chicken from pan; chop into ½-inch pieces.

5. Add chicken, tomatoes, and onion to oil mixture; toss gently to combine. Add greens; toss gently. Top crust evenly with chicken mixture, avocado, and 1½ tablespoons cheese. Cut pizza into 8 pieces. Serves 4 (serving size: 2 pieces)

CALORIES 380; FAT 14.8g (sat 3.8g, mono 7.9g, poly 1.8g); PROTEIN 21.2g; CARB 41.7g; FIBER 3.5g; CHOL 40mg; IRON 3mg; SODIUM 789mg; CALC 45mg

Give pizza a makeover by topping with fresh peach slices and two types of cheese.
A drizzle of tangy balsamic reduction perfectly balances the sweet summer fruit.

Peach and Gorgonzola Chicken Pizza

Hands-on time: 7 min.   Total time: 23 min.

1   (10-ounce) prebaked thin pizza crust
Cooking spray
1   teaspoon extra-virgin olive oil
½   cup (2 ounces) shredded part-skim
     mozzarella cheese, divided

1   cup shredded cooked chicken breast
⅓   cup (about 1½ ounces) crumbled
     Gorgonzola cheese
1   unpeeled medium peach, thinly sliced
⅓   cup balsamic vinegar

1. Preheat oven to 400°.

2. Place pizza crust on a baking sheet coated with cooking spray. Brush oil evenly over crust. Top evenly with ¼ cup mozzarella, chicken, Gorgonzola, and peach slices. Top with ¼ cup mozzarella. Bake at 400° for 11 minutes or until crust is golden.

3. Place vinegar in a small saucepan over medium-high heat; cook until reduced to 2 tablespoons (about 5 minutes). Drizzle balsamic reduction evenly over pizza. Cut pizza into 8 wedges. Serves 4 (serving size: 2 wedges)

CALORIES 384; FAT 12.5g (sat 4.9g, mono 4.7g, poly 1.1g); PROTEIN 24.3g; CARB 42.5g; FIBER 2.1g; CHOL 46mg; IRON 2.9mg; SODIUM 643mg; CALC 264mg

Brighten a homemade version of a take-out favorite with two different colors of bell peppers. Use your own color combo, or any bell peppers you have on hand.

Pizza Supreme

Hands-on time: 21 min.   Total time: 65 min.

1   pound refrigerated fresh pizza dough
Cooking spray
2   teaspoons olive oil
1   (4-ounce) link sweet turkey Italian sausage
1   cup sliced mushrooms
1   cup thinly sliced red bell pepper

1   cup thinly sliced orange bell pepper
1   cup thinly sliced red onion
¼   teaspoon crushed red pepper
3   garlic cloves, thinly sliced
¾   cup lower-sodium marinara sauce
4   ounces fresh mozzarella cheese, thinly sliced

1. Preheat oven to 500°.

2. Place dough in a bowl coated with cooking spray; let dough stand, covered, 30 minutes or until dough comes to room temperature.

3. Roll dough into a 14-inch circle on a lightly floured surface. Place dough on a 14-inch pizza pan or baking sheet coated with cooking spray.

4. Heat oil in a large nonstick skillet over medium-high heat. Remove casing from sausage. Add sausage to pan; cook 2 minutes, stirring to crumble. Add mushrooms, bell peppers, onion, crushed red pepper, and garlic; cook 4 minutes, stirring occasionally.

5. Spread sauce over dough, leaving a 1-inch border. Arrange cheese evenly over sauce. Arrange sausage mixture evenly over cheese. Bake at 500° for 15 minutes or until crust and cheese are browned. Cut pizza into 6 wedges. Serves 6 (serving size: 1 wedge)

CALORIES 320; FAT 9.5g (sat 3.4g, mono 4g, poly 1.1g); PROTEIN 13.7g; CARB 48.7g; FIBER 6.5g; CHOL 27mg; IRON 1.4mg; SODIUM 497mg; CALC 13mg

You only need half of the Homemade Pizza Dough recipe; refrigerate or freeze the other half for another use.

Sausage Pizza

Hands-on time: 34 min.   Total time: 26 hr. 4 min.

1½ teaspoons olive oil
¼ to ½ teaspoon crushed red pepper
1 (4-ounce) link sweet turkey Italian sausage
½ cup vertically sliced fennel bulb
½ cup thinly vertically sliced red onion (about 1 small onion)
¼ teaspoon kosher salt

⅔ cup chopped seeded tomato (about 2 tomatoes)
Homemade Pizza Dough (page 66)
Cooking spray
¼ cup (1 ounce) grated fresh Parmigiano-Reggiano cheese

1. Position oven rack in lowest setting. Place a pizza stone or heavy baking sheet on bottom rack in oven. Preheat oven to 500° (keep pizza stone or baking sheet in oven as it preheats). Preheat pizza stone or heavy baking sheet 30 minutes before baking pizza.

2. Heat oil in a large nonstick skillet over medium-high heat. Add pepper to pan; cook 10 seconds. Remove casing from sausage. Add sausage, fennel, and onion to pan; sauté 4 minutes or until browned, stirring to crumble sausage. Stir in salt. Add tomato; sauté 2 minutes or until tender. Remove from heat.

3. Roll dough into a 10-inch circle on a lightly floured surface. Place dough on a 10-inch pizza pan or baking sheet coated with cooking spray.

4. Spread sausage mixture over dough, leaving a ½-inch border. Slide dough onto preheated pizza stone or heavy baking sheet, using a spatula as a guide.

5. Bake at 500° for 8 minutes or until crust is golden. Sprinkle with cheese. Cut pizza into 6 wedges. Serves 6 (serving size: 1 wedge)

CALORIES 225; FAT 5.7g (sat 1.2g, mono 2.8g, poly 1.2g); PROTEIN 9.4g; CARB 33.6g; FIBER 1.8g; CHOL 17mg; IRON 2.2mg; SODIUM 373mg; CALC 26mg

Garlicky Clam Grilled Pizza

Hands-on time: 52 min.   Total time: 25 hr. 59 min.

1 cup warm water (100° to 110°), divided
10 ounces bread flour (about 2 cups plus 2 tablespoons)
1 package dry yeast (about 2¼ teaspoons)
10 teaspoons olive oil, divided
½ teaspoon kosher salt
Cooking spray
2 tablespoons yellow cornmeal
2 tablespoons butter

⅓ cup chopped shallots
6 garlic cloves, minced
½ cup dry white wine
5 dozen small clams in shells, scrubbed
½ cup (2 ounces) grated fresh Parmigiano-Reggiano cheese
1 tablespoon finely chopped fresh flat-leaf parsley
1 tablespoon finely chopped fresh oregano

1. Pour ¾ cup warm water in the bowl of a stand mixer with dough hook attached. Weigh or lightly spoon flour into dry measuring cups and spoons; level with a knife. Add flour to ¾ cup warm water; mix until combined. Cover and let stand 20 minutes. Combine ¼ cup warm water and yeast in a small bowl; let stand 5 minutes or until bubbly. Add yeast mixture, 4 teaspoons oil, and salt to flour mixture; mix 5 minutes or until a soft dough forms. Place dough in a large bowl coated with cooking spray; cover surface of dough with plastic wrap lightly coated with cooking spray. Refrigerate 24 hours.

2. Remove dough from refrigerator. Let stand, covered, 1 hour or until dough comes to room temperature. Punch dough down. Press dough into a 12-inch circle on a lightly floured baking sheet, without raised sides, sprinkled with cornmeal. Crimp edges to form a ½-inch border. Cover dough loosely with plastic wrap.

3. Preheat grill to high heat.

4. Heat a Dutch oven over medium-high heat. Add 2 tablespoons oil to pan; swirl to coat. Add butter; swirl until butter melts. Add shallots; sauté 2 minutes. Add garlic; sauté 1 minute. Stir in wine and clams; bring to a boil. Cover and cook 8 minutes or until shells open; discard any unopened shells. Remove clams from pan using a slotted spoon. Strain cooking liquid through a fine sieve over a bowl, reserving solids. Reserve cooking liquid for another use. Remove clams from shells; discard shells. Chop clams; toss with reserved solids.

5. Remove plastic wrap from dough. Place dough, cornmeal side up, on grill rack coated with cooking spray; grill 4 minutes or until blistered. Turn dough over; grill 3 minutes. Remove from grill. Spread clam mixture evenly over top side of crust, leaving a ½-inch border; top with cheese. Return pizza to grill rack; grill 4 minutes or until thoroughly cooked. Remove from grill. Sprinkle with parsley and oregano. Cut pizza into 10 wedges. Serves 5 (serving size: 2 wedges)

CALORIES 420; FAT 11.7g (sat 5.1g, mono 5.1g, poly 1.5g); PROTEIN 26.3g; CARB 51.2g; FIBER 2g; CHOL 50mg; IRON 18.4mg; SODIUM 435mg; CALC 201mg

The crisp cracker crust of this pizza makes a pleasing contrast to the velvety-soft salmon.

Smoked Salmon Thin-Crust Pizza

Hands-on time: 11 min.   Total time: 25 hr. 25 min.

½   cup warm water (100° to 110°)
½   teaspoon dry yeast
2   tablespoons olive oil
¼   teaspoon kosher salt
6   ounces bread flour (about 1¼ cups)
Cooking spray
1   tablespoon yellow cornmeal

⅓   cup (3 ounces) ⅓-less-fat cream cheese, softened
1   tablespoon capers, drained
4   (⅛-inch-thick) slices red onion, separated into rings
3   ounces cold-smoked salmon, thinly sliced
1   tablespoon chopped fresh dill

1. Combine ½ cup warm water and yeast in the bowl of a stand mixer with dough hook attached; let stand 5 minutes or until bubbly. Add oil and salt to yeast mixture. Weigh or lightly spoon flour into dry measuring cups; level with a knife. Sprinkle flour over yeast mixture; mix 2 minutes or until a soft dough forms. Place dough in a large bowl coated with cooking spray; cover surface of dough with plastic wrap lightly coated with cooking spray. Refrigerate 24 hours.

2. Remove dough from refrigerator. Let stand, covered, 1 hour or until dough comes to room temperature. Position oven rack in lowest setting. Place a pizza stone or heavy baking sheet on rack. Preheat oven to 550° (keep pizza stone or baking sheet in oven as it preheats). Preheat pizza stone or baking sheet 30 minutes before baking dough.

3. Punch dough down. Sprinkle cornmeal on a lightly floured baking sheet without raised edges. Roll dough into a very thin 14-inch circle on prepared baking sheet. Crimp edges to form a ½-inch border. Pierce dough several times with a fork.

4. Slide dough onto preheated pizza stone or heavy baking sheet, using a spatula as a guide. Bake at 550° for 4 minutes. Remove from oven; spread cheese evenly over dough. Arrange capers and onion over cheese. Bake an additional 5 minutes or until crust is golden. Top evenly with salmon; sprinkle with dill. Cut pizza into 8 wedges. Serves 4 (serving size: 2 wedges)

CALORIES 318; FAT 13.6g (sat 4g, mono 6.8g, poly 1.5g); PROTEIN 11.7g; CARB 36.7g; FIBER 1.6g; CHOL 21mg; IRON 2.4mg; SODIUM 424mg; CALC 37mg

Cremini and portobellos are actually the same mushroom; portobellos are the mature form. Marry them with a whole-wheat crust for a pizza with earthy, nutty flavor.

Double-Mushroom Pizza

Hands-on time: 29 min. Total time: 1 hr. 43 min.

1½ teaspoons olive oil
1 (8-ounce) package presliced cremini or button mushrooms
1 (6-ounce) package presliced portobello mushrooms, coarsely chopped
¼ teaspoon freshly ground black pepper
3 garlic cloves, minced
1 tablespoon yellow cornmeal

Whole-Wheat Pizza Dough (page 67) or 1 pound refrigerated fresh whole-wheat pizza dough
1 large plum tomato, thinly sliced
1¼ cups (5 ounces) shredded part-skim mozzarella cheese
1½ teaspoons chopped fresh thyme

1. Preheat oven to 500°.

2. Heat oil in a large nonstick skillet over medium-high heat. Add mushrooms and pepper to pan; cook 8 minutes or until liquid evaporates, stirring occasionally. Stir in garlic; sauté 30 seconds. Remove from heat.

3. Sprinkle cornmeal on a large baking sheet. Roll dough into a 12-inch circle on prepared pan. Arrange tomato slices over dough, leaving a ½-inch border. Spread mushroom mixture over tomatoes; sprinkle with cheese.

4. Bake at 500° for 14 minutes or until cheese melts and begins to brown. Remove pizza from oven; sprinkle with thyme. Cut pizza into 4 wedges. Serves 4 (serving size: 1 wedge)

CALORIES 416; FAT 12.1g (sat 4.5g, mono 5.6g, poly 1.2g); PROTEIN 19.2g; CARB 59.5g; FIBER 5.2g; CHOL 23mg; IRON 3.5mg; SODIUM 519mg; CALC 312mg

Four-Cheese Pizza

Hands-on time: 18 min.   Total time: 25 hr. 53 min.

1 cup warm water (100° to 110°), divided
10 ounces bread flour (about 2 cups plus 2 tablespoons)
1 package dry yeast (about 2¼ teaspoons)
7 teaspoons olive oil, divided
½ teaspoon kosher salt
Cooking spray
1 tablespoon yellow cornmeal
2 tablespoons chopped garlic

⅓ cup (about 3 ounces) part-skim ricotta cheese
3 tablespoons (¾ ounce) crumbled Gorgonzola cheese
1 ounce taleggio cheese, thinly sliced
¼ cup (1 ounce) finely grated Parmigiano-Reggiano cheese
2 tablespoons chopped fresh chives
Freshly ground black pepper (optional)

1. Pour ¾ cup warm water in the bowl of a stand mixer with dough hook attached. Weigh or lightly spoon flour into dry measuring cups and spoons; level with a knife. Add flour to ¾ cup warm water; mix until combined. Cover and let stand 20 minutes. Combine ¼ cup warm water and yeast in a small bowl; let stand 5 minutes or until bubbly. Add yeast mixture, 4 teaspoons oil, and salt to flour mixture; mix 5 minutes or until a soft dough forms. Place dough in a large bowl coated with cooking spray; cover surface of dough with plastic wrap lightly coated with cooking spray. Refrigerate 24 hours.

2. Remove dough from refrigerator. Let stand, covered, 1 hour or until dough comes to room temperature. Punch dough down. Sprinkle cornmeal on a lightly floured baking sheet without raised edges. Press dough into a 12-inch circle on prepared pan. Crimp edges to form a ½-inch border. Cover dough loosely with plastic wrap.

3. Position oven rack in lowest setting. Place a pizza stone or heavy baking sheet on bottom rack in oven. Preheat oven to 550° (keep pizza stone or baking sheet in oven as it preheats). Preheat pizza stone or baking sheet 30 minutes before baking pizza.

4. Remove plastic wrap from dough. Combine 1 tablespoon oil and garlic; gently brush garlic mixture evenly over dough, leaving a ½-inch border. Spread ricotta evenly over dough; arrange Gorgonzola and taleggio evenly over ricotta. Top with Parmigiano-Reggiano. Slide pizza onto preheated pizza stone or heavy baking sheet, using a spatula as a guide. Bake at 550° for 10 minutes or until crust is golden. Cut pizza into 5 wedges; sprinkle with chives and pepper, if desired. Serves 5 (serving size: 1 wedge)

CALORIES 362; FAT 13.3g (sat 4.8g, mono 6.4g, poly 1.3g); PROTEIN 14.1g; CARB 45.9g; FIBER 2.2g; CHOL 20mg; IRON 0.9mg; SODIUM 396mg; CALC 159mg

If olives are a deal breaker, leave them off; the pizza is still yummy. Draining the sliced tomatoes on paper towels will keep the crust from getting soggy.

Fresh Tomato–Feta Pizza

Hands-on time: 35 min.   Total time: 55 min.

1 pound refrigerated fresh pizza dough	1 tablespoon yellow cornmeal
Cooking spray	3 ounces feta cheese
4 plum tomatoes, sliced	1/3 cup pitted kalamata olives, halved
2 1/2 tablespoons olive oil, divided	1/4 cup basil leaves
2 garlic cloves, minced	

1. Place dough in a bowl coated with cooking spray. Let dough stand, covered, 30 minutes or until dough comes to room temperature.

2. Arrange tomato slices on a jelly-roll pan lined with paper towels; top with more paper towels. Let stand 30 minutes.

3. Position oven rack in lowest setting. Place a pizza stone or heavy baking sheet on bottom rack in oven. Preheat oven to 500° (keep pizza stone or baking sheet in oven as it preheats). Preheat pizza stone or heavy baking sheet 30 minutes before baking pizza.

4. Combine tomatoes, 2 tablespoons oil, and garlic. Sprinkle cornmeal on a lightly floured baking sheet without raised edges. Roll dough into a 14-inch circle on prepared baking sheet. Pierce dough liberally with a fork. Arrange tomato mixture over dough. Crumble cheese; sprinkle over pizza. Slide pizza onto preheated pizza stone or heavy baking sheet, using a spatula as a guide. Bake at 500° for 19 minutes or until crust is golden and cheese is lightly browned. Remove from oven; top with olives and basil. Brush edges of crust with 1½ teaspoons oil. Cut pizza into 6 wedges. Serves 6 (serving size: 1 wedge)

CALORIES 314; FAT 12g (sat 3.2g, mono 7.1g, poly 1.3g); PROTEIN 9.5g; CARB 40g; FIBER 6.1g; CHOL 13mg; IRON 1.4mg; SODIUM 608mg; CALC 82mg

For an out-of-the-ordinary first course, offer guests a wedge of this veggie-topped pizza with smoky flavor from the grill, or enjoy two wedges as a main course.

Grilled Pizza with Asparagus and Caramelized Onion

Hands-on time: 38 min. Total time: 38 min.

8 ounces refrigerated fresh pizza dough
Cooking spray
1 tablespoon extra-virgin olive oil, divided
2 cups thinly vertically sliced onion
2 cups (2-inch) sliced asparagus (about ½ pound)

1 tablespoon thinly sliced ready-to-use sun-dried tomatoes
⅛ teaspoon salt
¾ cup (3 ounces) shredded fontina cheese
1½ teaspoons fresh oregano leaves
¼ teaspoon freshly ground black pepper

1. Preheat grill to medium-high heat.

2. Place dough in a bowl coated with cooking spray. Let dough stand, covered, 30 minutes or until dough comes to room temperature.

3. Heat 2 teaspoons oil in a large nonstick skillet over medium-high heat. Add onion to pan; sauté 5 minutes. Reduce heat to medium-low; cook 5 minutes or until browned. Add asparagus to pan; cook 5 minutes or until asparagus is crisp-tender. Stir in tomatoes and salt.

4. Roll dough into a 12-inch circle on a lightly floured surface; brush each side of dough with ½ teaspoon oil.

5. Place dough on grill rack; grill 1½ minutes or until crust bubbles and is well marked. Reduce grill heat to low; turn dough over. Sprinkle cheese over crust; arrange onion mixture over cheese. Cover and grill over low heat 3½ minutes or until cheese melts; remove pizza from grill. Sprinkle with oregano and black pepper. Cut pizza into 8 wedges. Serves 8 (serving size: 1 wedge)

CALORIES 152; FAT 5.8g (sat 2.3g, mono 2.2g, poly 0.9g); PROTEIN 6.3g; CARB 19.4g; FIBER 1.7g; CHOL 12mg; IRON 1.7mg; SODIUM 314mg; CALC 74mg

Summer's best produce—including plump corn, crisp bell peppers, fragrant herbs, and sweet tomatoes—comes together to make this pizza a fun way to enjoy veggies.

Local Farmers' Market Pizza

Hands-on time: 28 min.   Total time: 58 min.

1 pound refrigerated fresh pizza dough	¼ teaspoon salt
Cooking spray	¼ teaspoon black pepper
1 tablespoon extra-virgin olive oil	5 ounces thinly sliced fresh mozzarella cheese
2 cups thinly sliced onion	⅓ cup (1½ ounces) grated Parmigiano-
1 teaspoon chopped fresh thyme	Reggiano cheese
2 cups thinly sliced red bell pepper	1 cup cherry tomatoes, halved
5 garlic cloves, thinly sliced	⅓ cup basil leaves
1 cup fresh corn kernels (about 2 ears)	

1. Preheat oven to 425°. Position oven rack in next-to-lowest setting. Place a 16-inch pizza pan on the rack.

2. Place dough in a bowl coated with cooking spray. Let dough stand, covered, 30 minutes or until dough comes to room temperature.

3. Heat a large nonstick skillet over medium-high heat. Add olive oil to pan; swirl to coat. Add onion and thyme to pan; cook 3 minutes or until onion is tender, stirring occasionally. Add bell pepper and garlic to pan; cook 2 minutes, stirring occasionally. Add corn, salt, and black pepper to pan; cook 1 minute or until thoroughly heated.

4. Roll dough into a 16-inch circle on a lightly floured surface. Remove pan from oven. Coat pan with cooking spray. Place dough on pan. Arrange mozzarella slices evenly over dough. Spread corn mixture evenly over mozzarella, and top with Parmigiano-Reggiano cheese. Bake at 425° for 23 minutes. Arrange tomatoes evenly over pizza; bake an additional 5 minutes or until crust is golden. Remove from oven; sprinkle with basil. Cut pizza into 6 wedges. Serves 6 (serving size: 1 wedge)

CALORIES 356; FAT 11.2g (sat 4.6g, mono 4.2g, poly 0.9g); PROTEIN 14.5g; CARB 48.4g; FIBER 7.8g; CHOL 23mg; IRON 1.6mg; SODIUM 472mg; CALC 91mg

Because this classic Neapolitan-style pizza is so simple, it depends on quality ingredients. Use the best fresh mozzarella and basil you can find.

Pizza Margherita

Hands-on time: 19 min. Total time: 25 hr. 55 min.

1 cup warm water (100° to 110°), divided
10 ounces bread flour (about 2 cups plus 2 tablespoons)
1 package dry yeast (about 2 1/4 teaspoons)
4 teaspoons olive oil
3/4 teaspoon kosher salt, divided

Cooking spray
1 tablespoon yellow cornmeal
3/4 cup Basic Pizza Sauce (page 73)
5 ounces thinly sliced fresh mozzarella cheese
1/3 cup small basil leaves

1. Pour ¾ cup warm water in the bowl of a stand mixer with dough hook attached. Weigh or lightly spoon flour into dry measuring cups and spoons; level with a knife. Add flour to ¾ cup warm water; mix until combined. Cover and let stand 20 minutes. Combine ¼ cup warm water and yeast in a small bowl; let stand 5 minutes or until bubbly. Add yeast mixture, oil, and ½ teaspoon salt to flour mixture; mix 5 minutes or until a soft dough forms. Place dough in a large bowl coated with cooking spray; cover surface of dough with plastic wrap lightly coated with cooking spray. Refrigerate 24 hours.

2. Remove dough from refrigerator. Let stand, covered, 1 hour or until dough comes to room temperature. Punch dough down. Sprinkle cornmeal on a lightly floured baking sheet without raised edges. Press dough into a 12-inch circle on prepared pan. Crimp edges to form a ½-inch border. Cover dough loosely with plastic wrap.

3. Position oven rack in lowest setting. Place a pizza stone or heavy baking sheet on the rack. Preheat oven to 550° (keep pizza stone or baking sheet in oven as it preheats). Preheat pizza stone or baking sheet 30 minutes before baking pizza.

4. Remove plastic wrap from dough. Sprinkle dough with ¼ teaspoon salt. Spread pizza sauce evenly over dough, leaving a ½-inch border. Arrange cheese slices evenly over pizza. Slide pizza onto preheated pizza stone or heavy baking sheet, using a spatula as a guide. Bake at 550° for 11 minutes or until crust is golden. Cut pizza into 10 wedges, and sprinkle evenly with basil. Serves 5 (serving size: 2 wedges)

CALORIES 360; FAT 13.6g (sat 4.9g, mono 6.3g, poly 1.2g); PROTEIN 13.3g; CARB 45.8g; FIBER 2.4g; CHOL 23mg; IRON 2.1mg; SODIUM 424mg; CALC 17mg

If you know someone who doesn't like beets, this pizza might convert them. Serve it as a first course. You'll only need half of the Homemade Pizza Dough recipe; save the rest for another use.

Roasted Beet Pizza
(Pizza alla Barbabietola Arrostito)

Hands-on time: 24 min.   Total time: 26 hr. 42 min.

1 (4-ounce) golden beet
1 tablespoon yellow cornmeal
Homemade Pizza Dough (page 66)
1 teaspoon olive oil
½ cup (2 ounces) crumbled feta cheese

¼ cup vertically sliced shallots
¼ teaspoon kosher salt
1 teaspoon honey
1 teaspoon rosemary leaves

1. Preheat oven to 450°.

2. Leave root and 1 inch of stem on beet; scrub with a brush. Wrap beet in foil. Bake at 450° for 40 minutes or until tender. Remove from oven; cool. Trim off beet root; rub off skin. Cut beet in half crosswise; thinly slice halves.

3. Position oven rack in lowest setting. Place a pizza stone or heavy baking sheet on the rack.

4. Increase oven temperature to 500° (keep pizza stone or baking sheet in oven as it preheats). Preheat pizza stone or baking sheet 30 minutes before baking pizza.

5. Sprinkle cornmeal on a baking sheet without raised edges. Roll dough into a 10-inch circle on prepared pan. Gently brush oil over dough. Arrange cheese, beet slices, and shallots evenly over dough, leaving a ½-inch border. Slide dough onto preheated pizza stone or heavy baking sheet, using a spatula as a guide.

6. Bake at 500° for 8 minutes or until crust is golden. Remove from pizza stone. Sprinkle with salt, and drizzle with honey. Sprinkle with rosemary. Cut pizza into 8 wedges. Serves 8 (serving size: 1 wedge)

CALORIES 176; FAT 4g (sat 1.4g, mono 1.8g, poly 0.5g); PROTEIN 5.8g; CARB 29.4g; FIBER 1.3g; CHOL 6mg; IRON 1.9mg; SODIUM 262mg; CALC 42mg

A slice of this pizza makes a tasty hors d'oeuvre, or serve two slices with a tossed salad for supper. You can roast the garlic a day ahead; cool, extract the pulp, and refrigerate until you're ready to assemble the pizza.

Roasted Garlic Pizza

Hands-on time: 12 min.   Total time: 2 hr. 17 min.

1 whole garlic head
½ teaspoon dry yeast
⅓ cup warm water (100° to 110°)
2¼ ounces all-purpose flour (about ½ cup)
2⅜ ounces bread flour (about ½ cup)
½ teaspoon kosher salt
1 teaspoon olive oil
Cooking spray

1 tablespoon yellow cornmeal
1 cup (4 ounces) shredded part-skim mozzarella cheese
¼ cup (1 ounce) grated Parmigiano-Reggiano cheese
2 teaspoons chopped fresh oregano
¼ teaspoon crushed red pepper

1. Preheat oven to 375°.

2. Remove white papery skin from garlic head (do not peel or separate the cloves). Wrap head in foil. Bake at 375° for 45 minutes; cool 10 minutes. Separate cloves; squeeze to extract garlic pulp. Discard skins.

3. Dissolve yeast in ⅓ cup warm water in a small bowl, and let stand 5 minutes. Weigh or lightly spoon flours into dry measuring cups; level with a knife. Place flours and salt in a food processor; pulse 2 times or until blended. Add oil to yeast mixture, stirring with a whisk. With processor on, slowly add yeast mixture through food chute; process until dough forms a ball. Process 1 minute. Turn dough out onto a floured surface; knead lightly 4 to 5 times. Place dough in a large bowl coated with cooking spray, turning to coat top. Cover and let rise in a warm place (85°), free from drafts, 1 hour or until doubled in size. (Gently press two fingers into dough. If indentation remains, dough has risen enough.)

4. Increase oven temperature to 400°.

5. Punch dough down; cover and let rest 5 minutes. Roll dough into a 10-inch circle on a floured surface. Place dough on pizza pan or baking sheet sprinkled with cornmeal. Spread roasted garlic evenly over pizza, leaving a ½-inch border; top with cheeses, oregano, and pepper. Bake at 400° for 12 minutes or until crust is golden. Cut pizza into 8 wedges. Serves 8 (serving size: 1 wedge)

CALORIES 127; FAT 3.9g (sat 2g, mono 1.3g, poly 0.3g); PROTEIN 6.7g; CARB 16.2g; FIBER 0.7g; CHOL 10mg; IRON 1mg; SODIUM 2mg; CALC 137mg

Roasting vegetables helps bring out their natural sweetness. Combined with two kinds of cheese, crushed red pepper, and basil, this is one satisfying pie.

Roasted Vegetable and Ricotta Pizza

Hands-on time: 15 min.   Total time: 1 hr. 11 min.

1 pound refrigerated fresh pizza dough	1 tablespoon yellow cornmeal
Cooking spray	1/3 cup tomato sauce
2 cups sliced cremini mushrooms	1 cup (4 ounces) shredded part-skim
1 cup (1/4-inch-thick) slices zucchini	mozzarella cheese
1/4 teaspoon black pepper	1/2 teaspoon crushed red pepper
1 medium-sized yellow bell pepper, sliced	1/3 cup part-skim ricotta cheese
1 medium-sized red onion, cut into thick slices	2 tablespoons small basil leaves
5 1/2 teaspoons olive oil, divided	

1. Position oven rack in lowest setting; place a pizza stone or heavy baking sheet on the rack. Preheat oven to 500° (keep pizza stone or baking sheet in oven as it preheats). Preheat pizza stone or heavy baking sheet 30 minutes before baking pizza.

2. Place dough in a bowl coated with cooking spray. Let dough stand, covered, 30 minutes or until dough comes to room temperature.

3. Combine mushrooms and next 4 ingredients (through onion) in a large bowl; drizzle with 1½ tablespoons oil. Toss. Arrange vegetables on a jelly-roll pan. Bake at 500° for 15 minutes.

4. Punch dough down. Sprinkle a lightly floured baking sheet with cornmeal; roll dough into a 15-inch circle on prepared baking sheet. Brush dough with 1 teaspoon oil. Spread sauce over dough, leaving a ½-inch border. Sprinkle ½ cup mozzarella over sauce; top with vegetables. Sprinkle ½ cup mozzarella and red pepper over zucchini mixture. Dollop with ricotta. Slide pizza onto preheated pizza stone or heavy baking sheet, using a spatula as a guide. Bake at 500° for 11 minutes or until crust is golden. Sprinkle with basil. Cut pizza into 12 wedges. Serves 6 (serving size: 2 wedges)

CALORIES 347; FAT 11.1g (sat 3.7g, mono 4.4g, poly 2g); PROTEIN 14.8g; CARB 48.5g; FIBER 2.7g; CHOL 15mg; IRON 3mg; SODIUM 655mg; CALC 193mg

Pizza for breakfast? This pie would certainly be a great one to try in the morning, or for any other meal of the day.

Sunny-Side-Up Pizza

Hands-on time: 30 min. Total time: 30 min.

1 pound refrigerated fresh pizza dough
2 tablespoons olive oil, divided
2 garlic cloves, minced
6 large eggs
⅛ teaspoon kosher salt
4 cups mâche or baby spinach

¼ cup thinly sliced red onion
3 tablespoons balsamic vinaigrette
½ cup (2 ounces) shaved fresh Parmesan cheese
⅜ teaspoon black pepper

1. Preheat oven to 450°.

2. Place dough in a microwave-safe bowl; microwave at MEDIUM (50% power) 45 seconds. Let stand 5 minutes. Roll dough into a 14-inch circle. Place on a pizza pan; pierce with a fork. Combine 1½ tablespoons oil and garlic; brush over dough. Bake at 450° for 14 minutes.

3. Heat a large nonstick skillet over medium heat. Add 1½ teaspoons oil; swirl to coat. Crack eggs into pan; cook 4 minutes or until whites are set. Sprinkle with salt.

4. Combine mâche, onion, and vinaigrette. Arrange on crust; top with eggs, cheese, and pepper. Cut pizza into 6 wedges. Serves 6 (serving size: 1 wedge)

CALORIES 371; FAT 14.6g (sat 3.4g, mono 8.3g, poly 1.9g); PROTEIN 17.2g; CARB 38.8g; FIBER 6.4g; CHOL 181mg; IRON 2.8mg; SODIUM 663mg; CALC 184mg

Homemade pizza dough is economical, fun, and healthful since you control the ingredients. This recipe yields enough dough to make two pizzas. When a pizza recipe calls for only half of the Homemade Pizza Dough, you can freeze the rest for up to two months.

Homemade Pizza Dough

Hands-on time: 15 min.   Total time: 25 hr. 15 min.

1   package dry yeast (about 2¼ teaspoons)
⅔   cup warm water (100° to 110°)
1   cup cold water
1½ tablespoons olive oil
18 ounces (about 4 cups) unbleached bread flour, divided
¾   teaspoon sugar
¾   teaspoon salt
Cooking spray

1. Dissolve yeast in ⅔ cup warm water in the bowl of a stand mixer; let stand 5 minutes. Stir in 1 cup cold water and oil.

2. Weigh or lightly spoon flour into dry measuring cups; level with a knife. Gradually add 9 ounces flour (about 2 cups), sugar, and salt to yeast mixture; beat at low speed until smooth. Gradually add 7.9 ounces flour (about 1¾ cups); beat until smooth. Turn dough out onto a floured surface. Knead until smooth and elastic (about 10 minutes); add enough of remaining flour, 1 tablespoon at a time, to prevent dough from sticking to hands (dough will feel sticky).

3. Divide dough in half; place each portion in a zip-top plastic bag coated with cooking spray. Seal. Chill overnight or up to 2 days. Let stand at room temperature 1 hour before using. Makes 2 (1-pound) balls of dough.

Totals given are for 1 (14-ounce) ball of dough: CALORIES 1,032; FAT 15.1g (sat 2.1g, mono 7.9g, poly 2.9g); PROTEIN 32g; CARB 188g; FIBER 7.1g; CHOL 0mg; IRON 11.4mg; SODIUM 892mg; CALC 39mg

You can make dough ahead; refrigerate it after allowing it to rise for 30 minutes. When you're ready to use it, let refrigerated dough stand, covered, in a bowl coated with cooking spray, 30 minutes or until it comes to room temperature.

or until doubled in size. (Gently press two fingers into dough. If indentation remains, dough has risen enough.) Punch dough down, and shape into a ball. Use as directed in pizza recipe. Makes 1 (14-ounce) ball pizza dough.

Totals given are for 1 (1-pound) ball of dough: CALORIES 1,031; FAT 18.3g (sat 2.5g, mono 10.4g, poly 3g); PROTEIN 28.8g; CARB 191.5g; FIBER 14.2g; CHOL 0mg; IRON 10.4mg; SODIUM 1,128mg; CALC 53mg

Whole-Wheat Pizza Dough

Hands-on time: 12 min.   Total time: 1 hr. 12 min.

1¼   teaspoons dry yeast
¼   teaspoon sugar
⅔   cup warm water (100° to 110°)
1   tablespoon olive oil
2   teaspoons honey
5.6   ounces all-purpose flour (about 1¼ cups)
3.2   ounces whole-wheat flour (about ⅔ cup)
½   teaspoon sea salt
Cooking spray

1. Dissolve yeast and sugar in ⅔ cup warm water in a small bowl; let stand 5 minutes. Stir in olive oil and honey.

2. Weigh or lightly spoon flours into dry measuring cups; level with a knife. Combine flours and salt in the bowl of a stand mixer, stirring with a whisk. Gradually add yeast mixture, beating at low speed until smooth. Turn dough out onto a lightly floured surface; knead until smooth and elastic (about 3 minutes). Place dough in a large bowl coated with cooking spray, turning to coat top. Cover and let rise in a warm place (85°), free from drafts, 1 hour

RESTING DOUGH

If you are using dough that has been refrigerated, let it stand, covered, until it comes to room temperature—usually 30 minutes, sometimes as long as 60 minutes. This allows it to relax so it will be easy to work with. To tell if your dough is ready to use, gently press two fingers into the dough. If an indentation remains (see the example on the right), the dough has risen enough, and you're ready to make a pizza.

SECRET TO A PERFECTLY CRISPY CRUST

Pizzerias bake their pies at high temperatures—sometimes as high as 900°. (No wonder those crusts are so crisp!) To get a crisp crust without a blazing wood-burning oven, pizza stone, or other special equipment, use this secret strategy: Sprinkle 1 tablespoon cornmeal onto a baking sheet, and then roll your dough on top. Bake as directed, and enjoy the crunch!

7 GOOD CRUSTS

Just about any flatbread can serve as an impromptu base for a pizza when you're in a hurry—you can shave cooking time down to the few minutes it takes to melt the cheese. Use lighter, drier ingredients when topping thinner breads, and save juicy, heavy goodies for sturdier breads.

1. Naan: Most associated with Indian cuisine, naan is a flat, slightly puffy bread from South Asia with a dense, chewy texture. Traditionally cooked in a tandoor oven, it's often brushed with clarified butter once it's done.

2. Lavash: A very thin bread from the Middle East often used as a wrap that can be up to 14 inches in diameter. Top sparingly and bake for a cracker-crisp crust.

3. Premade Pizza Crust: These fully baked crusts are a great stand-in when you don't want to make or use fresh dough.

4. Flatbread: Thin and flexible, commercial flatbreads come in a wide variety of flavors, giving you options for a tasty pizza.

5. Pita: A Middle Eastern pocket bread often stuffed with sandwich fillings or cut into wedges for dips and mezze. Split pita in half horizontally and build your pizza on the soft, white interior.

6. English Muffin: Go mini, and turn breakfast fare into a fun base for a pizza. The English muffin's crevices are great for sauce and melted cheese.

7. Wraps: Evolved from flour tortillas, wraps can also serve as thin pizza crusts. Some varieties have more fat than others.

8 GOOD CHEESES

Cheese is arguably the most important ingredient on a pizza: It can stand alone as a topping, and it can bring other ingredients together in a tasty harmony.

1. Feta: A brined, tangy cheese that isn't great for melting, but it makes up for it with lots of flavor.

2. Blue: Pungent blue cheese can be made with sheep's, goat's, or cow's milk. Its unique distinction is its blue veins, created by mold.

3. Parmesan: A hard, aged cheese with a grainy texture and a nutty taste. Splurge on Parmigiano-Reggiano, made only in Italy's Emilia-Romagna region, for a real treat.

4. Provolone: Often used on sandwiches, provolone is a dense, smooth cow's milk cheese that melts nicely and has a slight spicy-smoky flavor.

5. Jack: Also sold as Monterey Jack, Sonoma Jack, and California Jack, it's often mixed with other ingredients, such as peppers, onion, and herbs.

6. Fresh Mozzarella: A soft, white, mild unaged cheese that is sold in plastic containers with water or whey, or vacuum packed. Try it on pizzas with assertive toppings.

7. Aged Mozzarella: This is the cheese most associated with pizza. With a little more flavor and a denser texture than fresh mozzarella, it melts beautifully.

8. Goat Cheese: Slightly tangy, goat cheese—or chèvre—is made from goat's milk or a combo of goat's and cow's milk. It's sold in cylinders, disks, or cones and sometimes has added black pepper or herbs. It isn't a melting cheese, but it adds creamy texture to pizza.

5 GOOD PIZZA SAUCES

Put a fresh twist on a pizza recipe, and use one of these in place of another sauce. Ready to build your own pizza? Let these serve as a base for your creations: Each one is packed with plenty of its own unique flavor.

Sun-dried tomato flakes give this quick sauce a smoky essence. Try it with pasta, too.

Sun-Dried Tomato Pizza Sauce

Hands-on time: 14 min.   Total time: 14 min.

Heat 1 teaspoon olive oil in a small skillet over medium heat. Add 2 garlic cloves, minced; sauté 1 minute. Reduce heat to low; add 2 cups lower-sodium marinara sauce, ¼ cup thinly sliced fresh basil, 2 tablespoons sun-dried tomato flakes, and 2 tablespoons finely shredded fresh Parmesan cheese. Cook over medium heat 4 minutes or until thoroughly heated. Serves 36 (serving size: 1 tablespoon)

CALORIES 7; FAT 0.3g (sat 0.1g, mono 0.1g, poly 0g); PROTEIN 0.2g; CARB 0.9g; FIBER 0.1g; CHOL 0mg; IRON 0.2mg; SODIUM 15mg; CALC 6mg

Red Pepper, Arugula, and Pistachio Pesto

Hands-on time: 7 min.   Total time: 7 min.

Place 2 cups arugula, 1 cup roasted red bell pepper strips, 2 tablespoons unsalted shelled dry-roasted pistachios, 3 tablespoons extra-virgin olive oil, 1 teaspoon lemon juice, ¼ teaspoon each of salt and black pepper, and 1 peeled garlic clove in food processor; process until peppers are minced. Serves 16 (serving size: 1 tablespoon)

CALORIES 32; FAT 3.1g (sat 0.4g, mono 2.3g, poly 0.4g); PROTEIN 0.3g; CARB 1g; FIBER 0.2g; CHOL 0mg; IRON 0.1mg; SODIUM 73mg; CALC 6mg

Basic Pizza Sauce

Hands-on time: 9 min. Total time: 39 min.

Heat 2 tablespoons extra-virgin olive oil in a medium saucepan over medium heat. Add 5 minced garlic cloves to pan; cook 1 minute, stirring frequently. Remove tomatoes from 1 (28-ounce) can San Marzano tomatoes using a slotted spoon, reserving juices. Crush tomatoes. Stir tomatoes, juices, ½ teaspoon salt, and ½ teaspoon dried oregano into garlic mixture; bring to a boil. Reduce heat, and simmer 30 minutes, stirring occasionally. Serves 32 (serving size: 1 tablespoon)

CALORIES 13; FAT 0.9g (sat 0.1g, mono 0.7g, poly 0.1g); PROTEIN 0.5g; CARB 1g; FIBER 0.2g; CHOL 0mg; IRON 0.6mg; SODIUM 49mg; CALC 1mg

Cheesy White Sauce

Hands-on time: 6 min. Total time: 6 min.

Melt 1 tablespoon butter in a medium saucepan over medium heat. Add 2 minced garlic cloves; cook 30 seconds, stirring constantly. Add 2 tablespoons all-purpose flour and ½ teaspoon freshly ground black pepper; cook 1 minute, stirring constantly with a whisk. Gradually add ¾ cup 2% reduced-fat milk, stirring constantly with a whisk. Cook 3 minutes or until thick and bubbly, stirring constantly with a whisk. Remove from heat; add ½ cup (2 ounces) grated fresh pecorino Romano cheese, stirring until cheese melts. Serves 14 (serving size: 1 tablespoon)

CALORIES 34; FAT 2.1g (sat 1.5g, mono 0.5g, poly 0.1g); PROTEIN 1.6g; CARB 2g; FIBER 0.1g; CHOL 6mg; IRON 0.1mg; SODIUM 77mg; CALC 67mg

Asian BBQ Sauce

Hands-on time: 5 min. Total time: 5 min.

Combine ½ cup barbecue sauce, ¼ cup honey, 2 tablespoons rice vinegar, 2 tablespoons hoisin sauce, 1 tablespoon lower-sodium soy sauce, 2 teaspoons grated peeled fresh ginger, 1 teaspoon sambal oelek, 2 minced garlic cloves, and a pinch of five-spice powder in a small bowl. Serves 20 (serving size: 1 tablespoon)

CALORIES 21; FAT 0.1g (sat 0g, mono 0g, poly 0g); PROTEIN 0.4g; CARB 5g; FIBER 0.1g; CHOL 0mg; IRON 0mg; SODIUM 88mg; CALC 2mg

200-CALORIE PIZZA SLICES

Roll a 1-pound ball of fresh dough into a 14-inch circle. Top with one of these tasty topping combinations (wait until the pizza is out of the oven before adding fresh herbs, greens, or smoked salmon), bake on a baking sheet at 425° for 15 minutes or until the crust is golden, and cut into 8 wedges. *Buon appetito!*

THE BAGEL-AND-LOX TREATMENT

Base: 1 tablespoon fresh lemon juice + 1/2 cup 1/3-less-fat cream cheese
Toppings: 4 ounces sliced smoked salmon + 1/3 cup thinly sliced red onion + 1 tablespoon chopped fresh dill

THE CAN'T-BEET-THIS COMBO

Base: 1 1/2 tablespoons olive oil
Toppings: 8 ounces sliced roasted beets + 1/3 cup toasted walnut halves + 1/3 cup crumbled goat cheese + 2 tablespoons chopped flat-leaf parsley

THE CHICKEN PESTO PARTY

Base: 1/4 cup prepared pesto
Toppings: 3/4 cup shredded roasted chicken breast + 1/2 cup sliced red bell pepper + 1/3 cup grated fresh Parmigiano-Reggiano cheese

THE HAPPY HAWAIIAN

Base: ½ cup lower-sodium marinara sauce

Toppings: 4 ounces turkey pepperoni slices + 1 cup pineapple chunks (fresh or canned) + ½ cup shredded part-skim mozzarella cheese

THE FARMERS' MARKET

Base: ⅓ cup part-skim ricotta cheese

Toppings: 2 cups cut asparagus + ½ cup spring peas + 1½ tablespoons olive oil + 2 tablespoons grated lemon rind + ½ cup shaved fresh Parmigiano-Reggiano cheese

THE GREEK AUSTERITY CURE

Base: ¾ cup ready-made Greek-style hummus

Toppings: 6 sliced plum tomatoes + ⅓ cup black olives + ½ cup crumbled feta cheese + ½ cup chopped fresh basil

THE BBQ YARDBIRD

Base: ½ cup ready-made barbecue sauce

Toppings: ½ cup sliced roasted chicken breast + ½ cup shredded cheddar cheese + ½ cup sliced red onion + ½ cup chopped fresh cilantro

THE PEPPERY PIG

Base: 1½ tablespoons olive oil

Toppings: 4 ounces sliced prosciutto + ½ cup shaved Parmigiano-Reggiano cheese + 4 cups arugula + cracked black pepper

BURGERS

SEASON, GRILL, SQUIRT, BITE.

(extra onions. and pass the ketchup, would you?)

Small but loaded with flavor: Caramelized onions, blue cheese, arugula, and sirloin fill your mouth with sweetness and pungency.

Caramelized Onion–and–Blue Cheese Mini Burgers

Hands-on time: 28 min.   Total time: 28 min.

1   medium onion, thinly sliced
Cooking spray
½   teaspoon salt
½   teaspoon freshly ground black pepper
1   pound ground sirloin

2   tablespoons canola mayonnaise
1½   tablespoons crumbled blue cheese
8   slider buns, toasted
1½   cups arugula
8   thin tomato slices

1. Heat a medium nonstick skillet over medium-high heat. Add onion to pan; coat onion with cooking spray. Cook 15 minutes, stirring frequently, until tender and browned. Remove pan from heat. Finely chop ¼ cup onion, and place in a medium bowl, reserving remaining onion in pan.

2. Add salt, pepper, and beef to caramelized onion in bowl; mix well. Divide beef mixture into 8 equal portions, shaping each into a ¼-inch-thick patty.

3. Heat a grill pan over medium-high heat. Place patties on grill pan. Grill 3 minutes on each side, until a thermometer registers 160° or until desired degree of doneness.

4. Place mayonnaise and blue cheese in a food processor; process until smooth. Spread blue cheese mixture evenly on bottom halves of buns. Place 1 patty on bottom half of each bun. Top patties evenly with arugula, tomato slices, and remaining caramelized onion; cover with bun tops. Serves 8 (serving size: 1 burger)

CALORIES 198; FAT 6.6g (sat 1.9g, mono 2.2g, poly 1.4g); PROTEIN 16g; CARB 20.5g; FIBER 1.6g; CHOL 32mg; IRON 1.1mg; SODIUM 402mg; CALC 26mg

These top-rated burgers prove that you don't have to own a grill to enjoy juicy, amazingly flavorful hamburgers.

Cast-Iron Burgers

Hands-on time: 32 min.   Total time: 64 min.

Patties:
- 1 pound ground sirloin
- ½ teaspoon kosher salt

Horseradish spread:
- 1 tablespoon canola mayonnaise
- 1 tablespoon Dijon mustard
- 1 tablespoon prepared horseradish
- 2 teaspoons ketchup

Relish:
- 2 applewood-smoked bacon slices, chopped

- 3 cups vertically sliced yellow onion
- 1 tablespoon finely chopped fresh chives
- 1 teaspoon Worcestershire sauce
- ¼ teaspoon freshly ground black pepper

Remaining ingredients:
- Cooking spray
- 4 (1½-ounce) hamburger buns or Kaiser rolls
- 4 (¼-inch-thick) slices tomato

1. To prepare patties, divide beef into 4 equal portions, lightly shaping each into a ½-inch-thick patty. Press thumb in center of each patty, leaving a nickel-sized indentation. Sprinkle evenly with salt. Cover and refrigerate 30 minutes.

2. To prepare horseradish spread, combine mayonnaise and next 3 ingredients (through ketchup) in a small bowl. Set aside.

3. To prepare relish, cook bacon in a large nonstick skillet over medium-low heat until crisp. Remove bacon from pan with a slotted spoon. Add onion to drippings in pan; cook 15 minutes or until golden brown. Combine bacon, onion mixture, chives, Worcestershire sauce, and pepper in a small bowl.

4. Heat a large cast-iron skillet over medium-high heat. Coat pan with cooking spray. Add patties; cook 2 minutes on each side or until desired degree of doneness. Spread 1½ teaspoons horseradish spread on cut side of each bun half. Top bottom half of each bun with 1 patty, 1 tomato slice, and ¼ cup relish. Cover with bun tops. Serves 4 (serving size: 1 burger)

CALORIES 351; FAT 12g (sat 3.5g, mono 3.4g, poly 3.2g); PROTEIN 29.2g; CARB 32.7g; FIBER 3g; CHOL 66mg; IRON 3.7mg; SODIUM 788mg; CALC 91mg

Tender, golden shallots lend a lovely sweetness to this classic cheeseburger. Don't be afraid to cook the shallots to a deep golden brown: It will improve their flavor.

Cheddar Cheeseburgers with Caramelized Shallots

Hands-on time: 38 min.   Total time: 38 min.

1   tablespoon olive oil, divided
2   cups thinly sliced shallots
½   teaspoon kosher salt, divided
1   tablespoon white wine vinegar
2   garlic cloves, minced
1   pound 90% lean ground beef

½   cup (2 ounces) shredded sharp cheddar cheese
1   cup arugula
4   (1½-ounce) hamburger buns, toasted
3   tablespoons light mayonnaise

1. Heat a nonstick skillet over medium-low heat. Add 2 teaspoons oil; swirl to coat. Add shallots and ¼ teaspoon salt; cook 15 minutes or until golden brown, stirring occasionally. Stir in vinegar; cook 1 minute. Remove from heat; keep warm.

2. Gently combine garlic and beef. Divide meat mixture into 4 equal portions, gently shaping each into a ½-inch-thick patty. Press thumb in center of each patty, leaving a nickel-sized indentation. Sprinkle evenly with ¼ teaspoon salt.

3. Heat a large cast-iron skillet over medium-high heat. Add 1 teaspoon oil to pan; swirl to coat. Add patties, and cook 3 minutes on each side or until desired degree of doneness. Top each patty with 2 tablespoons cheese; cover and cook 1 minute or until cheese melts.

4. Place ¼ cup arugula on bottom half of each bun; top with 1 patty and one-fourth of shallot mixture. Spread about 2 teaspoons mayonnaise on cut side of top half of each bun; place on top of burgers. Serves 4 (serving size: 1 burger)

CALORIES 370; FAT 17.7g (sat 6.1g, mono 5.4g, poly 2.9g); PROTEIN 31.1g; CARB 31.7g; FIBER 8.1g; CHOL 77mg; IRON 2.2mg; SODIUM 654mg; CALC 113mg

Thyme, garlic, and Dijon mustard give these burgers a French twist. Pan-grilled tomatoes enhance the already-juicy texture.

Garlic-Thyme Burgers with Grilled Tomato

Hands-on time: 20 min.   Total time: 20 min.

1 tablespoon chopped fresh thyme	4 (½-inch-thick) slices beefsteak tomato
⅜ teaspoon kosher salt	1 tablespoon Dijon mustard
¼ teaspoon freshly ground black pepper	4 (2-ounce) Kaiser rolls or other sandwich rolls
2 garlic cloves, minced	
1 pound ground sirloin	4 baby romaine lettuce leaves

1. Heat a grill pan over medium-high heat. Combine first 5 ingredients in a medium bowl. Divide mixture into 4 equal portions, shaping each into a ½-inch-thick patty. Press thumb in center of each patty, leaving a nickel-sized indentation. Add patties to pan; cook 4 minutes on each side or until desired degree of doneness. Remove patties from pan. Add tomato slices to pan; cook 1 minute on each side. Spread ¾ teaspoon mustard over bottom half of each roll; top each with 1 lettuce leaf, 1 patty, 1 tomato slice, and top half of roll. Serves 4 (serving size: 1 burger)

CALORIES 354; FAT 12g (sat 4.4g, mono 4.6g, poly 1.5g); PROTEIN 28.5g; CARB 30.9g; FIBER 1.9g; CHOL 73mg; IRON 4.7mg; SODIUM 591mg; CALC 101mg

These saucy, family-friendly burgers might be best eaten with a knife and fork. If you'd like to go bunless, serve over spaghetti with extra sauce.

Italian Meatball Burgers

Hands-on time: 24 min.   Total time: 29 min.

6 (1.5-ounce) frozen ciabatta rolls with rosemary and olive oil
8 ounces sweet turkey Italian sausage
1 tablespoon chopped fresh basil
2 teaspoons chopped fresh oregano
½ teaspoon fennel seeds, crushed
¼ teaspoon salt
⅛ teaspoon garlic powder
1 pound ground sirloin
Cooking spray
½ cup (2 ounces) shredded sharp provolone cheese
6 large basil leaves
6 tablespoons lower-sodium marinara sauce

1. Preheat grill to medium-high heat.

2. Bake rolls according to package directions. Split rolls.

3. Remove casings from sausage. Combine sausage, chopped basil, and next 5 ingredients (through ground sirloin) in a medium bowl. Divide meat mixture into 6 equal portions with moist hands, shaping each into a ½-inch-thick patty. Press thumb in center of each patty, leaving a nickel-sized indentation.

4. Place patties on grill rack coated with cooking spray; grill 6 minutes. Turn patties over; grill 2 minutes. Sprinkle cheese evenly over patties, and grill 6 minutes or until a thermometer registers 160°. Remove from grill; let stand 5 minutes.

5. Place 1 basil leaf on bottom half of each roll; top each with 1 patty, 1 tablespoon marinara sauce, and roll top. Serves 6 (serving size: 1 burger)

CALORIES 292; FAT 11.5g (sat 3.9g, mono 3.8g, poly 0.9g); PROTEIN 26.8g; CARB 24g; FIBER 1.1g; CHOL 75mg; IRON 1.6mg; SODIUM 642mg; CALC 93mg

Mushroom Burgers with Fried Egg and Truffle Oil

Hands-on time: 29 min.   Total time: 29 min.

Cooking spray
3 cups finely chopped cremini mushrooms (about 8 ounces)
1/3 cup minced shallots
1 tablespoon chopped fresh thyme
5 garlic cloves, minced
1/3 cup cabernet sauvignon or other dry red wine
3/4 teaspoon freshly ground black pepper, divided
1/2 teaspoon kosher salt

1 pound ground beef, extra lean
4 large eggs
2 cups arugula
1/4 cup (1 ounce) grated fresh Parmigiano-Reggiano cheese
1 tablespoon white truffle oil
1 tablespoon minced fresh chives
1 tablespoon light canola mayonnaise
1 tablespoon no-salt-added ketchup
2 teaspoons Dijon mustard
4 (1½-ounce) hamburger buns, toasted

1. Preheat grill to medium-high heat.

2. Heat a large skillet over medium-high heat. Coat pan with cooking spray. Add mushrooms and next 3 ingredients (through garlic) to pan; sauté 5 minutes or until mushrooms are browned. Add wine; cook 3 minutes or until liquid evaporates. Remove from heat; cool completely.

3. Combine mushroom mixture, ½ teaspoon pepper, salt, and beef in a large bowl. Divide mixture into 4 equal portions, gently shaping each into a ½-inch-thick patty. Press thumb in center of each patty, leaving a nickel-sized indentation. Place patties on grill rack coated with cooking spray; grill 4 minutes. Carefully turn patties; grill 4 minutes or until desired degree of doneness.

4. Return pan to medium heat; coat with cooking spray. Crack eggs into pan; cook 4 minutes or until whites are set. Remove from heat.

5. Combine ¼ teaspoon pepper, arugula, cheese, and oil in a medium bowl; toss gently to coat. Combine chives and next 3 ingredients (through mustard) in a small bowl. Spread 2 teaspoons mayonnaise mixture on bottom half of each bun; top with 1 patty. Top each serving with 1 egg, ½ cup arugula mixture, and top half of bun. Serves 4 (serving size: 1 burger)

CALORIES 429; FAT 17.5g (sat 5.5g, mono 7.4g, poly 2g); PROTEIN 37.5g; CARB 31.2g; FIBER 1.8g; CHOL 244mg; IRON 4.7mg; SODIUM 767mg; CALC 185mg

Here is a crave-worthy, reasonable version of a fast-food icon. With a similarly addictive sauce, this tasty handful is made healthier with lean ground sirloin and lower-sodium, lighter cheese.

Out-n-In California Burgers

Hands-on time: 22 min. Total time: 22 min.

3 tablespoons ketchup
2 tablespoons canola mayonnaise
2 teaspoons sweet pickle relish
1 teaspoon Dijon mustard
1 pound extra lean ground beef
1/8 teaspoon salt
1/8 teaspoon freshly ground black pepper
Cooking spray
4 (0.67-ounce) thin slices reduced-fat cheddar cheese

4 green leaf lettuce leaves
4 (1 1/2-ounce) hamburger buns
8 (1/4-inch-thick) slices tomato
1/2 ripe peeled avocado, cut into 1/8-inch-thick slices
8 dill pickle chips
4 (1/4-inch-thick) slices red onion

1. Combine first 4 ingredients in a small bowl.

2. Divide beef into 4 equal portions, gently shaping each into a ½-inch-thick patty. Press thumb in center of each patty, leaving a nickel-sized indentation. Sprinkle patties evenly with salt and pepper. Heat a large skillet or grill pan over medium-high heat. Coat pan with cooking spray. Add patties to pan; cook 3 minutes on each side. Top each patty with 1 cheese slice; cook 2 minutes or until cheese melts and patties are desired degree of doneness.

3. Place 1 lettuce leaf on bottom half of each hamburger bun; top with 2 tomato slices, 1 patty, about 2 avocado slices, 2 pickle chips, 1 onion slice, about 1½ tablespoons sauce, and top half of bun. Serves 4 (serving size: 1 burger)

CALORIES 429; FAT 20.3g (sat 6.3g, mono 7.8g, poly 3.2g); PROTEIN 32.7g; CARB 30.8g; FIBER 3.7g; CHOL 75mg; IRON 3.9mg; SODIUM 822mg; CALC 223mg

Billions Served: **AMERICANS EAT** more than 14 billion hamburgers a year.

Mixing salt and pepper into the beef seasons it more thoroughly than sprinkling the surface of the patties. Make your own pesto when basil is in season.

Pesto Sliders

Hands-on time: 13 min.   Total time: 13 min.

¼   teaspoon salt
¼   teaspoon freshly ground black pepper
1   pound ground beef, extra lean
Cooking spray
8   basil leaves (optional)

1   large plum tomato, cut into 8 slices
8   slider buns
2   tablespoons commercial refrigerated pesto
2   tablespoons shaved Parmigiano-Reggiano cheese

1. Gently combine salt, pepper, and ground beef in a medium bowl. Divide beef mixture into 8 equal portions, shaping each into a ¼-inch-thick patty.

2. Heat a grill pan over medium-high heat. Coat pan with cooking spray. Add patties to pan; cook 3 minutes on each side or until desired degree of doneness. Place 1 basil leaf, if desired, 1 patty, and 1 tomato slice on bottom half of each bun. Top each serving with ¾ teaspoon pesto, ¾ teaspoon shaved Parmigiano-Reggiano cheese, and top half of bun. Serves 4 (serving size: 2 sliders)

CALORIES 416; FAT 16.5g (sat 6.2g, mono 6.9g, poly 2.3g); PROTEIN 29.7g; CARB 38.8g; FIBER 2.3g; CHOL 65mg; IRON 4.4mg; SODIUM 754mg; CALC 149mg

We loved the flavorful patty we got from grinding inexpensive beef brisket. Ask for the flat cut of brisket for the leanest choice. Traditional condiments like ketchup and mustard are an option; or try a homemade spread (like the Jalapeño-Cilantro Mayo on page 136).

Simple, Perfect Fresh-Ground Brisket Burgers

Hands-on time: 19 min.   Total time: 49 min.

1   (1-pound) beef brisket, trimmed and cut into
    1-inch pieces
2   tablespoons olive oil
1/4 teaspoon kosher salt
1/8 teaspoon freshly ground black pepper

Cooking spray
4   (1/2-ounce) slices cheddar cheese
4   (1 1/2-ounce) hamburger buns, toasted
4   green leaf lettuce leaves
4   (1/4-inch-thick) slices tomato

1. To prepare grinder, place feed shaft, blade, and 1/4-inch die plate in freezer 30 minutes or until well chilled. Assemble grinder just before grinding.

2. Arrange meat in a single layer on a jelly-roll pan, leaving space between each piece. Freeze 15 minutes or until meat is firm but not frozen. Combine meat and oil in a large bowl, and toss to combine. Pass meat through meat grinder completely. Immediately pass meat through grinder a second time. Divide mixture into 4 equal portions, gently shaping each into a 1/2-inch-thick patty. Press thumb in center of each patty, leaving a nickel-sized indentation. Cover and chill until ready to grill.

3. Preheat grill to medium-high heat.

4. Sprinkle patties with salt and pepper. Place on grill rack coated with cooking spray; grill 2 minutes. Carefully turn patties; grill 3 minutes or until beef reaches desired degree of doneness. Place 1 cheese slice and 1 patty on bottom half of each bun; top each serving with 1 lettuce leaf, 1 tomato slice, and top half of bun. Serves 4 (serving size: 1 burger)

CALORIES 386; FAT 17.9g (sat 6.1g, mono 8.7g, poly 1.9g); PROTEIN 32.4g; CARB 22.1g; FIBER 1.2g; CHOL 64mg; IRON 4mg; SODIUM 496mg; CALC 181mg

A Lot o' Burger: **A SINGLE COW WILL PROVIDE ENOUGH GROUND BEEF** to make 720 quarter-pound hamburger patties.

Sautéed mushrooms, steak sauce, and Worcestershire sauce create robust flavors in this knife-and-fork burger.

Smothered Steak Burgers

Hands-on time: 32 min.   Total time: 32 min.

Cooking spray
2 tablespoons finely chopped shallots
1 garlic clove, minced
1 (8-ounce) package presliced mushrooms
½ cup fat-free, lower-sodium beef broth
1 tablespoon lower-sodium steak sauce
1 teaspoon cornstarch
½ teaspoon freshly ground black pepper, divided

2 tablespoons ketchup
1 tablespoon Worcestershire sauce
1 pound ground sirloin
¼ teaspoon salt
4 green leaf lettuce leaves
4 (½-inch-thick) slices tomato (optional)
4 (2-ounce) bakery rolls, toasted

1. Heat a large skillet over medium heat. Coat pan with cooking spray. Add shallots and garlic to pan; cook 1 minute or until tender, stirring frequently. Increase heat to medium-high. Add mushrooms to pan; cook 10 minutes or until moisture evaporates, stirring occasionally. Combine broth, steak sauce, and cornstarch, stirring with a whisk. Add broth mixture to pan; bring to a boil. Cook 1 minute or until thick, stirring constantly. Stir in ¼ teaspoon pepper. Remove mushroom mixture from pan; cover and keep warm. Wipe pan with paper towels.

2. Combine ¼ teaspoon pepper, ketchup, and Worcestershire sauce in a large bowl, stirring with a whisk. Add beef to bowl; toss gently to combine. Shape beef mixture into 4 equal portions, shaping each into a ½-inch-thick patty. Press thumb in center of each patty, leaving a nickel-sized indentation. Sprinkle evenly with salt.

3. Heat pan over medium-high heat. Coat pan with cooking spray. Add patties to pan; cook 4 minutes. Turn and cook 3 minutes or until desired degree of doneness. Place 1 lettuce leaf and 1 tomato slice, if desired, on bottom half of each roll. Top each serving with 1 patty, about ¼ cup mushroom mixture, and top half of roll. Serves 4 (serving size: 1 burger)

CALORIES 398; FAT 12.9g (sat 4.4g, mono 5.1g, poly 1.4g); PROTEIN 30.7g; CARB 38.4g; FIBER 1.9g; CHOL 41mg; IRON 4.9mg; SODIUM 747mg; CALC 79mg

Chipotle chiles and fresh salsa give these burgers a Southwestern kick that will heat up the dinner table in just 20 minutes.

Southwest Salsa Burgers

Hands-on time: 20 min. Total time: 20 min.

¼ cup finely chopped shallots
⅜ teaspoon salt
¼ teaspoon ground chipotle chile pepper
⅛ teaspoon black pepper
1 pound 90% lean ground sirloin
¼ cup refrigerated fresh salsa, divided

Cooking spray
4 (0.67-ounce) slices reduced-fat Monterey Jack cheese with jalapeño peppers
4 Boston lettuce leaves
4 (1½-ounce) hamburger buns, toasted

1. Combine first 5 ingredients and 2 tablespoons salsa in a medium bowl. Divide mixture into 4 equal portions, shaping each into a ½-inch-thick patty. Press thumb in center of each patty, leaving a nickel-sized indentation.

2. Heat a large skillet or grill pan over medium-high heat. Coat pan with cooking spray. Add patties to pan; cook 5 minutes on each side or until desired degree of doneness. Top each patty with 1 cheese slice; cook 1 minute or until cheese melts.

3. Place 1 lettuce leaf on bottom half of each bun; top with 1 patty, 1½ teaspoons salsa, and bun top. Serves 4 (serving size: 1 burger)

CALORIES 328; FAT 11.3g (sat 4.9g, mono 3.5g, poly 1.6g); PROTEIN 32g; CARB 26g; FIBER 1.7g; CHOL 74mg; IRON 3.7mg; SODIUM 696mg; CALC 209mg

Slime on the Side? **THE ANNUAL SLUGBURGER FESTIVAL IN CORINTH, MISSISSIPPI,** honors a local delicacy: the slugburger, a deep-fried patty that's a mix of beef and a lot of filler, usually potato flour. The name doesn't come from a critter—it comes from the original price of 5 cents, or a slug.

Spicy Poblano Burgers with Pickled Red Onions and Chipotle Cream

Hands-on time: 27 min.   Total time: 65 min.

Pickled red onions:
- ½ cup sugar
- ½ cup rice vinegar
- ½ cup water
- 1 jalapeño pepper, halved lengthwise
- 2½ cups thinly vertically sliced red onion

Burgers:
- 2 large poblano chiles
- 1 (1-ounce) slice white bread
- 1 tablespoon 1% low-fat milk
- 3 tablespoons minced fresh cilantro, divided
- 1 teaspoon ground cumin
- ½ teaspoon ground coriander
- ½ teaspoon paprika
- ½ teaspoon kosher salt, divided
- ½ teaspoon freshly ground black pepper, divided
- 1 pound 93% extra-lean ground beef
- ½ cup light sour cream
- 1 tablespoon minced shallots
- 2 teaspoons fresh lime juice
- 1 (7-ounce) can chipotle chiles in adobo sauce
- Cooking spray
- 4 (1½-ounce) hamburger buns, toasted

1. To prepare pickled red onions, place first 4 ingredients in a medium saucepan. Bring to a boil, stirring until sugar dissolves. Stir in onion. Cover and remove from heat. Cool to room temperature. Place in an airtight container. Store in refrigerator up to 2 weeks.

2. Preheat broiler.

3. Place poblano chiles on a foil-lined baking sheet. Broil 10 minutes or until blackened, turning after 6 minutes. Place in a paper bag; fold to close tightly. Let stand 15 minutes. Peel chiles, discarding seeds and membranes. Finely chop chiles to measure ¾ cup.

4. Trim crusts from bread, and tear into ½-inch pieces. Combine bread and milk in a large bowl, mashing with a fork until smooth. Stir in poblano chile, 1½ tablespoons cilantro, next 3 ingredients (through paprika), ¼ teaspoon salt, and ¼ teaspoon black pepper. Add beef to milk mixture, stirring gently to combine. Divide mixture into 4 equal portions; shape each portion into a ½-inch-thick patty. Press thumb in center of each patty, leaving a nickel-sized indentation. Cover and chill while grill preheats.

5. Preheat grill to medium-high heat.

6. Combine 1½ tablespoons cilantro, ¼ teaspoon salt, and ¼ teaspoon black pepper in a medium bowl. Stir in sour cream, shallots, and juice. Remove 1 chipotle pepper and 2 teaspoons adobo sauce from can; reserve remaining chipotle peppers and adobo sauce for another use. Chop chipotle chile. Stir chopped chipotle chile and 2 teaspoons adobo sauce into sour cream mixture. Set aside.

7. Place patties on grill rack coated with cooking spray; grill 3 to 4 minutes on each side or until a thermometer registers 160°. Spread 3 tablespoons chipotle cream on bottom half of each bun; top each with 1 patty, 1 tablespoon drained pickled red onions, and bun top. Serves 4 (serving size: 1 burger)

CALORIES 365; FAT 8.9g (sat 3.5g, mono 3g, poly 1.5g); PROTEIN 31.4g; CARB 42g; FIBER 2.4g; CHOL 70mg; IRON 4mg; SODIUM 649mg; CALC 121mg

Lamb Burgers with Indian Spices and Yogurt-Mint Sauce

Hands-on time: 39 min.   Total time: 1 hr. 18 min.

1 pound boneless lamb shoulder, trimmed and cut into 1-inch pieces
2 tablespoons canola oil, divided
³⁄₄ cup finely chopped onion
¼ cup finely chopped shallots
2 tablespoons minced garlic, divided
³⁄₄ teaspoon ground cumin
³⁄₄ teaspoon ground coriander
¼ teaspoon ground cardamom
¼ teaspoon dry mustard
¼ teaspoon ground turmeric
⅛ teaspoon ground red pepper

Dash of grated whole nutmeg
2 tablespoons finely chopped fresh mint, divided
³⁄₄ teaspoon kosher salt, divided
2 red bell peppers
½ cup plain 2% reduced-fat Greek yogurt
1 tablespoon fresh lemon juice
¼ teaspoon freshly ground black pepper, divided
Cooking spray
4 (1½-ounce) hamburger buns, toasted
2 cups thinly sliced radicchio
Chopped fresh mint (optional)

1. To prepare grinder, place feed shaft, blade, and ¼-inch die plate in freezer 30 minutes or until well chilled. Assemble grinder just before grinding.

2. Arrange lamb pieces in a single layer on a jelly-roll pan, leaving space between each piece. Freeze 15 minutes or until meat is firm but not frozen. Combine lamb and 1 tablespoon oil in a large bowl; toss to combine. Pass lamb through meat grinder completely. Immediately pass meat through grinder a second time. Cover and chill.

3. Heat 1 tablespoon oil in a medium nonstick skillet over medium heat. Add onion and shallots; cook 15 minutes or until golden, stirring frequently. Stir in 1½ tablespoons garlic, cumin, and next 6 ingredients (through nutmeg); cook 1 minute. Remove from heat; cool to room temperature.

4. Combine lamb mixture, onion mixture, 1 tablespoon mint, and ¼ teaspoon salt. Divide mixture into 4 equal portions, gently shaping each into a ½-inch-thick patty. Press thumb in center of each patty, leaving a nickel-sized indentation. Cover and chill until ready to grill.

5. Preheat broiler.

6. Cut bell peppers in half lengthwise; discard seeds and membranes. Place pepper halves, skin sides up, on a foil-lined baking sheet; flatten with hand. Broil 9 minutes or until blackened. Place in a paper bag; fold to close tightly. Let stand 10 minutes. Peel, and cut each pepper portion in half.

7. Preheat grill to medium-high heat.

8. Combine 1½ teaspoons garlic, 1 tablespoon mint, yogurt, juice, ¼ teaspoon salt, and ⅛ teaspoon black pepper in a medium bowl. Set aside.

9. Sprinkle patties evenly with ¼ teaspoon salt and ⅛ teaspoon black pepper. Place patties on grill rack coated with cooking spray; grill 4 minutes. Carefully turn patties; grill 3 minutes or until desired degree of doneness. Place 1 patty on bottom half of each bun; top each serving with 2 tablespoons yogurt mixture, 2 bell pepper strips, ½ cup radicchio, chopped mint, if desired, and top half of bun. Serves 4 (serving size: 1 burger)

CALORIES 412; FAT 16.6g (sat 4.2g, mono 7.8g, poly 3.2g); PROTEIN 31.4g; CARB 33.7g; FIBER 3.2g; CHOL 72mg; IRON 4.2mg; SODIUM 680mg; CALC 140mg

Cinnamon, ginger, and cumin give these burgers the warm, spicy flavor of the eastern Mediterranean. The burgers would pair nicely with a simple cucumber or cucumber-tomato salad.

Lamb and Turkey Pita Burgers

Hands-on time: 30 min.   Total time: 30 min.

Sauce:
- ¼ cup reduced-fat mayonnaise
- 2 teaspoons fresh lemon juice
- ¼ teaspoon ground cumin
- ⅛ teaspoon ground red pepper

Burgers:
- ¼ cup prechopped onion
- 1 tablespoon tomato paste

- ¼ teaspoon salt
- ⅛ teaspoon ground cinnamon
- ⅛ teaspoon ground ginger
- 8 ounces lean ground lamb
- 8 ounces ground turkey breast
- Cooking spray
- 12 small lettuce leaves
- 6 (4-inch) pitas, cut in half

1. To prepare sauce, combine first 4 ingredients; cover and chill.

2. To prepare burgers, combine onion and next 6 ingredients (through turkey) in a large bowl. Divide mixture into 12 equal portions, shaping each into a ⅓-inch-thick oval patty.

3. Heat a large grill pan over medium-high heat. Coat pan with cooking spray. Add patties to pan; cook 5 minutes on each side or until well marked and done. Arrange 1 lettuce leaf, 1 patty, and about 1½ teaspoons sauce in each pita half. Serves 6 (serving size: 2 stuffed pita halves)

CALORIES 370; FAT 15.3g (sat 5.5g, mono 5.4g, poly 2.7g); PROTEIN 31.8g; CARB 27.5g; FIBER 3.7g; CHOL 78mg; IRON 3mg; SODIUM 623mg; CALC 28mg

Turn the usual weeknight chicken dinner into fun, tasty burgers, and serve them with a simple side salad. For an extra hit of flavor and a little crunch, try topping them with capers fried for a minute in a little olive oil.

Chicken Burgers

Hands-on time: 26 min.   Total time: 26 min.

 1 tablespoon capers, drained
 ¼ teaspoon black pepper
 2 shallots, trimmed and peeled
 1 pound skinless, boneless chicken breasts
Cooking spray
 8 slices sourdough bread, toasted

 ¼ cup canola mayonnaise
 4 green leaf lettuce leaves
 8 slices plum tomato
 4 slices red onion
 2 tablespoons Dijon mustard

1. Place first 4 ingredients in a food processor; process until finely ground. Divide chicken mixture into 4 equal portions; shape each into a ½-inch-thick patty. Press thumb in the center of each patty, leaving a nickel-sized indentation. Heat a large grill pan over medium-high heat. Coat pan with cooking spray. Add patties to pan; cook 5 minutes on each side.

2. Place 1 slice of toast on each of 4 plates, and spread 1 tablespoon mayonnaise over each. Top each slice with 1 lettuce leaf, 1 patty, 2 tomato slices, and 1 onion slice. Spread 1½ teaspoons mustard over each of remaining toast slices, and place on burgers. Serves 4 (serving size: 1 burger)

CALORIES 387; FAT 8.9g (sat 1g, mono 3.7g, poly 2.5g); PROTEIN 33g; CARB 42g; FIBER 2.2g; CHOL 73mg; IRON 3mg; SODIUM 816mg; CALC 47mg

Get out of your burger rut with these grilled ground-chicken burgers that are a twist on a popular Italian-American dish. Serve on ciabatta rolls, and top with marinara sauce and mozzarella.

Chicken Parmesan Burgers

Hands-on time: 16 min.   Total time: 24 min.

2 (3-ounce) square ciabatta rolls
1 garlic clove, halved
8 ounces ground chicken
⅓ cup plus 2 tablespoons lower-sodium
   marinara sauce, divided
½ teaspoon chopped fresh rosemary
½ teaspoon chopped fresh thyme

¼ teaspoon crushed red pepper
⅛ teaspoon kosher salt
⅛ teaspoon black pepper
Cooking spray
¼ cup (1 ounce) shredded part-skim
   mozzarella cheese
8 basil leaves

1. Preheat broiler.

2. Cut rolls in half. Place rolls, cut sides up, on a baking sheet. Broil 3 minutes or until lightly browned. Remove bread from pan. Rub each half with cut side of garlic. Set aside.

3. Reduce oven temperature to 375°.

4. Combine chicken, ⅓ cup marinara sauce, and next 5 ingredients (through black pepper). Divide into 2 portions, shaping each into a ¼-inch-thick patty. Heat an ovenproof skillet over medium-high heat. Coat pan with cooking spray. Add patties to pan; cook 3 minutes. Turn patties, and place pan in oven. Bake at 375° for 8 minutes. Top each patty with 2 tablespoons cheese; bake 1 minute.

5. Layer bottom half of each roll with 2 basil leaves, 1 patty, 1 tablespoon marinara sauce, 2 basil leaves, and roll top. Serves 2 (serving size: 1 burger)

CALORIES 427; FAT 14.4g (sat 4.5g, mono 5.3g, poly 2.3g); PROTEIN 28.9g; CARB 55.4g; FIBER 1.2g; CHOL 83mg; IRON 2.9mg; SODIUM 742mg; CALC 112mg

A small amount of tangy goat cheese flavors the creamy spread. Double the spread and use it on grilled chicken or turkey sandwiches.

Grilled Turkey Burgers with Goat Cheese Spread

Hands-on time: 18 min.   Total time: 18 min.

2   teaspoons grated lemon rind
½   teaspoon salt
2   garlic cloves, minced
1   pound ground turkey breast
1   (10-ounce) package frozen chopped spinach, thawed, drained, and squeezed dry
1   large egg white
¼   teaspoon freshly ground black pepper, divided
Cooking spray

½   cup plain 2% reduced-fat Greek yogurt
¼   cup (1 ounce) crumbled goat cheese
2   tablespoons chopped fresh flat-leaf parsley
1   tablespoon chopped fresh oregano
1   tablespoon chopped fresh mint
6   (2-ounce) whole-wheat hamburger buns, toasted
6   green leaf lettuce leaves
6   (⅛-inch-thick) slices red onion (optional)

1. Combine first 6 ingredients and ⅛ teaspoon pepper in a large bowl, mixing gently. Divide turkey mixture into 6 equal portions, shaping each into a ¼-inch-thick patty. Heat a grill pan over medium-high heat. Coat pan with cooking spray. Add patties to pan; cook 3 minutes on each side or until done.

2. Combine ⅛ teaspoon pepper, yogurt, and next 4 ingredients (through mint) in a small bowl, stirring well. Layer bottom half of each bun with 1 lettuce leaf, 1 onion slice, if desired, 1 patty, 1½ tablespoons yogurt mixture, and top half of bun. Serves 6 (serving size: 1 burger)

CALORIES 269; FAT 5.7g (sat 2.2g, mono 1g, poly 1.4g); PROTEIN 23.9g; CARB 33.9g; FIBER 6.2g; CHOL 28mg; IRON 3mg; SODIUM 588mg; CALC 182mg

Dark green poblano chiles have mild to moderate heat. The darker the chile, the more fiery it will be.

Southwest Turkey Burgers

Hands-on time: 21 min.   Total time: 46 min.

2 poblano chiles (about 1/2 pound)
1 ounce French bread baguette, about 1 (2-inch) slice
1/4 cup 1% low-fat milk
1 teaspoon ground cumin
1/2 teaspoon chili powder, divided
1/2 teaspoon salt
1/4 teaspoon black pepper

1/4 teaspoon ground red pepper
1 pound ground turkey breast
Cooking spray
2 tablespoons canola mayonnaise
4 (1 1/2-ounce) hamburger buns, toasted
4 green leaf lettuce leaves
4 (1/2-inch-thick) slices tomato

1. Preheat grill to medium-high heat.

2. Cut poblanos in half lengthwise; discard seeds and membranes. Place poblanos, skin sides down, on grill rack; grill 10 minutes or until blackened. Place poblanos in a paper bag; fold to close tightly. Let stand 15 minutes. Peel and dice.

3. Place bread in a food processor; pulse 5 times or until coarse crumbs measure 1/2 cup. Combine breadcrumbs and milk in a large bowl; let stand 5 minutes. Add cumin, 1/4 teaspoon chili powder, and next 4 ingredients (through turkey); mix gently just until combined. Divide turkey mixture into 4 equal portions; shape each portion into a 1/2-inch-thick patty. Press thumb in center of each patty, leaving a nickel-sized indentation. Place patties on grill rack coated with cooking spray; grill 3 minutes on each side or until done.

4. Combine 1/4 teaspoon chili powder and mayonnaise. Top bottom half of each bun with 1 lettuce leaf, 1 tomato slice, 1 patty, about 1 1/2 teaspoons mayonnaise mixture, and bun top. Serves 4 (serving size: 1 burger)

CALORIES 321; FAT 8.5g (sat 1.1g, mono 4.2g, poly 2.9g); PROTEIN 27.8g; CARB 32.5g; FIBER 2.6g; CHOL 56mg; IRON 3.5mg; SODIUM 658mg; CALC 108mg

Leftover eggplant puree from this recipe is perfect as a dip for toasted pita wedges. Marmite is a concentrated yeast paste that helps give this burger meaty flavor—find it in supermarket baking aisles and health-food stores. The Marmite and eggplant also help make the burger juicy (see page 132).

Turkey Burgers with Roasted Eggplant

Hands-on time: 30 min. Total time: 66 min.

1 (8-ounce) eggplant
Cooking spray
2 tablespoons finely chopped fresh parsley, divided
4 teaspoons olive oil, divided
1 teaspoon fresh lemon juice
1 garlic clove, minced
³⁄₄ teaspoon kosher salt, divided

¹⁄₂ teaspoon freshly ground black pepper, divided
1 pound turkey tenderloins, cut into 1-inch pieces
1 teaspoon lower-sodium soy sauce
¹⁄₄ teaspoon Marmite
4 (1¹⁄₂-ounce) hamburger buns, toasted
4 Bibb lettuce leaves
8 (¹⁄₄-inch-thick) slices tomato

1. Preheat oven to 400°.

2. Lightly coat eggplant with cooking spray; wrap in foil. Place eggplant on a jelly-roll pan; bake at 400° for 45 minutes or until very tender, turning once. Remove from foil; cool slightly. Cut eggplant in half. Carefully scoop out pulp to measure 1¼ cups; discard skin. Place pulp in a food processor; process until smooth. Reserve ¼ cup pureed pulp. Combine remaining pulp, 1 tablespoon parsley, 2 teaspoons oil, juice, and garlic. Stir in ½ teaspoon salt and ¼ teaspoon pepper; set aside.

3. To prepare grinder, place feed shaft, blade, and ¼-inch die plate in freezer 30 minutes or until well chilled. Assemble grinder just before grinding.

4. Arrange turkey pieces in a single layer on a jelly-roll pan, leaving space between each piece. Freeze 15 minutes or until meat is firm but not frozen. Combine meat and 2 teaspoons oil in a large bowl; toss to combine. Pass meat through meat grinder completely. Immediately pass meat through grinder a second time. Combine reserved ¼ cup eggplant puree, turkey, 1 tablespoon parsley, soy sauce, and Marmite in a large bowl. Divide mixture into 4 equal portions, gently shaping each into a ½-inch-thick patty. Press thumb in center of each patty, leaving a nickel-sized indentation. Cover and chill until ready to grill.

5. Preheat grill to medium-high heat.

6. Lightly coat patties with cooking spray; sprinkle with ¼ teaspoon salt and ¼ teaspoon pepper. Place patties on grill rack, and grill 4 minutes. Carefully turn patties over, and grill 3 minutes or until done. Place 1 patty on bottom half of each bun; top each serving with 1 lettuce leaf, 2 tomato slices, 1 tablespoon eggplant mixture, and top half of bun. (Reserve remaining eggplant mixture for another use.) Serves 4 (serving size: 1 burger)

CALORIES 291; FAT 8.2g (sat 1.6g, mono 4g, poly 1.8g); PROTEIN 32.7g; CARB 23.3g; FIBER 1.5g; CHOL 45mg; IRON 3.2mg; SODIUM 689mg; CALC 69mg

This burger has some of the same flavors as a popular sushi roll. Be sure to process the tuna using quick pulses to prevent the meat from being overworked and overheated by the blade.

Asian Tuna Burgers
Hands-on time: 46 min.   Total time: 51 min.

  6   tablespoons canola mayonnaise
 ¼   teaspoon grated lime rind
 1½ teaspoons fresh lime juice
  1   teaspoon sugar, divided
 4½ tablespoons seasoned rice vinegar, divided
 1½ cups thinly sliced English cucumber
 ¾   cup vertically sliced red onion
 1½ pounds tuna steaks, cut into 1-inch cubes

 ½   cup minced green onions
 1½ tablespoons lower-sodium soy sauce
  1   tablespoon grated peeled fresh ginger
 ¼   teaspoon salt
Cooking spray
  6   (1.6-ounce) sandwich buns
 ½   cup small cilantro sprigs

1. Preheat grill to medium-high heat.

2. Combine first 3 ingredients in a small bowl. Cover and chill.

3. Dissolve ¼ teaspoon sugar in 3 tablespoons vinegar in a medium bowl, stirring with a whisk. Add cucumber and red onion; toss to coat. Cover and chill.

4. Place tuna in a food processor; pulse until finely chopped. Combine chopped tuna, green onions, next 3 ingredients (through salt), 1½ tablespoons vinegar, and ¾ teaspoon sugar in a bowl. Divide mixture into 6 equal portions with moist hands, shaping each into a ½-inch-thick patty. Press thumb in center of each patty, leaving a nickel-sized indentation.

5. Place patties on grill rack coated with cooking spray; grill 4 minutes. Turn patties over; grill 4 minutes or until desired degree of doneness. Remove from grill; cover and let stand 5 minutes.

6. Spread 1 tablespoon mayonnaise mixture evenly on cut sides of each bun. Top bottom halves of buns with patties. Spoon cucumber mixture evenly on top of patties, using a slotted spoon. Arrange cilantro evenly over cucumber mixture. Cover with bun tops. Serve immediately. Serves 6 (serving size: 1 burger)

CALORIES 325; FAT 8.8g (sat 1.3g, mono 3.1g, poly 2.5g); PROTEIN 32g; CARB 28g; FIBER 1.8g; CHOL 51mg; IRON 2mg; SODIUM 772mg; CALC 73mg

Quick-pickled cukes give these burgers tart crunch. Panko and egg white hold the patties together. Use cilantro leaves as you would lettuce for herby freshness. For a sustainable seafood choice, purchase frozen or wild-caught fresh Alaskan salmon.

Hoisin-Glazed Salmon Burgers
with Pickled Cucumber

Hands-on time: 30 min. Total time: 38 min.

⅓ cup water
¼ cup cider vinegar
1 teaspoon sugar
½ teaspoon minced garlic
½ teaspoon minced peeled fresh ginger
¼ teaspoon crushed red pepper
24 thin English cucumber slices
½ cup panko (Japanese breadcrumbs)
⅓ cup thinly sliced green onions
2 tablespoons chopped fresh cilantro

1 tablespoon lower-sodium soy sauce
1½ teaspoons grated peeled fresh ginger
1 teaspoon grated lime rind
1 (1-pound) skinless center-cut salmon fillet, finely chopped
1 large egg white
1½ teaspoons dark sesame oil
1 tablespoon hoisin sauce
4 (1½-ounce) hamburger buns, toasted

1. Combine first 6 ingredients in a small saucepan; bring to a boil. Remove from heat; add cucumber. Let stand 30 minutes. Drain.

2. Combine panko and next 7 ingredients (through egg white) in a bowl, and stir well. Divide mixture into 4 equal portions, gently shaping each into a ½-inch-thick patty. Press thumb in center of each patty, leaving a nickel-sized indentation.

3. Heat a large cast-iron skillet over medium-high heat. Add sesame oil to pan; swirl to coat. Add patties; cook 3 minutes on each side or until desired degree of doneness. Brush tops of patties evenly with hoisin sauce; cook 30 seconds.

4. Place 1 patty on bottom half of each bun; top each patty with 6 cucumber slices and top half of bun. Serves 4 (serving size: 1 burger)

CALORIES 355; FAT 11.3g (sat 1.9g, mono 3.6g, poly 4.6g); PROTEIN 29.1g; CARB 31.2g; FIBER 1.9g; CHOL 63mg; IRON 2.6mg; SODIUM 502mg; CALC 89mg

For best results, choose salmon from the meaty center of the fish, and avoid portions cut from the tail section (where the body starts to taper). Tail-end flesh contains more connective tissue than center-cut fillets. Use black sesame seed buns, if available.

Salmon Burgers

Hands-on time: 17 min.   Total time: 17 min.

2 tablespoons Dijon mustard, divided
2 teaspoons grated lemon rind
1 (1-pound) skinless center-cut salmon fillet, cut into 1-inch pieces, divided
2 tablespoons minced fresh tarragon
1 tablespoon finely chopped shallots (about 1 small)
½ teaspoon kosher salt
¼ teaspoon freshly ground black pepper
1 tablespoon honey
1 cup arugula
½ cup thinly sliced red onion
1 teaspoon fresh lemon juice
1 teaspoon extra-virgin olive oil
Cooking spray
4 (1½-ounce) hamburger buns, toasted

1. Place 1 tablespoon mustard, rind, and ¼ pound salmon in a food processor; process until smooth. Spoon puree into a large bowl. Place ¾ pound salmon in food processor; pulse 6 times or until coarsely chopped. Fold chopped salmon, tarragon, shallots, salt, and pepper into puree. Divide mixture into 4 equal portions, gently shaping each into a ½-inch-thick patty. Cover and chill until ready to grill.

2. Preheat grill to medium heat.

3. Combine 1 tablespoon mustard and honey in a small bowl; set aside.

4. Combine arugula, onion, juice, and oil in a medium bowl; set aside.

5. Lightly coat both sides of patties with cooking spray. Place patties on grill rack; grill 2 minutes. Carefully turn patties, and grill 1 minute or until desired degree of doneness. Spread 1½ teaspoons honey mixture on bottom half of each bun; top each serving with 1 patty, ¼ cup arugula mixture, and top half of bun. Serves 4 (serving size: 1 burger)

CALORIES 372; FAT 16g (sat 3.2g, mono 5.9g, poly 5.8g); PROTEIN 27.3g; CARB 28.2g; FIBER 1.5g; CHOL 67mg; IRON 2.1mg; SODIUM 569mg; CALC 92mg

Marinated tofu slices acquire a golden crust when grilled; the olive-garlic mayonnaise adds a Mediterranean flavor. Serve with grilled asparagus for a simple side.

Grilled Lemon-Basil Tofu Burgers

Hands-on time: 28 min.   Total time: 1 hr. 28 min.

1/3 cup finely chopped fresh basil
  2 teaspoons grated lemon rind
1/4 cup fresh lemon juice
  2 tablespoons Dijon mustard
  2 tablespoons honey
  1 tablespoon extra-virgin olive oil
1/2 teaspoon salt
1/4 teaspoon freshly ground black pepper
  4 garlic cloves, minced and divided

  1 pound firm or extra-firm tofu, drained
Cooking spray
1/3 cup finely chopped pitted kalamata olives
  3 tablespoons reduced-fat sour cream
  3 tablespoons light mayonnaise
  6 (1½-ounce) hamburger buns
  6 (¼-inch-thick) slices tomato
  1 cup trimmed watercress

1. Combine first 8 ingredients and 3 garlic cloves in a small bowl. Cut tofu crosswise into 6 slices. Pat each slice dry with paper towels. Place tofu slices on a jelly-roll pan. Brush both sides of tofu slices with lemon juice mixture; reserve remaining juice mixture. Let tofu stand 1 hour.

2. Preheat grill to medium-high heat.

3. Place tofu slices on grill rack coated with cooking spray; grill 3 minutes on each side. Brush tofu with reserved juice mixture.

4. Combine 1 minced garlic clove, chopped olives, sour cream, and mayonnaise in a small bowl; stir well. Spread about 1½ tablespoons mayonnaise mixture over bottom half of each bun; top each with 1 tomato slice, 1 tofu slice, about 2 tablespoons watercress, and bun top. Serves 6 (serving size: 1 burger)

CALORIES 276; FAT 11.3g (sat 1.9g, mono 5.7g, poly 2.2g); PROTEIN 10.5g; CARB 35g; FIBER 1.5g; CHOL 5mg; IRON 2.4mg; SODIUM 743mg; CALC 101mg

Homemade Quick Black Bean Burgers

Hands-on time: 19 min.   Total time: 19 min.

1 (15.25-ounce) can black beans, rinsed, drained, and divided
5 (1½-ounce) hamburger buns, divided
3 tablespoons olive oil, divided
1 teaspoon grated lime rind
¾ teaspoon chili powder
½ teaspoon chopped fresh oregano
¼ teaspoon salt
2 garlic cloves, minced

1 large egg white, lightly beaten
¼ cup mashed avocado
2 tablespoons salsa
½ teaspoon hot sauce (optional)
4 (0.67-ounce) slices reduced-fat Monterey Jack cheese with jalapeño peppers
4 (¼-inch-thick) slices red onion
16 spinach leaves

1. Place ½ cup beans in a medium bowl; mash slightly with a potato masher. Tear 1 bun into large pieces, and place in a food processor; pulse 4 times or until crumbs measure 1 cup. Stir crumbs, 1 tablespoon oil, next 6 ingredients (through egg white), and remaining beans into mashed beans.

2. Preheat broiler.

3. Divide bean mixture into 4 equal portions with moist hands, shaping each into a 3-inch-round patty.

4. Heat 2 tablespoons oil in a large nonstick skillet over medium-high heat. Add patties to pan. Reduce heat to medium, and cook 3 minutes or until bottoms are browned. Carefully turn patties over; cook 3 minutes or until bottoms are browned.

5. While patties cook, arrange 4 buns, cut sides up, on a baking sheet. Broil 1 to 2 minutes or until toasted.

6. Combine avocado, salsa, and, if desired, hot sauce in a small bowl. Spread 1½ tablespoons avocado mixture on bottom half of each bun; top each serving with 1 patty, 1 cheese slice, 1 onion slice, 4 spinach leaves, and bun top. Serves 4 (serving size: 1 burger)

CALORIES 400; FAT 19.1g (sat 5g, mono 10.5g, poly 2.6g); PROTEIN 15.7g; CARB 40g; FIBER 6g; CHOL 14mg; IRON 3.9mg; SODIUM 740mg; CALC 144mg

Melty Topping: **THE TOP-RATED BITE AT FLORIDA'S STATE FAIR IN 2011** was a cheeseburger topped with bacon, lettuce, tomato, and a scoop of ice cream coated with crushed cereal and deep fried.

Satisfy your burger craving with a meatless mushroom stacker layered with Gorgonzola cheese. If you're not a fan of blue cheese, substitute crumbled goat cheese and omit the mayo.

Portobello Cheeseburgers

Hands-on time: 14 min.   Total time: 14 min.

2   teaspoons olive oil
4   (4-inch) portobello mushroom caps
¼   teaspoon salt
¼   teaspoon black pepper
1   tablespoon minced fresh garlic

¼   cup (1 ounce) crumbled Gorgonzola cheese
3   tablespoons reduced-fat mayonnaise
4   (2-ounce) sandwich rolls
2   cups arugula
½   cup sliced bottled roasted red bell peppers

1. Heat oil in a large nonstick skillet over medium-high heat. Sprinkle mushrooms with salt and pepper. Add mushrooms to pan; cook 4 minutes or until tender, turning once. Add garlic to pan; sauté 30 seconds. Remove from heat.

2. Combine cheese and mayonnaise, stirring well. Spread about 2 tablespoons mayonnaise mixture over bottom half of each roll; top each serving with ½ cup arugula and 1 mushroom. Top evenly with peppers, and cover with top halves of rolls. Serves 4 (serving size: 1 burger)

CALORIES 262; FAT 9.9g (sat 3g, mono 3.6g, poly 2.3g); PROTEIN 8.5g; CARB 33.8g; FIBER 1.7g; CHOL 9mg; IRON 2.4mg; SODIUM 689mg; CALC 159mg

These vegetable patties are meant to be soft. Prepare through step 2 the day before, since the mixture is easier to work with once it has been refrigerated overnight and the flavors have had time to marry. Amchur (or amchoor) powder is a tart, green mango–based seasoning. Omit it if you can't find it. Serve with a spicy tomato or mango chutney.

Vegetable Burgers

Hands-on time: 30 min.   Total time: 9 hr.

1   cup canned chickpeas (garbanzo beans), rinsed and drained
1   cup chopped fresh cilantro
½   cup coarsely chopped carrot
1¼ teaspoons kosher salt
1   teaspoon garam masala
1   teaspoon amchur powder
½   teaspoon freshly ground black pepper
¼   teaspoon ground red pepper

1   jalapeño pepper, seeded and quartered
2   pounds red potatoes, peeled and cut into 2-inch pieces
¼   cup coarsely chopped red onion
1   cup dry breadcrumbs
2   tablespoons canola oil, divided
2⅔ cups spinach
8   red onion slices
4   (6-inch) whole-grain pitas, cut in half

1. Place first 9 ingredients in a food processor; process until finely chopped.

2. Place potatoes in a large saucepan; cover with water. Bring to a boil; cook 13 minutes. Add chopped onion; cook 2 minutes or until potatoes are tender. Drain; cool 10 minutes. Place mixture in a large bowl; mash with a potato masher or fork. Stir in chickpea mixture and breadcrumbs; cover and chill 8 hours or overnight.

3. Divide potato mixture into 8 equal portions (about ⅔ cup mixture), shaping each portion into a ½-inch-thick patty. Heat 1 tablespoon oil in a large skillet over medium heat. Add 4 patties to pan; cook 5 minutes on each side or until browned and heated through. Repeat procedure with 1 tablespoon oil and 4 patties. Place ⅓ cup spinach, 1 patty, and 1 onion slice in each pita half. Serves 8 (serving size: 1 stuffed pita half)

CALORIES 300; FAT 5.5g (sat 0.6g, mono 2.6g, poly 1.8g); PROTEIN 8.4g; CARB 56.4g; FIBER 6.7g; CHOL 0mg; IRON 2.7mg; SODIUM 628mg; CALC 63mg

Sage and feta give this burger a Mediterranean flavor, and there's crunch, too, from toasted almonds. The bean mixture is sticky, so it helps to wet the measuring cup before scooping to form patties.

White Bean and Sage Pita Burgers

Hands-on time: 27 min.   Total time: 27 min.

1 tablespoon extra-virgin olive oil, divided
½ cup chopped onion
2 garlic cloves, minced
⅓ cup old-fashioned rolled oats
⅓ cup sliced almonds, toasted
2 tablespoons cornstarch
1½ teaspoons chopped fresh sage
2 teaspoons Dijon mustard
½ teaspoon salt
¼ teaspoon freshly ground black pepper

2 (15-ounce) cans cannellini beans, rinsed and drained
1 large egg, lightly beaten
½ cup reduced-fat sour cream
2 tablespoons grated fresh onion
2 tablespoons crumbled feta cheese
3 (6-inch) pitas, cut in half
6 green leaf lettuce leaves
6 (¼-inch-thick) slices tomato

1. Heat a large nonstick skillet over medium heat. Add 1 teaspoon oil to pan, and swirl to coat. Add ½ cup chopped onion and garlic; cook 2 minutes, stirring frequently. Place mixture in food processor. Add oats and next 8 ingredients (through egg); process until smooth.

2. Wipe pan with a paper towel. Return pan to medium heat. Add 2 teaspoons oil to pan, and swirl to coat. Spoon bean mixture into a ½-cup measuring cup, 1 portion at a time. Using a rubber spatula, carefully remove bean mixture into pan. (Bean mixture will be very soft and sticky.) Using spatula, shape mixture into a ¾-inch-thick round patty. Repeat procedure 5 times to form 6 patties. Cook 8 minutes or until golden, turning after 4 minutes.

3. Combine sour cream, 2 tablespoons grated onion, and cheese in a small bowl. Spread about 2 tablespoons sour cream mixture in each pita half. Arrange 1 lettuce leaf, 1 tomato slice, and 1 bean patty in each pita half. Serves 6 (serving size: 1 stuffed pita half)

CALORIES 315; FAT 10g (sat 3.1g, mono 4.7g, poly 1.5g); PROTEIN 13.2g; CARB 43.8g; FIBER 6g; CHOL 40mg; IRON 3.8mg; SODIUM 471mg; CALC 158mg

SECRETS TO A TASTY, JUICY, HEALTHY BURGER

Mastering a light burger is a bit tricky: Without help, lean meat often leads to dry patties, and ground poultry often tastes bland. Try these secrets to make a better burger.

SECRET #1:
GRIND YOUR OWN MEAT

There's no question: Fresh-ground beef, lamb, or turkey yields a superior, juicier burger. That includes meat you've had ground to order at a butcher shop or supermarket and loosely wrapped (tight wraps compress the meat).

Preground supermarket beef is often made from trim and scraps. The result can be inconsistent flavor. Not only that, but preground meat compresses the longer it sits in tight packaging, which affects texture. So it's much better to start with whole cuts of beef and grind them yourself, or get the butcher to do it at the shop or supermarket.

At home, an old-fashioned hand grinder or a grinder attachment for your stand mixer is ideal. You can also use your food processor; in that case, be sure to work in small batches, pulsing the meat 8 to 10 times or until the meat is finely chopped. (Be careful that the meat doesn't turn into a puree.)

No matter what grinding tool you use, it's important to keep the meat and the grinding equipment as cold as possible. If the meat gets too warm, it will begin to smear rather than grind cleanly, giving the finished product a nasty mashed texture. Putting the meat and grinding equipment in the freezer for 30 minutes beforehand helps guarantee optimum results.

No time? In a pinch, you can, of course, use preground beef, lamb, or turkey for these recipes. The spices and condiments will still produce a better, lighter burger.

SECRET #2:
MAKE A PANADE

Steal a trick from meatball recipes, and make a panade, a mash of milk and bread that keeps meatballs tender and moist. You can also use a panade as an opportunity to add flavor. For example, the recipe for Spicy Poblano Burgers with Pickled Red Onions and Chipotle Cream (page 100) calls for a panade mixed with warm spices often found in Mexican chorizo sausage, such as coriander, paprika, and cumin.

SECRET #3:
ADD FLAVOR-ENHANCING, JUICY INGREDIENTS

 You can give a burger made from mild, low-fat meats like turkey some of the meaty richness of beef: Just add some rich, meaty flavors! Here's the kitchen science: Beef and other red meats contain compounds called glutamates. So do soy sauce and Marmite, which is a powerfully strong yeast extract found in supermarkets. You'll see both used in the Turkey

Burgers with Roasted Eggplant (page 114), lending the burger the umami flavors of real red meat. Try this trick with other poultry, too.

To add juiciness to ground poultry and lean meats, try adding a cooked, pureed vegetable. The Turkey Burgers with Roasted Eggplant get their moisture from roasted eggplant mixed with olive oil. You don't have to keep your veg bland, either: In the turkey burger recipe, the eggplant is flavored with parsley, lemon, and garlic—the same ingredients found in baba ghanoush, a popular Middle Eastern dip.

SECRET #4:
THE THUMBPRINT TRICK

Overworking and compressing the meat results in dense, dry hamburgers. Form the patty gently; then make a small indentation in the center of each one with your thumb, as shown below (a grill pan is a good backup on a day too rainy for the barbecue). The indentation helps the patty hold its shape—rather than swelling—during cooking.

8 GOOD BREADS

Shake up your burger routine and reach for a different roll: A variety of sizes and toppings can add fun and flavor. Split and toast buns for a sturdier, less squishy bite.

1. Onion Roll: Topped with onions, onion rolls have a subtle pungency.

2. Kaiser Roll: With a distinctive star shape on top, the Kaiser roll has a crisp crust, giving a burger a little chew.

3. Sesame Seed Bun: A fast-food-joint staple. Sesame seeds top the standard soft burger bun.

4. Slider Bun: They're the perfect size for a mini burger, so stock up on these for a party. Keep the patties thin—about ¼-inch thick before cooking—to prevent burgers that slide apart.

5. Poppy Seed Bun: Poppy seeds add a fun crunch.

6. Bakery Roll: Wander away from the bread aisle and over to a bakery for fun options: You'll find different shapes and textures to complement your creation.

7. Whole-Wheat Bun: A healthy choice with a slightly nutty flavor, whole-wheat breads can come off a little dry, so choose a juicy burger or condiments that will compensate.

8. Deli-Style Bun: Perfect for Sloppy Joes and hearty burgers, deli-style hard rolls are crunchy outside, light and chewy inside.

6 GOOD CHEESES

Sure, you can always rely on American for a classic cheeseburger, but why not experiment with something new? Cheese can marry burger ingredients together or bring its own personality to the mix, with nuttiness, tang, pungency, and even heat.

1. Pepper-Jack: Monterey Jack cheese mixed with chile peppers, pepper-Jack adds a spicy kick to burgers. Try it for a Southwestern flair.

2. Blue: A classic combo with beef, blue cheese is a great partner with rich, meaty flavors. In general, older blue cheese is stronger and more pungent, so choose a young cheese if you want a mild hit.

3. Cheddar: A great melting, semi-hard cow's milk cheese available in a range of flavors and colors. Cheddar can be subtle enough to simply pull a burger together, or sharp enough to make an otherwise bland sandwich sing. Seek out artisanal cheddar for a treat.

4. Brick: Smooth and slightly sweet, especially when young (the flavor gets stronger as the cheese ages). It's available mild, aged, and with caraway seeds.

5. Swiss: Pale, slightly nutty, and famous for its eyes, Swiss melts beautifully and pairs well with beef, chicken, and turkey.

6. Colby-Jack: Bright orange colby and off-white Jack cheese are marbled together for a fun-to-look-at effect. Colby-Jack melts well.

6 GOOD BURGER TOPPINGS

Make your own backyard burger special with these toppings—many also taste great on a sandwich or as a dip for fries and chips.

Jalapeño-Cilantro Mayo

Hands-on time: 18 min.   Total time: 18 min.

Combine 1 tablespoon fresh lime juice and 1 garlic clove, minced, in a small bowl; let stand 5 minutes. Stir in 1 cup canola mayonnaise, ¼ cup finely chopped seeded jalapeño pepper, and 2 tablespoons chopped fresh cilantro. Cover and chill. Serves 18 (serving size: 1 tablespoon)

CALORIES 41; FAT 4g (sat 0g, mono 2.2g, poly 1.3g); PROTEIN 0g; CARB 0.2g; FIBER 0g; CHOL 0mg; IRON 0mg; SODIUM 80mg; CALC 1mg

Tonkatsu Mayo

Hands-on time: 5 min.   Total time: 5 min.

Combine ½ cup organic ketchup with agave nectar, ⅓ cup canola mayonnaise, 1 tablespoon Worcestershire sauce, 1 teaspoon dry mustard, and 1 tablespoon lower-sodium soy sauce in a small bowl, stirring with a whisk. Serves 13 (serving size: 1 tablespoon)

CALORIES 56; FAT 4.6g (sat 0.4g, mono 2.5g, poly 1.2g); PROTEIN 0.1g; CARB 2.8g; FIBER 0g; CHOL 2mg; IRON 0.1mg; SODIUM 161mg; CALC 2mg

Pomegranate-Rosemary Ketchup

Hands-on time: 5 min.   Total time: 5 min.

Combine ¾ cup organic ketchup with agave nectar, 2 tablespoons pomegranate molasses, and 1 tablespoon chopped fresh rosemary in a small bowl. Serves 14 (serving size: 1 tablespoon)

CALORIES 35; FAT 0g; PROTEIN 0g; CARB 7.3g; FIBER 0g; CHOL 0mg; IRON 0.3mg; SODIUM 107mg; CALC 9mg

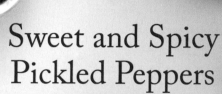

Sambal Ketchup

Hands-on time: 7 min. Total time: 7 min.

Combine ¾ cup organic ketchup, 1 tablespoon sambal oelek (ground fresh chile paste), and 2 teaspoons grated shallots. Serves 12 (serving size: about 1 tablespoon)

CALORIES 20; FAT 0g; PROTEIN 0g; CARB 4.1g; FIBER 0g; CHOL 0mg; IRON 0mg; SODIUM 153mg; CALC 0mg

Quick Pickled Onion Relish

Hands-on time: 12 min. Total time: 12 min.

Combine ½ cup rice vinegar, ¼ cup water, 3 tablespoons sugar, ¼ teaspoon salt, and ¼ teaspoon freshly ground black pepper in a medium bowl. Add 1 cup diced red onion, 1 cup diced English cucumber, and 1 cup diced multicolored cherry tomatoes; stir well. Cover and refrigerate until ready to serve or up to 24 hours. Serve with a slotted spoon. Serves 40 (serving size: 1 tablespoon)

CALORIES 6; FAT 0g; PROTEIN 0.1g; CARB 1.5g; FIBER 0.1g; CHOL 0mg; IRON 0mg; SODIUM 15mg; CALC 2mg

Sweet and Spicy Pickled Peppers

Hands-on time: 19 min. Total time: 2 hr. 26 min.

Remove stems and seeds from 1 (8-ounce) package mini bell peppers (assorted colors) and 2 small jalapeño peppers; cut peppers into thin rings. Combine ⅓ cup cider vinegar, ⅓ cup water, 3 tablespoons sugar, and ⅛ teaspoon salt in a 2-quart saucepan. Bring to a boil, and stir in pepper rings. Remove from heat. Cool to room temperature. Cover and chill 2 to 3 hours. Serve with a slotted spoon. Serves 32 (serving size: 1 tablespoon)

CALORIES 8; FAT 0g; PROTEIN 0.1g; CARB 2g; FIBER 0.1g; CHOL 0mg; IRON 0mg; SODIUM 10mg; CALC 1mg

100-CALORIE BURGER COMBOS

A quarter-pound of lean ground sirloin and a hearty whole-grain bun start you out at 250 calories. Now you're ready for some tasty toppings.

HOW DO PATTY PROTEINS COMPARE?

QUARTER-POUND PATTIES, COOKED:

Lamb (23% fat)
240 calories, 9g sat fat

Chuck (20% fat)
209 calories, 5g sat fat

Turkey (13% fat)
193 calories, 3g sat fat

Bison (grass-fed)
124 calories, 2.5g sat fat

Lean Sirloin (5% fat)
140 calories, 2g sat fat

Turkey Breast (1% fat)
91 calories, 0.5g sat fat

Soy Crumbles
90 calories, 0g sat fat

THE AMERICAN STANDARD

2 teaspoons ketchup +
3 dill pickle chips + 1 thin slice
sharp cheddar cheese +
green leaf lettuce +
1 heirloom tomato slice

ZESTY PESTO & TOMATO

1 tablespoon pesto +
2 heirloom tomato slices +
1 tablespoon crumbled feta

THE POACHED EGGER

1 large poached egg +
1 tablespoon fresh salsa +
green leaf lettuce +
1 tablespoon queso fresco

AVOCADO-MANGO TANGO

2 thin slices avocado +
2 tablespoons mango salsa +
1 tablespoon chopped cilantro +
2 tablespoons shredded
Monterey Jack cheese

BEEFY CAPRESE

1 ounce fresh buffalo mozzarella +
½ teaspoon drizzle extra-virgin olive
oil + 2 heirloom tomato slices +
6 basil leaves

GRECIAN GOURMET

1 tablespoon chopped red onion +
2 tablespoons crumbled feta +
¼ cup fresh spinach tossed with
½ teaspoon extra-virgin olive oil +
1 ounce tzatziki sauce

SUN-DRIED SUMMER

2 tablespoons chopped sun-dried
tomatoes + ¼ cup fresh spinach +
1 ounce goat cheese

SANDWICHES

SLICE, SLATHER, STUFF, SAVOR.

(swipe that bit of mustard
that's squishing out on the side...)

Your family won't believe this comforting sandwich is light. For the kids, use beef broth instead of beer, and try mild wheat bread.

Mushroom and Provolone Patty Melts

Hands-on time: 27 min.   Total time: 27 min.

¾ cup thinly sliced onion, divided
1 pound 93% lean ground beef
¼ teaspoon salt, divided
¼ teaspoon freshly ground black pepper, divided
1 tablespoon olive oil, divided
1 (8-ounce) package presliced cremini mushrooms

1½ teaspoons all-purpose flour
¼ cup dark lager beer
8 (1.1-ounce) slices rye bread
Cooking spray
4 (0.67-ounce) slices reduced-fat provolone cheese

1. Chop enough of the sliced onion to measure ¼ cup. Combine chopped onion, beef, ⅛ teaspoon salt, and ⅛ teaspoon pepper in a medium bowl. Divide beef mixture into 4 equal portions with moist hands, shaping each into a 4-inch oval patty. Press thumb in center of each patty, leaving a nickel-sized indentation.

2. Heat a large nonstick skillet over medium-high heat. Add 1 teaspoon oil to pan, swirling to coat. Add patties; cook 4 minutes on each side or until done.

3. Heat 2 teaspoons oil in a medium skillet over medium-high heat. Add mushrooms, remaining onion, ⅛ teaspoon salt, and ⅛ teaspoon pepper; sauté 3 minutes. Sprinkle flour over mushroom mixture; cook 1 minute, stirring constantly. Stir in beer; cook 30 seconds or until thick. Remove from heat; keep warm.

4. When patties are done, remove from large pan. Wipe pan clean; heat over medium-high heat. Coat 1 side of each bread slice with cooking spray. Place 4 bread slices, coated sides down, in pan. Top each with 1 patty, 1 cheese slice, and one-fourth of mushroom mixture. Top with remaining bread slices; coat with cooking spray. Cook 2 minutes on each side or until browned. Serves 4 (serving size: 1 sandwich)

CALORIES 407; FAT 13g (sat 4.4g, mono 5.8g, poly 1.5g); PROTEIN 36.2g; CARB 37g; FIBER 4.5g; CHOL 70mg; IRON 3.9mg; SODIUM 770mg; CALC 213mg

Meaty, gooey, and delightfully messy, our lightened version of a Philly cheesesteak is the type of sandwich you'll crave all year. Two kinds of cheese make the sauce creamy and flavorful.

Philly Cheesesteaks

Hands-on time: 35 min. Total time: 45 min.

- 1 (12-ounce) flank steak, trimmed
- ¼ teaspoon kosher salt
- ¼ teaspoon freshly ground black pepper
- 2 (5-inch) portobello mushroom caps
- 2 teaspoons olive oil, divided
- 1 cup thinly sliced onion
- 1½ cups thinly sliced green bell pepper
- 2 teaspoons minced garlic
- ½ teaspoon Worcestershire sauce
- ½ teaspoon lower-sodium soy sauce
- 2 teaspoons all-purpose flour
- ½ cup 1% low-fat milk
- 2 tablespoons grated Parmigiano-Reggiano cheese
- 1 ounce provolone cheese, torn into small pieces
- ¼ teaspoon dry mustard
- 4 (3-ounce) hoagie rolls, toasted

1. Place beef in freezer 15 minutes. Cut beef across grain into thin slices. Sprinkle beef with salt and black pepper. Remove brown gills from undersides of mushroom caps using a spoon; discard gills. Remove stems; discard. Thinly slice mushroom caps; cut slices in half crosswise.

2. Heat a large nonstick skillet over medium-high heat. Add 1 teaspoon oil to pan; swirl to coat. Add beef to pan; sauté 2 minutes or until beef loses its pink color, stirring constantly. Remove beef from pan. Add 1 teaspoon oil to pan. Add onion; sauté 3 minutes. Add mushrooms, bell pepper, and garlic; sauté 6 minutes. Return beef to pan; sauté 1 minute or until thoroughly heated and vegetables are tender. Remove from heat. Stir in Worcestershire sauce and soy sauce; keep warm.

3. Place flour in a small saucepan; gradually add milk, stirring with a whisk until blended. Bring to a simmer over medium heat; cook 1 minute or until slightly thick. Remove from heat. Add cheeses and mustard, stirring until smooth. Keep warm (mixture will thicken as it cools).

4. Hollow out top and bottom halves of bread, leaving a ½-inch-thick shell; reserve torn bread for another use. Divide beef mixture evenly among bottom halves of hoagies. Drizzle sauce evenly over beef mixture; replace top halves. Serves 4 (serving size: 1 sandwich)

CALORIES 397; FAT 12.4g (sat 4.9g, mono 4.7g, poly 1.6g); PROTEIN 30.8g; CARB 44.1g; FIBER 3.7g; CHOL 37mg; IRON 4.6mg; SODIUM 637mg; CALC 213mg

With sauerkraut, corned beef, and rye bread, sodium is a serious issue in a traditional Reuben. Add dressing and cheese, and the saturated fat and calories start to climb, too. Not to fear: Our lighter, lower-sodium version is just as delicious. Chili sauce is a ketchup-based sauce. If you can't find it, substitute ketchup.

Reuben Sandwiches

Hands-on time: 18 min.   Total time: 18 min.

Dressing:
- ¼ cup canola mayonnaise
- 1 tablespoon chili sauce
- 2 teaspoons finely minced dill pickle
- 1 teaspoon Worcestershire sauce
- ½ teaspoon grated onion

Sandwiches:
- 8 (¾-ounce) slices rye bread
- 3 ounces Swiss cheese, shaved (about ¾ cup)
- 4 ounces lower-sodium corned beef, thinly sliced
- 1 cup organic sauerkraut, drained well

1. Preheat broiler.

2. To prepare dressing, combine first 5 ingredients in a small bowl, stirring well.

3. To prepare sandwiches, place bread slices in a single layer on a heavy baking sheet. Broil bread 1½ minutes or until toasted. Turn bread over; broil 1 minute or until lightly toasted. Remove 4 slices. Divide cheese evenly among remaining 4 slices, sprinkling it over lightly toasted sides. Broil 1 minute or until cheese melts. Spread about 1½ tablespoons dressing over cheese-coated side of each bread slice; top each serving with 1 ounce corned beef, ¼ cup sauerkraut, and remaining bread slices. Serve immediately. Serves 4 (serving size: 1 sandwich)

CALORIES 336; FAT 19.9g (sat 5.6g, mono 8.1g, poly 3.6g); PROTEIN 14.7g; CARB 24.2g; FIBER 3.4g; CHOL 40mg; IRON 1.9mg; SODIUM 790mg; CALC 212mg

Serve up mini versions of a weeknight favorite. Make the sauce ahead of time, if you like. Just reheat it and toast the buns to finish the sliders.

Sloppy Joe Sliders
Hands-on time: 17 min.   Total time: 17 min.

1 large carrot	1 tablespoon Dijon mustard
¾ cup prechopped onion	1 tablespoon Worcestershire sauce
10 ounces 92% lean ground beef	1 tablespoon tomato paste
1 teaspoon garlic powder	1 teaspoon red wine vinegar
1 teaspoon chili powder	1 (8-ounce) can no-salt-added tomato sauce
¼ teaspoon freshly ground black pepper	8 slider buns
¼ cup ketchup	

1. Preheat broiler.

2. Heat a large nonstick skillet over medium-high heat. While pan is heating, grate carrot. Add carrot, onion, and beef to pan; cook 6 minutes or until beef is browned and vegetables are tender. Add garlic powder, chili powder, and pepper; cook 1 minute.

3. Combine ketchup and next 5 ingredients (through tomato sauce) in a small bowl. Add ketchup mixture to pan, stirring to coat beef mixture evenly. Simmer 5 minutes or until thick.

4. While sauce thickens, arrange buns, cut sides up, in a single layer on a baking sheet. Broil 2 minutes or until lightly toasted. Place about ¼ cup beef mixture on bottom half of each of 8 buns; top each slider with top half of bun. Serves 4 (serving size: 2 sliders)

CALORIES 373; FAT 10g (sat 3.6g, mono 3.5g, poly 2.3g); PROTEIN 23.1g; CARB 52.2g; FIBER 4.2g; CHOL 38mg; IRON 4mg; SODIUM 736mg; CALC 111mg

Piled high with steak and veggies, the real treat on this sandwich is the sauce, a pesto mayonnaise. Use sirloin for a more tender bite than you get with cuts like flank steak.

Steak Baguettes with Pesto Mayo

Hands-on time: 20 min.   Total time: 20 min.

1 (12-ounce) boneless beef sirloin steak (about 1 inch thick), trimmed
¼ teaspoon kosher salt
⅛ teaspoon freshly ground black pepper
2 tablespoons canola mayonnaise
2 tablespoons refrigerated pesto

1 (12-ounce) piece white or whole-grain baguette, split in half horizontally
1 cup packed arugula (about 1 ounce)
3 (⅛-inch-thick) slices red onion
2 plum tomatoes, thinly sliced lengthwise

1. Heat a grill pan over medium-high heat. Sprinkle steak with salt and pepper. Add steak to pan, and cook 2½ minutes on each side or until desired degree of doneness. Remove steak from pan, and let stand 5 minutes. Cut steak across grain into thin slices.

2. Combine mayonnaise and pesto, stirring until well blended. Spread mayonnaise mixture evenly over cut sides of bread. Layer bottom half of bread with arugula, red onion, steak, and tomato; top with top half of bread. Cut sandwich diagonally into 4 equal pieces. Serves 4 (serving size: 1 sandwich piece)

CALORIES 346; FAT 9.1g (sat 1.6g, mono 4.6g, poly 1.4g); PROTEIN 21g; CARB 41.4g; FIBER 2.3g; CHOL 26mg; IRON 3.3mg; SODIUM 701mg; CALC 41mg

This upscale twist on the traditional breakfast sandwich features sweet caramelized onion and peppery arugula. A fresh fruit salad would be a good accompaniment. Skip the hot sauce for a family-friendly version.

Bacon and Egg Sandwiches with Caramelized Onions and Arugula

Hands-on time: 32 min. Total time: 32 min.

4 center-cut bacon slices
2 cups thinly sliced onion
1 tablespoon water
1/2 teaspoon Mexican hot sauce
1 1/2 teaspoons butter
Dash of sugar

1 teaspoon canola oil, divided
4 (1/2-ounce) slices whole-wheat bread
2 large eggs
1/8 teaspoon salt
1/4 teaspoon freshly ground black pepper
1 cup arugula

1. Cook bacon in a nonstick skillet over medium heat until crisp (about 8 minutes). Remove bacon from pan, reserving drippings; drain on paper towels. Add onion, 1 tablespoon water, and hot sauce to drippings in pan; cover and cook 3 minutes. Stir in butter and sugar; cover and cook 3 minutes. Uncover and cook 5 minutes or until golden brown, stirring frequently. Set aside; keep warm.

2. Heat a large nonstick skillet over medium-high heat. Add 1/2 teaspoon oil to pan; swirl to coat. Place bread in pan, and cook 3 minutes on each side or until lightly browned. Set aside, and keep warm.

3. Recoat pan with 1/2 teaspoon oil. Crack eggs into pan, and cook 2 minutes. Gently turn eggs, 1 at a time; cook 1 minute or until desired degree of doneness. Sprinkle evenly with salt and black pepper.

4. Place 1 bread slice on each of 2 plates; arrange arugula evenly over bread. Place onion mixture, 2 bacon slices, and 1 egg over each serving; top with remaining bread slices. Serve immediately. Serves 2 (serving size: 1 sandwich)

CALORIES 278; FAT 13.8g (sat 4.8g, mono 5.8g, poly 2.3g); PROTEIN 15.6g; CARB 23.6g; FIBER 4.1g; CHOL 204mg; IRON 2mg; SODIUM 587mg; CALC 103mg

Use this recipe as a panini template, and customize it to your liking. Use hollowed-out focaccia or ciabatta, or try different herbs and cheese, for example. You can use the cast-iron skillet trick whenever you need to improvise a panini press.

Classic Italian Panini with Prosciutto and Fresh Mozzarella

Hands-on time: 21 min. Total time: 21 min.

1 (12-ounce) loaf French bread, cut in half horizontally
¼ cup reduced-fat mayonnaise
1 cup (4 ounces) shredded fresh mozzarella cheese, divided

2 tablespoons chopped fresh basil
2 ounces very thinly sliced prosciutto
2 plum tomatoes, thinly sliced
Cooking spray

1. Hollow out top and bottom halves of bread, leaving a ½-inch-thick shell; reserve torn bread for another use. Spread 2 tablespoons mayonnaise over cut side of each bread half. Sprinkle ½ cup cheese and basil on bottom half of loaf. Top evenly with tomato slices, prosciutto, and ½ cup cheese. Cover with top half of loaf. Cut filled loaf crosswise into 4 equal pieces.

2. Heat a grill pan over medium heat. Coat pan with cooking spray. Add sandwiches to pan. Place a cast-iron or other heavy skillet on top of sandwiches; press gently to flatten sandwiches. Cook 3 minutes on each side or until bread is toasted (leave cast-iron skillet on sandwiches while they cook). Remove from heat and serve immediately. Serves 4 (serving size: 1 sandwich)

CALORIES 316; FAT 10.6g (sat 4.8g, mono 2.3g, poly 1.9g); PROTEIN 16.1g; CARB 39.9g; FIBER 2g; CHOL 31mg; IRON 2.8mg; SODIUM 799mg; CALC 196mg

Straight from the Funnies: **CARTOONIST MURAT "CHIC" YOUNG INTRODUCED THE DAGWOOD SANDWICH** in his 1936 comic strip *Blondie* when his character, Dagwood Bumstead, created a towering sandwich with everything in the fridge.

A Dagwood sandwich, popularized by the comic strip character Dagwood Bumstead, is characterized by layers of sodium- and fat-laden meats and cheeses. We've slimmed ours down by using no-salt-added and lower-sodium deli meats and lower-fat cheeses held together with a tasty homemade spread.

Dagwood Sandwiches

Hands-on time: 17 min.   Total time: 17 min.

¼ cup canola mayonnaise
1 tablespoon Dijon mustard
2 teaspoons dill pickle relish
8 (1-ounce) slices 10-grain bread, cut in half diagonally
4 small curly leaf lettuce leaves
8 (¼-inch-thick) slices tomato
3 ounces thinly sliced deli no-salt-added roasted turkey breast
2 (0.7-ounce) slices reduced-fat cheddar cheese, cut in half diagonally

3 ounces thinly sliced deli 25%-lower-sodium Black Forest ham
2 (¾-ounce) slices reduced-fat Swiss cheese, cut in half diagonally
8 thinly sliced green bell pepper rings
16 thin slices cucumber
4 pimiento-stuffed olives
8 grape tomatoes (optional)

1. Combine first 3 ingredients. Spread about 1 tablespoon mayonnaise mixture on 1 side of each of 4 bread triangles. Top with 1 lettuce leaf, 2 tomato slices, ¾ ounce turkey, 1 cheddar cheese triangle, ¾ ounce ham, 1 Swiss cheese triangle, 2 bell pepper rings, and 4 cucumber slices. Cover sandwiches with remaining bread triangles.

2. Thread 1 olive and 2 grape tomatoes, if desired, alternately onto each of 4 long wooden picks; secure sandwiches with picks. Serves 4 (serving size: 1 sandwich)

CALORIES 300; FAT 11.1g (sat 2.3g, mono 3.8g, poly 2.6g); PROTEIN 23.7g; CARB 26g; FIBER 3.1g; CHOL 48mg; IRON 1.5mg; SODIUM 693mg; CALC 282mg

Two breakfast classics merge in this dish, perfect for weekend brunch or a light dinner. Toss any leftover hollandaise sauce; because it is made with egg yolks, it doesn't keep well.

Eggs Benedict Waffle Sandwiches

Hands-on time: 24 min. Total time: 32 min.

Hollandaise:
½ cup unsalted butter
2 tablespoons cold water
2 large egg yolks
1 tablespoon fresh lemon juice
⅜ teaspoon salt, divided

Remaining ingredients:
12 thin asparagus spears
6 large eggs
Cooking spray
6 ounces shaved lower-sodium deli ham
6 frozen whole-grain waffles, toasted
½ teaspoon freshly ground black pepper

1. To prepare hollandaise, place butter in a small saucepan over medium-low heat; cook 5 minutes or until completely melted. Carefully skim solids off top with a spoon; discard solids. Slowly pour remaining butter out of pan into a small bowl, leaving remaining solids in pan; discard solids, and set clarified butter aside.

2. Combine 2 tablespoons cold water and egg yolks in a small saucepan, stirring with a whisk until foamy. Place pan over low heat, stirring constantly until mixture thickens slightly. Gradually add ¼ cup clarified butter, about 1 tablespoon at a time, stirring with a whisk until each addition is incorporated and mixture is thick. Reserve remaining clarified butter for another use.

3. Stir lemon juice and ⅛ teaspoon salt into butter mixture, whisking until blended. Remove pan from heat.

4. To prepare sandwich, snap off tough ends of asparagus. Cook asparagus in boiling water to cover 3 minutes. Drain and plunge asparagus into ice water; drain.

5. Add water to a large skillet, filling two-thirds full; bring to a boil. Reduce heat; simmer. Break 1 egg into each of 6 (6-ounce) custard cups coated with cooking spray. Place custard cups in simmering water in pan. Cover pan; cook 6 minutes. Remove custard cups from water.

6. Place 1 ounce ham and 1 poached egg on each waffle; sprinkle eggs evenly with remaining ¼ teaspoon salt. Top each serving with 2 asparagus spears and 1 tablespoon hollandaise. Sprinkle evenly with pepper. Serves 6 (serving size: 1 sandwich)

CALORIES 257; FAT 15.5g (sat 5.8g, mono 5.6g, poly 2.2g); PROTEIN 14.4g; CARB 17g; FIBER 3.9g; CHOL 292mg; IRON 1.9mg; SODIUM 654mg; CALC 52mg

Try a slightly new interpretation of the classic BLT with a flavored mayo. You can prepare the mayonnaise mixture and cook the bacon up to one day ahead. Heirloom tomatoes can vary in size, so use your judgment: If your tomatoes are small, add a slice or two more (just be sure not to stack so high the filling will slip).

Heirloom Tomato, Arugula, and Bacon Sandwiches

Hands-on time: 10 min.   Total time: 20 min.

2 tablespoons light mayonnaise
1 tablespoon minced shallots
2 teaspoons Dijon mustard
½ teaspoon minced fresh sage
8 (1-ounce) slices sourdough bread, toasted

3 medium heirloom tomatoes, each cut into 4 (½-inch-thick) slices
8 center-cut bacon slices, cooked
1 cup arugula

1. Combine first 4 ingredients in a bowl.

2. Spread mayonnaise mixture evenly over 1 side of each toast slice. Top each of 4 toast slices with 3 tomato slices, 2 bacon slices, and ¼ cup arugula. Top with remaining 4 toast slices. Serves 4 (serving size: 1 sandwich)

CALORIES 263; FAT 6.8g (sat 1.7g, mono 1.8g, poly 2g); PROTEIN 11.7g; CARB 39g; FIBER 2.2g; CHOL 13mg; IRON 2.5mg; SODIUM 667mg, CALC 53mg

This update on a traditional Cuban sandwich adds a spicy black bean spread and sweet mango, which balances the salty ham. If mango isn't your thing, use low-acid tomatoes.

Nuevo Cubano

Hands-on time: 14 min.   Total time: 14 min.

4	(3-ounce) whole-wheat submarine rolls, cut in half lengthwise
¼	cup chopped fresh cilantro
1½	tablespoons fresh lime juice
¼	teaspoon chili powder
2	garlic cloves, minced
1	(15-ounce) can no-salt-added black beans, rinsed and drained
4	ounces thinly sliced deli reduced-sodium ham
1	peeled mango or 2 large tomatoes, thinly sliced
3	ounces thinly sliced provolone cheese
2	teaspoons olive oil, divided

1. Hollow out top and bottom halves of bread, leaving a ½-inch-thick shell; reserve torn bread for another use.

2. Combine cilantro, lime juice, chili powder, garlic, and black beans in a food processor; process until almost smooth and spreadable, adding a few drops of water, if necessary. Spread bean mixture evenly on bottom halves of prepared rolls. Layer rolls evenly with ham, mango or tomato, and provolone cheese; replace top halves of rolls.

3. Heat 1 teaspoon olive oil in a large skillet over medium heat 5 minutes. Add 2 sandwiches to pan. Place a cast-iron or other heavy skillet on top of sandwiches; press gently. Cook 2 to 3 minutes on each side or until sandwiches are golden brown (leave cast-iron skillet on sandwiches while they cook). Remove sandwiches from pan; repeat procedure with remaining 1 teaspoon oil and 2 sandwiches. Serves 4 (serving size: 1 sandwich)

CALORIES 383; FAT 11g (sat 4.4g, mono 4.5g, poly 1g); PROTEIN 21g; CARB 53.6g; FIBER 7.7g; CHOL 27mg; IRON 3.2mg; SODIUM 724mg; CALC 278mg

Pimiento cheese is a Southern tradition. A little Parmesan added to the standard cheddar-mayo mixture creates extra savory depth. You can make the pimiento cheese ahead of time. Store it in an airtight container in the refrigerator for up to three days.

Open-Faced Pimiento Cheese BLTs

Hands-on time: 12 min.   Total time: 12 min.

1   cup (4 ounces) reduced-fat shredded sharp cheddar cheese
$\frac{1}{3}$ cup (about 1.25 ounces) grated fresh Parmesan cheese
2   tablespoons bottled diced pimientos, drained
1   tablespoon grated peeled shallots
2   tablespoons canola mayonnaise

1   teaspoon cider vinegar
$\frac{1}{4}$ teaspoon freshly ground black pepper
4   (1-ounce) slices sourdough bread, toasted
12   tomato slices
$\frac{1}{4}$ teaspoon kosher salt
4   center-cut bacon slices, cooked and halved
1   cup arugula

1. Combine first 7 ingredients in a large bowl. Top each toast slice with 3 tomato slices. Sprinkle tomato slices evenly with salt. Spread 3 tablespoons cheese mixture on top of tomatoes. Top each sandwich with 2 bacon halves and ¼ cup arugula. Serves 4 (serving size: 1 sandwich)

CALORIES 266; FAT 14.9g (sat 5.5g, mono 6.1g, poly 2.2g); PROTEIN 16.4g; CARB 19.3g; FIBER 2.2g; CHOL 31mg; IRON 1.7mg; SODIUM 743mg; CALC 139mg

Fit for a King: **IN 1976, ELVIS PRESLEY FLEW FROM HIS HOME IN MEMPHIS TO DENVER (MORE THAN 800 MILES)** just to eat a Fool's Gold sandwich from a restaurant called the Colorado Gold Mine Company. The recipe for this $50 sandwich? An entire loaf of warm Italian bread, hollowed out and filled with peanut butter, grape jelly, and a pound of bacon.

Sweet fig preserves balance the tartness of the plums. Choose red or purple plums that have bright, unblemished skins and are firm and plump to the touch.

Open-Faced Prosciutto and Plum Sandwiches

Hands-on time: 7 min.   Total time: 7 min.

¼   cup fig preserves
1   tablespoon fresh lemon juice
¼   teaspoon grated peeled fresh ginger
⅓   cup (3 ounces) soft goat cheese
4   (2-ounce) slices country wheat bread, toasted

1   cup loosely packed arugula
2   ripe plums, cut into thin wedges
3   ounces very thinly sliced prosciutto

1. Combine first 3 ingredients, stirring with a whisk; set aside.

2. Spread ¾ ounce cheese evenly over each toast slice; divide arugula, plum wedges, and prosciutto evenly among sandwiches. Drizzle each sandwich with about 1 tablespoon fig preserves mixture. Serves 4 (serving size: 1 sandwich)

CALORIES 318; FAT 9.1g (sat 5.1g, mono 3.1g, poly 0.6g); PROTEIN 13.1g; CARB 45.5g; FIBER 1.9g; CHOL 26mg; IRON 4.4mg; SODIUM 689mg; CALC 161mg

Pulled pork is the barbecue meat of choice in North and South Carolina, but when it comes to sauce, the preferences are intensely different. The mustard sauce in this recipe is inspired by South Carolina's sauce of choice.

Pulled Pork Sandwiches with Mustard Sauce

Hands-on time: 60 min. Total time: 7 hr. 20 min.

7 to 8 cups hickory wood chips
2 tablespoons brown sugar
1 tablespoon dry mustard
1 tablespoon smoked paprika
1 tablespoon black pepper
1½ teaspoons kosher salt
1 (5-pound) boneless pork shoulder (Boston butt)
2 tablespoons olive oil

¾ cup finely chopped onion
⅓ cup packed brown sugar
⅔ cup Dijon mustard
⅔ cup cider vinegar
⅓ cup molasses
1 teaspoon hot sauce
½ teaspoon kosher salt
16 (1½-ounce) whole-wheat hamburger buns

1. Soak wood chips in water at least 1 hour; drain.

2. Combine sugar and next 4 ingredients (through 1½ teaspoons salt) in a bowl. Pat pork dry, and rub with sugar mixture.

3. Remove grill rack, and set aside. Prepare grill for indirect grilling, heating 1 side to high and leaving 1 side with no heat. Pierce bottom of a disposable foil pan several times with the tip of a knife. Place pan on heat element on heated side of grill; add 1½ cups wood chips to pan. Place another disposable foil pan (do not pierce pan) on unheated side of grill. Pour 2 cups water in pan. Let chips stand 15 minutes or until smoking; reduce heat to medium. Maintain temperature at 300°. Place grill rack on grill. Place pork on grill rack over unheated side. Close lid; cook 6 hours at 300° or until a meat thermometer registers 195°, covering pork loosely with foil after 5 hours. Drain and add 1 cup additional wood chips every 45 minutes. Refill water pan and add charcoal to fire as needed. Remove pork from grill; let stand 20 minutes. Unwrap pork; trim and discard fat. Shred pork.

4. Heat oil in a medium saucepan over medium heat; swirl to coat. Add onion; cook 2 minutes, stirring frequently. Add ⅓ cup sugar and next 5 ingredients (through ½ teaspoon salt); bring to a simmer. Cook 15 minutes or until thick. Arrange about 3 ounces pork and 2 tablespoons sauce on each bun. Serves 16 (serving size: 1 sandwich)

CALORIES 390; FAT 16.1g (sat 5g, mono 7.2g, poly 2.2g); PROTEIN 24.7g; CARB 36.3g; FIBER 3.6g; CHOL 73mg; IRON 2.9mg; SODIUM 739mg; CALC 93mg

Prosciutto and fresh figs are a classic Italian combination. Here, along with cheese and jam, they create a sweet-savory sandwich that's simple yet memorable. Great ingredients make all the difference here, so look for a fine loaf of artisan bread and quality prosciutto. Use a sharp vegetable peeler to shave the Manchego, a Spanish cheese similar to pecorino Romano (which you can substitute).

Prosciutto, Fresh Fig, and Manchego Sandwiches

Hands-on time: 20 min.   Total time: 20 min.

4 teaspoons Dijon mustard
8 (¾-ounce) slices Italian bread, toasted
1 cup arugula
2 ounces very thinly sliced prosciutto

2 ounces Manchego cheese, shaved
8 fresh figs, cut into thin slices
2 tablespoons fig jam

1. Spread 1 teaspoon mustard over each of 4 bread slices. Arrange ¼ cup arugula over each bread slice. Divide prosciutto evenly among bread slices; top evenly with cheese and fig slices. Spread 1½ teaspoons jam over each of the remaining 4 bread slices, and place on sandwiches jam side down. Serves 4 (serving size: 1 sandwich)

CALORIES 295; FAT 5.3g (sat 2.6g, mono 2.1g, poly 0.6g); PROTEIN 11.5g, CARB 52.3g; FIBER 4.2g; CHOL 18mg; IRON 1.8mg; SODIUM 805mg; CALC 114mg

Put together a quick pulled chicken barbecue sandwich: Make your own sauce (it gets a nice smoky depth from ancho chile powder), and mix it with shredded roasted or rotisserie chicken. You can make the sauce ahead, if you like.

Barbecue Chicken Sandwiches

Hands-on time: 11 min.   Total time: 21 min.

½ cup no-salt-added ketchup
2 tablespoons honey mustard
2 tablespoons water
¾ teaspoon ancho chile powder
¾ teaspoon smoked paprika
½ teaspoon garlic powder
½ teaspoon onion powder
½ teaspoon ground cumin
½ teaspoon Worcestershire sauce
⅛ teaspoon kosher salt
3 cups shredded skinless, boneless rotisserie chicken breast
3 tablespoons canola mayonnaise
2 tablespoons cider vinegar
1 teaspoon sugar
3 cups packaged coleslaw
⅓ cup chopped green onions
6 (1½-ounce) hamburger buns, toasted

1. Combine first 10 ingredients in a saucepan. Bring to a simmer; cook 10 minutes. Combine sauce and chicken. Combine mayonnaise, vinegar, and sugar. Add coleslaw and onions; toss.

2. Place about ½ cup chicken mixture on bottom half of each bun. Top each serving with about ½ cup coleslaw mixture; top with top half of bun. Serves 6 (serving size: 1 sandwich)

CALORIES 316; FAT 9.9g (sat 1.5g, mono 4.3g, poly 2.7g); PROTEIN 21.4g; CARB 35.3g; FIBER 2.1g; CHOL 53mg; IRON 2.1mg; SODIUM 548mg; CALC 91mg

If you can't find tahini, substitute an equal amount of peanut butter to make the sauce for these Middle East–inspired sandwiches. You can prepare the sauce and chicken ahead of time and stuff the pitas when you're ready to eat.

Chicken Souvlaki Pitas with Tahini Sauce

Hands-on time: 25 min.   Total time: 25 min.

6 tablespoons plain fat-free Greek yogurt
2 tablespoons shredded cucumber
4½ teaspoons tahini (roasted sesame seed paste)
5 teaspoons fresh lemon juice, divided
5 garlic cloves, minced
1 tablespoon extra-virgin olive oil
1 teaspoon dried oregano
¼ teaspoon salt

¼ teaspoon freshly ground black pepper
1 pound skinless, boneless chicken breast halves, cut into 1-inch pieces
Cooking spray
4 (6-inch) pitas, cut in half
1 cup shredded iceberg lettuce
½ cup thinly sliced red onion
16 (¼-inch-thick) slices cucumber
16 (¼-inch-thick) slices plum tomato

1. Combine yogurt, shredded cucumber, tahini, 1 tablespoon lemon juice, and garlic in a small bowl; set aside.

2. Combine 2 teaspoons lemon juice, olive oil, and next 4 ingredients (through chicken) in a small bowl. Heat a grill pan over medium-high heat. Thread chicken pieces evenly onto 4 (8-inch) skewers. Coat grill pan with cooking spray. Add chicken to pan; cook 10 minutes or until done, turning every 2 minutes. Remove chicken from skewers.

3. Divide chicken evenly among pita halves. Fill each half with 2 tablespoons lettuce, 1 tablespoon onion, 2 cucumber slices, 2 tomato slices, and 1 tablespoon sauce. Serves 4 (serving size: 2 stuffed pita halves)

CALORIES 390; FAT 8g (sat 1.3g, mono 4g, poly 2.1g); PROTEIN 37.3g; CARB 41.9g; FIBER 2.9g; CHOL 66mg; IRON 4.3mg; SODIUM 398mg; CALC 103mg

Tarragon and rye bread make a classic chicken salad sandwich extra special. You can make the chicken salad ahead. If you're packing it to go, keep the salad cold, and make your sandwich right before you're ready to eat to keep the bread from getting soggy.

Herbed Chicken Salad Sandwiches

Hands-on time: 14 min.   Total time: 14 min.

1   tablespoon finely chopped fresh tarragon
3   tablespoons canola mayonnaise
3   tablespoons plain 2% reduced-fat Greek yogurt
1   tablespoon fresh lemon juice
⅛   teaspoon kosher salt

2   cups chopped skinless, boneless rotisserie chicken breast
¼   cup minced sweet onion
8   (1½-ounce) slices rye sandwich bread
4   red leaf lettuce leaves (optional)
1   cup microgreens or arugula

1. Combine first 5 ingredients in a large bowl. Stir in chicken and onion. Top each of 4 bread slices with 1 lettuce leaf, if desired, about ½ packed cup chicken salad, ¼ cup microgreens, and 1 bread slice. Serves 4 (serving size: 1 sandwich)

CALORIES 382; FAT 9g (sat 1.4g, mono 3.9g, poly 2.4g); PROTEIN 30.2g; CARB 42.9g; FIBER 5.1g; CHOL 60mg; IRON 3.2mg; SODIUM 745mg; CALC 89mg

Eats for the Rich and Famous: **NOW CONSIDERED A HUMBLE BROWN-BAG LUNCH ITEM,** the chicken salad sandwich was a lavish meal reserved only for the wealthy in the 1880s, when the recipe was first recorded.

Grab a fork and knife for this sandwich, which doesn't skimp on goodies: A mayo-avocado spread and bacon make it decadent.

Open-Faced Chicken Club Sandwiches

Hands-on time: 23 min.   Total time: 23 min.

1 tablespoon olive oil
4 (6-ounce) skinless, boneless chicken breast halves
¼ teaspoon kosher salt, divided
¼ teaspoon freshly ground black pepper
3 tablespoons canola mayonnaise

2 teaspoons fresh lemon juice
1 ripe peeled avocado, coarsely mashed
4 (1-ounce) slices sourdough bread, toasted
4 green leaf lettuce leaves
2 plum tomatoes, each cut into 6 slices
4 center-cut bacon slices, cooked and drained

1. Heat a large skillet over medium-high heat. Add oil to pan; swirl to coat. Sprinkle chicken evenly with ⅛ teaspoon salt and pepper. Add chicken to pan; cook 6 minutes on each side or until done. Remove from pan; let stand 5 minutes. Slice.

2. Combine mayonnaise, juice, avocado, and ⅛ teaspoon salt in a small bowl; stir until well blended. Spread about 3 tablespoons avocado mixture over each bread slice. Top each sandwich with 1 lettuce leaf, 1 chicken breast half, 3 tomato slices, and 1 bacon slice. Serves 4 (serving size: 1 sandwich)

CALORIES 400; FAT 18g (sat 3.3g, mono 9.2g, poly 3.4g); PROTEIN 36g; CARB 22.5g; FIBER 4.8g; CHOL 85mg; IRON 2.5mg; SODIUM 597mg; CALC 45mg

Here's a tasty way to use up leftover roast chicken. Dark meat stands up to the intense flavors in the dressing. For a change, try using a wrap or naan instead of a pita.

Peanut-Sauced Chicken Pitas

Hands-on time: 24 min.   Total time: 24 min.

1   cup shredded skinless, boneless rotisserie chicken thigh or drumstick meat
1/3 cup thinly sliced green onions
2   tablespoons thin red bell pepper strips
2   tablespoons peanut satay sauce
1/8 teaspoon kosher salt

1   teaspoon chile paste with garlic (optional)
1   (6-inch) whole-wheat pita, cut in half
1/2 cup fresh mung bean sprouts, rinsed, drained, and patted dry
1/4 cup diagonally cut carrot
2   tablespoons chopped fresh cilantro

1. Combine first 5 ingredients, tossing well to coat. Stir in chile paste, if desired. Fill each pita half with about ½ cup chicken mixture, ¼ cup bean sprouts, half of the carrots, and 1 tablespoon cilantro. Serves 2 (serving size: 1 stuffed pita half)

CALORIES 299; FAT 11g (sat 2.8g, mono 4.2g, poly 2.8g); PROTEIN 23.3g; CARB 26.4g; FIBER 4.1g; CHOL 67mg; IRON 2.5mg; SODIUM 621mg; CALC 36mg

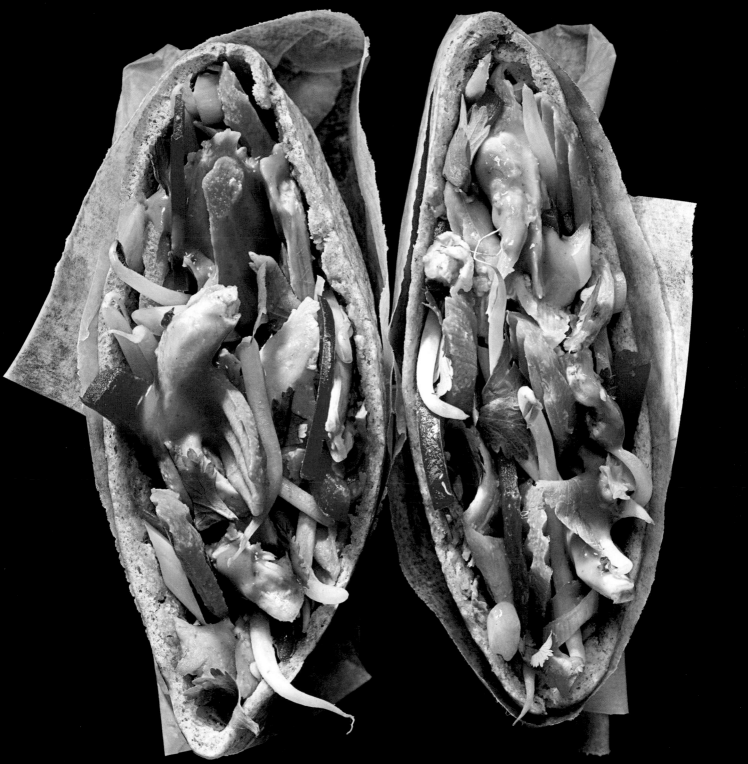

Satisfy a craving for a hot, Italian-style sub. Sausage stands in for traditional meatballs in this sandwich, and sliced fennel adds an herbal note.

Sausage-Fennel Subs

Hands-on time: 21 min.   Total time: 21 min.

1   teaspoon olive oil
1½ cups vertically sliced onion
1   cup thinly sliced fennel bulb
4   garlic cloves, thinly sliced
6   ounces chicken and sun-dried tomato
    sausage, thinly diagonally sliced

4   (2-ounce) submarine rolls or hoagie rolls
½   cup tomato-basil pasta sauce
4   (½-ounce) slices provolone cheese

1. Preheat broiler.

2. Heat oil in a large nonstick skillet over medium-high heat, swirling to coat. Add onion, fennel, and garlic; sauté 4 minutes. Add sausage; sauté 3 minutes or until sausage is lightly browned and vegetables begin to brown.

3. Arrange rolls, cut sides up, in a single layer on a baking sheet; broil 2 minutes or until toasted. Spoon about ⅔ cup sausage mixture on bottom half of each roll, and top each with 2 tablespoons sauce. Place 1 cheese slice over sauce. Arrange sandwiches on baking sheet; broil 2 minutes or until cheese melts. Serves 4 (serving size: 1 sandwich)

CALORIES 326; FAT 12.3g (sat 4.7g, mono 3.4g, poly 2.4g); PROTEIN 17.7g; CARB 41g; FIBER 3.7g; CHOL 54mg; IRON 1.4mg; SODIUM 822mg; CALC 185mg

Get a satisfying crunch by crusting the chicken cutlets with tortilla chip crumbs.
If you don't have green onions on hand, use red onion slices.

Spicy Chicken Sandwiches with Cilantro-Lime Mayo

Hands-on time: 22 min. Total time: 2 hr. 22 min.

Mayo:
- ¼ cup reduced-fat mayonnaise
- 2 tablespoons minced fresh cilantro
- 1 teaspoon fresh lime juice
- 1 garlic clove, minced

Chicken:
- 3 tablespoons hot pepper sauce
- 1 teaspoon dried oregano
- ⅛ teaspoon salt
- 2 large egg whites, lightly beaten
- 4 (3-ounce) chicken cutlets
- 4½ ounces baked tortilla chips (about 6 cups)
- 1 tablespoon olive oil

Remaining ingredients:
- 4 (2-ounce) Kaiser rolls, split
- 4 lettuce leaves
- 2 tablespoons sliced green onions

1. To prepare mayo, combine mayonnaise, cilantro, lime juice, and garlic in a small bowl.

2. To prepare chicken, combine hot pepper sauce, oregano, salt, and egg whites in a large zip-top plastic bag. Add chicken cutlets to bag; seal bag, turning to coat. Marinate in refrigerator for at least 2 hours, turning bag occasionally.

3. Place tortilla chips in a food processor; process 1 minute or until ground. Place chips in a shallow dish.

4. Working with 1 cutlet at a time, remove chicken from bag; discard marinade. Dredge chicken in ground chips.

5. Heat a large nonstick skillet over medium heat. Add oil to pan, swirling to coat. Add chicken to pan; cook 4 minutes on each side or until browned and done. Spread mayo evenly over cut sides of rolls. Layer bottom half of each roll with 1 lettuce leaf, 1 chicken cutlet, and ½ tablespoon sliced green onions; cover with roll tops. Serves 4 (serving size: 1 sandwich)

CALORIES 412; FAT 9.7g (sat 1.8g, mono 4g, poly 3.3g); PROTEIN 31g; CARB 56g; FIBER 7.9g; CHOL 49mg; IRON 1.5mg; SODIUM 759mg; CALC 413mg

You can substitute tilapia for the catfish, if desired; check for doneness a few minutes early because tilapia fillets are usually thinner than catfish fillets.

Oven-Fried Catfish Sandwiches

Hands-on time: 19 min.   Total time: 31 min.

¼ cup light mayonnaise
1 tablespoon sweet pickle relish
2 teaspoons capers, chopped
⅜ teaspoon salt, divided
¼ teaspoon hot pepper sauce
2 tablespoons all-purpose flour
1 teaspoon paprika
¾ teaspoon garlic powder, divided
¼ teaspoon black pepper

2 large egg whites, lightly beaten
⅔ cup yellow cornmeal
4 (4-ounce) catfish fillets
Cooking spray
4 (2-ounce) hoagie rolls, toasted
1 cup shredded romaine lettuce
8 (¼-inch-thick) slices tomato
4 (¼-inch-thick) slices red onion

1. Preheat oven to 450°. Place baking sheet in oven.

2. Combine mayonnaise, relish, capers, ⅛ teaspoon salt, and hot pepper sauce in a small bowl, stirring well. Set aside.

3. Combine flour, paprika, ½ teaspoon garlic powder, ⅛ teaspoon salt, and pepper in a shallow dish. Place egg whites in a shallow bowl. Combine cornmeal, ⅛ teaspoon salt, and ¼ teaspoon garlic powder in a shallow dish. Working with 1 fillet at a time, dredge in flour mixture. Dip in egg whites; dredge in cornmeal mixture. Place fillet on a plate; repeat procedure with remaining fillets, flour mixture, egg whites, and cornmeal mixture.

4. Transfer fillets to preheated baking sheet coated with cooking spray. Lightly coat fillets with cooking spray. Bake at 450° for 6 minutes. Turn fillets and coat with cooking spray; bake an additional 6 minutes, until fish flakes easily when tested with a fork or until desired degree of doneness.

5. Place 1 bottom half of roll on each of 4 plates. Top each serving with ¼ cup lettuce, 2 tomato slices, 1 fillet, and 1 onion slice. Spread 4 teaspoons mayonnaise mixture on cut side of each roll top; place on top of sandwiches. Serve immediately. Serves 4 (serving size: 1 sandwich)

CALORIES 431; FAT 16.2g (sat 3.5g, mono 5.5g, poly 5.6g); PROTEIN 25.4g; CARB 45.2g; FIBER 4.8g; CHOL 60mg; IRON 2.9mg; SODIUM 785mg; CALC 91mg

Serve a New Orleans classic featuring a homemade five-ingredient tartar sauce made with pantry staples.

Pan-Seared Shrimp Po' Boys

Hands-on time: 20 min.   Total time: 20 min.

⅓ cup canola mayonnaise
2 tablespoons sweet pickle relish
1 tablespoon chopped shallots
½ teaspoon capers, chopped
¼ teaspoon hot pepper sauce (optional)
1½ teaspoons salt-free Cajun seasoning

1 pound peeled and deveined large shrimp
2 teaspoons olive oil
4 (2-ounce) hoagie rolls
½ cup shredded romaine lettuce
12 thin slices tomato
4 thin slices red onion

1. Combine first 4 ingredients and hot pepper sauce, if desired, in a small bowl. Heat a large nonstick skillet over medium-high heat. Combine Cajun seasoning and shrimp in a bowl; toss well. Add olive oil to pan, and swirl to coat. Add shrimp to pan; cook 2 minutes on each side or until done.

2. Cut each roll in half horizontally. Top bottom half of each roll with 2 tablespoons lettuce, 3 tomato slices, 1 onion slice, and one-fourth of shrimp. Spread top half of each roll with about 2 tablespoons mayonnaise mixture; place on top of sandwich. Serves 4 (serving size: 1 sandwich)

CALORIES 401; FAT 14.5g (sat 1.6g, mono 6.3g, poly 4g); PROTEIN 34.7g; CARB 32.4g; FIBER 2.5g; CHOL 230mg; IRON 1.5mg; SODIUM 783mg; CALC 74mg

Legendary Leftovers: **THE PO' BOY SANDWICH WAS INVENTED BY BENNY AND CLOVIS MARTIN IN NEW ORLEANS IN 1929.** The Martin brothers showed their support of the streetcar strike by serving free sandwiches stuffed with leftovers to picketing strikers who couldn't afford to buy lunch—the "poor boys."

This classic New England sandwich comes together in a snap if you purchase lobster tails and have them steamed at the fish counter. You can make the lobster salad a few hours in advance; fill the sandwiches right before they're served.

Picnic-Perfect Lobster Rolls

Hands-on time: 12 min.   Total time: 1 hr. 12 min.

$1/3$ cup chopped celery
   2   tablespoons chopped green onions
   1   tablespoon finely chopped fresh tarragon
   3   tablespoons canola mayonnaise
$1/2$ teaspoon grated lemon rind
$1 1/2$ tablespoons fresh lemon juice
$1/2$ teaspoon Dijon mustard

$1/4$ teaspoon kosher salt
$1/4$ teaspoon black pepper
$1/8$ teaspoon ground red pepper
$3/4$ pound lobster meat, steamed and chopped
   4   (1½-ounce) New England–style hot dog buns, toasted

1. Combine first 11 ingredients in a large bowl, stirring well; cover and chill at least 1 hour. Divide lobster mixture evenly among buns. Serves 4 (serving size: 1 sandwich)

CALORIES 284; FAT 10.3g (sat 0.8g, mono 4.9g, poly 2.7g); PROTEIN 21.7g; CARB 22.4g; FIBER 0.3g; CHOL 65mg; IRON 1.5mg; SODIUM 731mg; CALC 61mg

This decadent sandwich would be perfect for brunch. Look for salmon that's labeled "wild Alaskan," and you can be sure you're getting sustainable seafood. You can also use soft-boiled eggs in place of the poached eggs.

Smoked Salmon and Egg Sandwich

Hands-on time: 14 min.   Total time: 14 min.

4 cups water	$3/8$ teaspoon kosher salt
1 tablespoon white vinegar	4 (1-ounce) slices whole-grain bread, toasted
4 large eggs	1 cup arugula
1/4 cup (2 ounces) 1/3-less-fat cream cheese	4 ounces smoked wild salmon
2 tablespoons minced red onion	1/4 teaspoon black pepper
1 tablespoon chopped fresh dill	

1. Add 4 cups water to a large skillet, filling two-thirds full; bring to a boil. Reduce heat; simmer. Add vinegar to pan. Break eggs into custard cups. Gently pour eggs into pan; cook 3 minutes or until desired degree of doneness. Carefully remove eggs from pan using a slotted spoon; set aside.

2. Combine cheese, onion, dill, and 1/8 teaspoon salt; spread 1 tablespoon cheese mixture over each toast slice. Top each serving with 1/4 cup arugula and 1 ounce salmon. Top each sandwich with 1 egg. Sprinkle with 1/4 teaspoon salt and pepper. Serves 4 (serving size: 1 sandwich)

CALORIES 219; FAT 10.5g (sat 4.1g, mono 2.7g, poly 1.5g); PROTEIN 16.5g; CARB 14.4g; FIBER 2.3g; CHOL 228mg; IRON 2mg; SODIUM 649mg; CALC 79mg

You can serve these with cornichons (small pickles), or with carrot and celery sticks and a bit of light ranch dressing on the side for dipping.

Tuna Melts

Hands-on time: 12 min.   Total time: 12 min.

2   tablespoons thinly sliced green onions
1   tablespoon olive oil
1   tablespoon Dijon mustard
2   teaspoons fresh lemon juice
1/8 teaspoon salt
1/4 teaspoon black pepper
1   (5-ounce) can solid white tuna in water, drained and flaked

1   (3-ounce) piece French bread, halved lengthwise and toasted
4   (1/4-inch-thick) slices plum tomato
1/4 cup (about 1 ounce) shredded Swiss cheese
2   teaspoons thinly sliced green onions (optional)

1. Preheat broiler.

2. Combine first 6 ingredients in a medium bowl. Add tuna; stir gently.

3. Hollow out top and bottom halves of bread, leaving a 1-inch-thick shell; reserve torn bread for another use. Place bread, cut sides up, on a baking sheet. Broil 1 minute or until toasted.

4. Spoon tuna mixture evenly into bread shells; top each with 2 tomato slices and 2 tablespoons cheese. Broil 2 minutes or until cheese melts. Sprinkle 1 teaspoon green onions on each sandwich, if desired. Serves 2 (serving size: 1 sandwich)

CALORIES 295; FAT 13g (sat 3.9g, mono 6.4g, poly 1.7g); PROTEIN 17.4g; CARB 25.7g; FIBER 1.8g; CHOL 30mg; IRON 2mg; SODIUM 787mg; CALC 145mg

A favorite in southern France, *pan bagnat* (pan ban-YAH) means "bathed bread." The bread is meant to absorb some liquid from the filling, so it's fine to assemble the entire sandwich ahead of time.

Tuna Pan Bagnat

Hands-on time: 28 min.   Total time: 48 min.

⅓ cup finely chopped red onion
 2 tablespoons chopped pitted niçoise olives
 1 tablespoon fresh lemon juice
¼ teaspoon kosher salt
¼ teaspoon freshly ground black pepper
 1 · (6-ounce) can premium tuna, packed in oil, drained

 1 hard-cooked large egg, chopped
¼ cup thinly sliced fresh basil
 2 teaspoons extra-virgin olive oil
 1 (8-ounce) whole-wheat French bread baguette
 1 garlic clove, halved
 1 cup thinly sliced plum tomato (about 2)

1. Combine first 7 ingredients in a medium bowl. Combine basil and oil; stir with a whisk. Cut bread in half horizontally. Hollow out top and bottom halves of bread, leaving a 1-inch-thick shell; reserve torn bread for another use. Rub cut sides of garlic clove over cut sides of bread; discard garlic. Drizzle basil mixture evenly over cut sides of bread. Arrange tomato slices over bottom half of baguette. Spoon tuna mixture over tomatoes. Cover with top half of baguette. Wrap filled baguette in plastic wrap, and let stand 20 minutes. Cut filled baguette into 4 (3-inch) equal portions. Serves 4 (serving size: 1 sandwich piece)

CALORIES 248; FAT 9.3g (sat 1.4g, mono 4.6g, poly 2g); PROTEIN 14.5g; CARB 26.3g; FIBER 2.2g; CHOL 63mg; IRON 2mg; SODIUM 589mg; CALC 84mg

A toasty bagel takes the place of croutons in this switch on a classic salad. To brown-bag, pack sandwich components separately—the lettuce and cheese, a mixture of the dressing and pepper, and the toasted bagel. For the vegetarians in your crew, choose a dressing that doesn't contain anchovies.

Caesar Salad Bagels

Hands-on time: 6 min.   Total time: 6 min.

3 tablespoons organic creamy Caesar dressing
2 (4-ounce) whole-grain, onion, or "everything" bagels, split and toasted
½ teaspoon black pepper

2 thin slices red onion
1 cup torn or shredded romaine lettuce
½ cup (2 ounces) shaved Parmigiano-Reggiano cheese

1. Spread dressing evenly on cut sides of bagels. Sprinkle with pepper.

2. Arrange half of red onion, romaine lettuce, and cheese on bottom halves of bagels. Repeat layers with remaining onion, lettuce, and cheese. Top with top halves of bagels. Serves 2 (serving size: 1 sandwich)

CALORIES 394; FAT 16g (sat 4.2g, mono 5.4g, poly 2.7g); PROTEIN 16.6g; CARB 51.9g; FIBER 8.6g; CHOL 18mg; IRON 1.9mg; SODIUM 757mg; CALC 396mg

A touch of lemon rind and sour cream adds a bright note to creamy egg salad. To pack for lunch, keep the egg salad chilled, and store the bread and lettuce separately; build your sandwich when you're ready to eat.

Egg Salad Sandwich

Hands-on time: 12 min.   Total time: 12 min.

¼ cup canola mayonnaise
3 tablespoons thinly sliced green onions
3 tablespoons reduced-fat sour cream
2 teaspoons whole-grain Dijon mustard
½ teaspoon freshly ground black pepper

¼ teaspoon grated lemon rind
8 hard-cooked large eggs
8 (1½-ounce) slices peasant bread or firm sandwich bread, toasted
4 large Boston lettuce leaves

1. Combine first 6 ingredients in a medium bowl, stirring well.

2. Cut 2 eggs in half lengthwise; reserve 2 yolks for another use. Coarsely chop egg whites and whole eggs. Add eggs to mayonnaise mixture; stir gently to combine.

3. Arrange 4 toast slices on a cutting board or work surface. Top each toast slice with 1 lettuce leaf, ½ cup egg mixture, and 1 toast slice. Serve immediately. Serves 4 (serving size: 1 sandwich)

CALORIES 404; FAT 16.5g (sat 4.2g, mono 7g, poly 3g); PROTEIN 20.8g; CARB 40.6g; FIBER 1.2g; CHOL 430mg; IRON 3.6mg; SODIUM 746mg; CALC 79mg

What kid (or grown-up, for that matter) wouldn't love this ooey-gooey sandwich? Serve these souped-up PB&Js with fresh fruit.

French Toast Peanut Butter and Jelly Sandwiches

Hands-on time: 15 min.   Total time: 15 min.

$2/3$ cup 2% reduced-fat milk
$1/2$ teaspoon baking powder
$1/2$ teaspoon vanilla extract
$1/8$ teaspoon salt
1 large egg, lightly beaten

8 (1-ounce) slices white whole-wheat bread
$1/2$ cup strawberry preserves
6 tablespoons creamy peanut butter
1 tablespoon canola oil, divided
1 tablespoon powdered sugar

1. Combine first 5 ingredients in a medium shallow dish, stirring well with a whisk. Place bread slices on a flat surface. Spread 2 tablespoons preserves over each of 4 bread slices, and spread 1½ tablespoons peanut butter over each of remaining 4 bread slices. Assemble sandwiches.

2. Carefully dip 2 sandwiches in milk mixture, turning to coat. Heat a large skillet over medium-high heat. Add 1½ teaspoons canola oil to pan; swirl to coat. Place coated sandwiches in pan; cook 2 minutes on each side or until toasted. Remove sandwiches from pan. Repeat procedure with remaining 2 sandwiches, milk mixture, and oil. Sprinkle powdered sugar evenly over sandwiches; cut each sandwich in half diagonally. Serves 4 (serving size: 1 sandwich)

CALORIES 394; FAT 19.4g (sat 4.6g, mono 8.7g, poly 5.1g); PROTEIN 14.9g; CARB 43.2g; FIBER 5.4g; CHOL 48mg; IRON 1.6mg; SODIUM 519mg; CALC 124mg

That'll Stick to the Roof of Your Mouth! **CAN'T GET ENOUGH PEANUT BUTTER AND JELLY?** Grand Saline, Texas, holds the world record for the biggest PB&J sandwich, weighing in at 1,342 pounds.

The stack of grilled eggplant, red onion, and zucchini is quite a tasty mouthful. You can, of course, change the vegetable mix according to what you find in the markets.

Grilled Farmers' Market Sandwiches

Hands-on time: 33 min. Total time: 33 min.

2   tablespoons olive oil, divided
8   (½-inch-thick) slices eggplant
2   (½-inch-thick) slices red onion
1   large zucchini, cut lengthwise into 4 pieces
2   teaspoons chopped fresh rosemary
¼   teaspoon black pepper
⅛   teaspoon salt

1   tablespoon white balsamic vinegar
4   (2½-ounce) ciabatta rolls, cut in half horizontally
Cooking spray
4   (1-ounce) slices provolone cheese, halved
8   (¼-inch-thick) slices tomato
8   basil leaves

1. Preheat grill to medium-high heat.

2. Brush 1 tablespoon olive oil evenly over both sides of eggplant, onion, and zucchini. Sprinkle with rosemary, pepper, and salt.

3. Combine 1 tablespoon oil and vinegar in a bowl. Brush vinegar mixture over cut sides of bread.

4. Place onion on grill rack coated with cooking spray, and grill 6 minutes on each side or until tender. Remove from grill, and separate into rings. Grill eggplant and zucchini 4 minutes on each side or until tender. Cut zucchini pieces in half crosswise.

5. Place bread, cut sides down, on grill rack; grill 2 minutes. Remove from grill. Place 1 piece of cheese on bottom half of each bread portion; top each serving with 1 eggplant slice, 1 tomato slice, 1 basil leaf, 2 pieces zucchini, one-fourth of onion rings, 1 eggplant slice, 1 tomato slice, 1 basil leaf, 1 piece of cheese, and top half of bread. Place sandwiches on grill rack; grill 2 minutes, covered, or until cheese melts. Serves 4 (serving size: 1 sandwich)

CALORIES 386; FAT 16.2g (sat 5.9g, mono 7.1g, poly 1.1g); PROTEIN 15.8g; CARB 45.5g; FIBER 6.4g; CHOL 20mg; IRON 3.2mg; SODIUM 670mg; CALC 249mg

You can easily shave thin slices of cheese using an inexpensive kitchen tool: a vegetable peeler. This is a perfect technique for many hard cheeses like Gruyère. Enjoy these sandwiches with cornichons, if you like.

Grilled Gruyère and Olive Tapenade Sandwiches

Hands-on time: 20 min.   Total time: 20 min.

1 (8.5-ounce) jar oil-packed sun-dried tomatoes
12 pitted kalamata olives
2 garlic cloves
8 (1-ounce) slices multigrain bread

¼ cup (1 ounce) grated Parmigiano-Reggiano cheese
8 (¼-inch-thick) slices large tomato
2 ounces Gruyère cheese, shaved

1. Remove 4 sun-dried tomatoes and 2 tablespoons oil from jar. Reserve remaining tomatoes and oil for another use. Combine tomatoes, 1 tablespoon oil, olives, and garlic in a mini food processor; process until mostly smooth, scraping sides of bowl once.

2. Brush 1 side of each bread slice with reserved 1 tablespoon oil. Spread 1½ tablespoons olive mixture on each of 4 bread slices, oil side down. Top each bread slice with 1 tablespoon Parmigiano-Reggiano, 2 tomato slices, and ½ ounce Gruyère. Top with remaining 4 bread slices, oil side up.

3. Heat a skillet over medium-high heat. Add sandwiches to pan. Place a cast-iron or other heavy skillet on top of sandwiches; press gently to flatten sandwiches (leave cast-iron skillet on sandwiches while they cook). Cook 2 minutes on each side or until cheese melts and bread is toasted. Serves 4 (serving size: 1 sandwich)

CALORIES 346; FAT 20.2g (sat 5.1g, mono 8.9g, poly 1.4g); PROTEIN 14.7g; CARB 28.9g; FIBER 5.8g; CHOL 21mg; IRON 1.6mg; SODIUM 618mg; CALC 290mg

Cheese Challenge: **APRIL IS NATIONAL GRILLED CHEESE MONTH.** Each year at the Grilled Cheese Invitational, cooks compete in the ultimate slice-to-slice competition full of melty, cheesy-liciousness.

Make the most of juicy, flavorful summer tomatoes by combining them with luscious Brie. (Remember that the rind on Brie is edible.) Serve with grapes or carrot sticks.

Grilled Tomato and Brie Sandwiches

Hands-on time: 9 min.   Total time: 9 min.

8   (1-ounce) slices 100% whole-grain bread (about ¼ inch thick)
1   teaspoon olive oil
1   garlic clove, halved
2   teaspoons country-style Dijon mustard

4   ounces Brie cheese, thinly sliced
1⅓   cups packaged baby arugula and spinach mix
8   (¼-inch-thick) slices beefsteak tomato
Cooking spray

1. Preheat grill to high heat.

2. Brush 1 side of each bread slice with oil; rub cut sides of garlic over oil. Spread ½ teaspoon mustard on each of 4 bread slices, oil side down. Top each bread slice with 1 ounce cheese, ⅓ cup greens, and 2 tomato slices. Top with remaining 4 bread slices, oil side up.

3. Place sandwiches on grill rack coated with cooking spray; grill 2 minutes on each side or until lightly toasted and cheese melts. Serves 4 (serving size: 1 sandwich)

CALORIES 234; FAT 10.1g (sat 5.1g, mono 3.1g, poly 1g); PROTEIN 11g; CARB 26.9g; FIBER 6.5g; CHOL 28mg; IRON 1.8mg; SODIUM 445mg; CALC 210mg

The classic Caprese salad of juicy tomatoes with fresh mozzarella and fragrant basil makes for a fantastic vegetarian sandwich. Grilled zucchini makes it more substantial and brings in some smoky flavor, too. Gooey mozzarella puts it over the top. Crunch is key with the bread, but you can sub a crusty baguette.

Grilled Zucchini Caprese Sandwiches

Hands-on time: 15 min.   Total time: 15 min.

1	medium zucchini, trimmed and cut lengthwise into 6 slices	$\frac{1}{8}$	teaspoon black pepper
4	teaspoons extra-virgin olive oil, divided	4	(2-ounce) ciabatta rolls, split and toasted
1	garlic clove, minced	8	large basil leaves
$1\frac{1}{2}$	teaspoons balsamic vinegar	1	medium tomato, thinly sliced
$\frac{1}{8}$	teaspoon kosher salt	6	ounces fresh mozzarella cheese, thinly sliced

1. Heat a large grill pan over medium-high heat. Place zucchini in a shallow dish. Add 2 teaspoons oil and garlic; toss to coat. Arrange zucchini in grill pan; cook 2 minutes on each side or until grill marks appear. Cut each zucchini piece in half crosswise. Return zucchini to shallow dish. Drizzle with vinegar. Sprinkle with salt and black pepper.

2. Brush bottom halves of rolls with 2 teaspoons oil. Top evenly with zucchini, basil leaves, tomato slices, and mozzarella.

3. Brush cut side of roll tops with remaining liquid from shallow dish, and place on sandwiches. Heat sandwiches in pan until warm. Serves 4 (serving size: 1 sandwich)

CALORIES 343; FAT 16.8g (sat 6.6g, mono 8g, poly 1.3g); PROTEIN 15.4g; CARB 35.3g; FIBER 2g; CHOL 34mg; IRON 2.3mg; SODIUM 722mg; CALC 229mg

Mini Falafel Pocket Sandwiches

Hands-on time: 28 min.   Total time: 1 hr. 28 min.

Tahini-Yogurt Sauce:
- 1/3 cup plain low-fat yogurt
- 2 tablespoons tahini (roasted sesame seed paste)
- 2 tablespoons cold water
- 1 tablespoon fresh lemon juice
- 1/4 teaspoon salt
- 1/4 teaspoon freshly ground black pepper

Falafel:
- 1 1/3 cups boiling water
- 2/3 cup uncooked bulgur
- 2 garlic cloves
- 1/3 cup fresh parsley leaves
- 1/4 cup fresh cilantro leaves
- 3/4 teaspoon ground cumin
- 1/4 teaspoon salt
- 1/4 teaspoon ground red pepper
- 1 (15-ounce) can chickpeas (garbanzo beans), rinsed and drained
- 1 large egg white
- 3 tablespoons olive oil, divided
- 2 (6-inch) whole-wheat pitas, halved crosswise
- 1 cup chopped tomato (1 medium tomato)
- 1/2 cup thinly sliced English cucumber
- 1/3 cup thinly sliced red onion

1. To prepare Tahini-Yogurt Sauce, combine first 6 ingredients in a small bowl. Cover and chill until ready to serve.

2. To prepare falafel, combine 1⅓ cups boiling water and bulgur in a small bowl. Cover and let stand 25 to 30 minutes or until tender. Drain.

3. Drop garlic through food chute with processor on; process until minced. Add bulgur, parsley, and next 6 ingredients (through egg white); process until smooth. Divide mixture into 8 equal portions, shaping each into a ½-inch-thick patty. Place patties on a baking sheet; cover and chill 30 minutes.

4. Heat 1½ tablespoons oil in a large nonstick skillet over medium-high heat. Add 4 patties; cook 3 minutes on each side or until golden brown. Repeat procedure with remaining 1½ tablespoons oil and 4 patties.

5. Spread 1 tablespoon Tahini-Yogurt Sauce inside each pita. Fill each pita half with 2 patties. Divide tomato, cucumber, and red onion evenly among pita halves, and drizzle evenly with 1 tablespoon sauce. Serves 4 (serving size: 1 pita half)

CALORIES 406; FAT 16.3g (sat 2.2g, mono 9.3g, poly 3.6g); PROTEIN 14.3g; CARB 55.1g; FIBER 10.7g; CHOL 1mg; IRON 3.5mg; SODIUM 542mg; CALC 116mg

You'll need a knife and fork to dig into these filling sandwiches—try them for a twist on breakfast-for-dinner. The runny yolk is a delicious sauce, but cook the eggs through for anyone whose health makes it a no-no.

Open-Faced Sandwiches with Ricotta, Arugula, and Fried Egg

Hands-on time: 15 min.   Total time: 15 min.

4   (2-ounce) slices whole-wheat country bread
Cooking spray
2   cups arugula
1   tablespoon extra-virgin olive oil, divided
1½   teaspoons fresh lemon juice
½   teaspoon salt, divided
½   teaspoon freshly ground black pepper, divided
4   large eggs
¾   cup part-skim ricotta cheese
¼   cup (1 ounce) grated fresh Parmigiano-Reggiano cheese
1   teaspoon chopped fresh thyme

1. Preheat broiler.

2. Coat both sides of bread with cooking spray. Broil 2 minutes on each side or until lightly toasted.

3. Combine arugula, 2 teaspoons oil, juice, ⅛ teaspoon salt, and ¼ teaspoon pepper; toss gently.

4. Heat 1 teaspoon oil in a large nonstick skillet over medium heat. Crack eggs into pan; cook 2 minutes. Cover and cook 2 minutes or until whites are set. Remove from heat.

5. Combine ¼ teaspoon salt, ricotta, Parmigiano-Reggiano, and thyme; spread over toast slices. Divide salad and eggs evenly among toast slices. Sprinkle with ⅛ teaspoon salt and ¼ teaspoon pepper. Serves 4 (serving size: 1 sandwich)

CALORIES 337; FAT 15.8g (sat 5.9g, mono 6.9g, poly 1.6g); PROTEIN 21.8g; CARB 27.2g; FIBER 4.1g; CHOL 231mg; IRON 2.8mg; SODIUM 807mg; CALC 316mg

Intensify everyday balsamic vinegar (not the expensive stuff) by reducing it. It will get syrupy, with a great balance of sweetness and tang—a perfect dressing for this Caprese salad–inspired sandwich.

Summer Tomato, Mozzarella, and Basil Panini with Balsamic Syrup

Hands-on time: 20 min.   Total time: 20 min.

½ cup balsamic vinegar
1 (8-ounce) piece Cuban bread, cut in half horizontally
1 tablespoon extra-virgin olive oil
12 large basil leaves

5 ounces fresh mozzarella cheese, thinly sliced
2 medium tomatoes, thinly sliced
¼ teaspoon salt
⅛ teaspoon freshly ground black pepper
Cooking spray

1. Bring balsamic vinegar to a boil in a small saucepan over medium-high heat; cook until reduced to 3 tablespoons (about 8 minutes).

2. While vinegar reduces, brush cut side of top half of bread with oil. Top evenly with basil, cheese, and tomatoes. Sprinkle evenly with salt and pepper. Brush cut side of bottom half of bread with reduced vinegar; place on top of sandwich. Invert sandwich.

3. Heat a large grill pan over medium-high heat. Coat pan with cooking spray. Add sandwich to pan. Place a cast-iron or other heavy skillet on top of sandwich; press gently to flatten. Cook 3 minutes on each side or until cheese melts and bread is toasted (leave cast-iron skillet on sandwich while it cooks). Cut sandwich into 4 equal pieces. Serves 4 (serving size: 1 sandwich piece)

CALORIES 325; FAT 13.4g (sat 5.5g, mono 5.5g, poly 1.1g); PROTEIN 13.6g; CARB 37.4g; FIBER 2.5g; CHOL 28mg; IRON 2.1mg; SODIUM 726mg; CALC 225mg

Saigon's Late-Night Eats: **IT'S ALWAYS BANH MI HOUR IN HO CHI MINH CITY, FORMERLY SAIGON,** where this sublime sandwich originated. "Banh mi," which means "foreign wheat," reflects Vietnam's history, combining the French baguette with traditional Vietnamese toppings. A perfect street food, these sandwiches are wrapped in scrap paper and sold hot by pushcart vendors at all hours of the day and night.

The bread and the Vietnamese filling—carrot, daikon radish, cilantro, mayonnaise, and cucumber—are traditional in this vegetarian take on the classic.

Lemongrass Tofu Banh Mi

Hands-on time: 26 min.   Total time: 50 min.

1 (14-ounce) package water-packed extra-firm tofu, drained
2 tablespoons finely chopped peeled fresh lemongrass
2 tablespoons water
1 tablespoon lower-sodium soy sauce
2 teaspoons sesame oil, divided
¼ cup rice vinegar
¼ cup water
1 tablespoon sugar
¼ teaspoon salt
1¼ cups matchstick-cut carrots
1¼ cups matchstick-cut peeled daikon radish
1½ tablespoons chopped fresh cilantro
3 tablespoons canola mayonnaise
1½ teaspoons Sriracha (hot chile sauce)
1 (12-ounce) French bread baguette, halved lengthwise and toasted
Cooking spray
1 cup thinly sliced English cucumber

1. Cut tofu crosswise into 6 (⅔-inch-thick) slices. Arrange tofu on several layers of paper towels. Cover with additional paper towels; top with a cast-iron skillet or other heavy pan. Let stand 15 minutes. Remove tofu from paper towels.

2. Combine lemongrass, 2 tablespoons water, soy sauce, and 1 teaspoon sesame oil in a 13 x 9–inch glass or ceramic baking dish. Arrange tofu slices in a single layer in soy mixture, turning to coat. Let stand 15 minutes.

3. Combine vinegar and next 3 ingredients (through salt) in a medium bowl, stirring until sugar and salt dissolve. Add carrot and radish; toss well. Let stand 30 minutes, stirring occasionally. Drain; stir in cilantro.

4. Combine 1 teaspoon sesame oil, mayonnaise, and Sriracha in a small bowl, stirring with a whisk. Spread mayonnaise mixture evenly on cut sides of bread.

5. Heat a large nonstick skillet over medium-high heat. Coat pan with cooking spray. Remove tofu from marinade; discard marinade. Pat tofu slices dry with paper towels. Add tofu slices to pan; cook 4 minutes on each side or until crisp and golden. Arrange tofu slices on bottom half of bread; top tofu slices with carrot mixture and cucumber slices. Cut baguette crosswise into 6 equal pieces. Serves 6 (serving size: 1 sandwich piece)

CALORIES 297; FAT 12g (sat 1.1g, mono 4.3g, poly 4g); PROTEIN 12g; CARB 34.9g; FIBER 3.1g; CHOL 3mg; IRON 2.8mg; SODIUM 499mg; CALC 91mg

6 GOOD BREADS

Good bread is the essential foundation here. If you're working with a saucy mix, you want sturdy bread that resists turning soggy. If fillings are subtle, avoid bread with too much flavor (such as rye).

1. Bagel: A real bagel is chewy, substantial, and flavorful. Look for modest ones, not monsters. Plain is best for many sandwiches, but seeded varieties can add a nice note. Don't fill too high—contents squeeze out.

2. Focaccia: This bread often comes as large, flat rounds or rectangles that you can cut into wedges for interesting shapes and then slice open for filling. Focaccia's herbs, olive oil, and toasty flavors pair well with Italian and other Mediterranean ingredients.

3. Boule: The rounded loaf shape yields large, flat slices—ideal for open-faced sandwiches, where you want more surface area.

4. Sandwich Loaves: The difference between a flabby white supermarket loaf and a substantial Pullman loaf is staggering. Try 100% whole grains and multigrains when you want grainy flavors. Dense bread, toasted and served hot with tuna salad, is delicious.

5. Baguette: Oh, that all the limp, fake baguettes were banished and only the sturdy, crusty loaves survived. The crunch factor counterpoints nicely with creamy or soft fillings, cheeses, or grilled vegetables.

6. Flatbreads: Beyond pita, blistered Indian naan and pliable tortilla-like wraps make for a nice change. One large flatbread might equal two or three regular bread servings.

7 GOOD CHEESES

Cheese can shine as the star of a sandwich (as in a great grilled cheese). Choose aged cheeses when you want a warm or toasted sandwich with an oozy melt. Fresh cheeses add richness to cold sandwiches.

1. Provolone: Provolone has a subtle hint of smoke, which makes it perfect for pairing with boldly flavored ingredients, as on a classic muffaletta.

2. Cheddar: Because cheddars range in flavor from mild to sharp, choose your cheddar with your other sandwich fillings in mind. Sharp cheddar pairs nicely with sweet ingredients like sliced apples and pears.

3. Mozzarella: Aged mozzarella is great as a melting cheese or in a stacked sandwich, where its mild flavor can play a supporting role with other fillings. Use fresh mozzarella in smaller stacks or on sub rolls to keep the sandwich from slipping apart.

4. Brie: This is a decadent French cheese with a runny center at room temperature. The rind is edible and can add a pungent flavor.

5. Goat Cheese: Goat cheese adds creaminess and a tart flavor. Pair it with stronger-flavored ingredients such as herbs, roasted or grilled vegetables, lamb, or beef.

6. Manchego: A sheep's milk cheese originally from Spain, Manchego is a good melting cheese with a bit of zip. It can pair with salty meats like serrano ham or prosciutto, or with fruits like apples, pears, and figs.

7. Swiss: Ham is the classic sandwich partner for Swiss cheese, but it can also work with other ingredients, such as chicken, vegetables, fruit, or fruit spreads.

5 GOOD CONDIMENTS

Spice up your sandwich with these homemade spreads and relishes. Some are also great on burgers or as dips. All can be made in advance and stored in airtight containers in the refrigerator.

Double Pepper–Cucumber Relish

Hands-on time: 20 min. Total time: 20 min.

Combine 1 cup halved and thinly sliced English cucumber, ½ cup vertically sliced red onion, ¼ cup sliced pickled pepperoncini peppers, ¼ cup coarsely chopped drained hot cherry peppers, 3 tablespoons crumbled feta cheese, 2 tablespoons chopped fresh parsley, 2 tablespoons pepperoncini pickling liquid, and 1½ tablespoons olive oil in a medium bowl; toss well. Serves 11 (serving size: ¼ cup)

CALORIES 33; FAT 2.5g (sat 0.6g, mono 1.5g, poly 0.3g); PROTEIN 0.5g; CARB 2.4g; FIBER 0.2g; CHOL 2mg; IRON 0.1mg; SODIUM 128mg; CALC 16mg

Inspired by traditional mint chutney, a condiment in Indian cuisine, this piquant spread adds a burst of flavor to sandwiches and wraps.

Mint-Cilantro Spread

Hands-on time: 6 min. Total time: 6 min.

With processor on, drop 1 peeled garlic clove and 1 (¼-inch-thick) slice peeled fresh ginger through food chute; process until minced. Add ½ cup fresh mint leaves; ½ cup fresh cilantro leaves; 1 teaspoon sugar; 2 teaspoons fresh lime juice; ¼ teaspoon salt; and 1 serrano chile, halved lengthwise, seeded, and sliced. Process until finely chopped. Add ½ cup plain 2% reduced-fat Greek yogurt and ¼ cup canola mayonnaise; process 20 seconds or until blended. Cover and chill. Serves 16 (serving size: 1 tablespoon)

CALORIES 19; FAT 1.3g (sat 0.1g, mono 0.7g, poly 0.4g); PROTEIN 0.7g; CARB 1.1g; FIBER 0.1g; CHOL 1mg; IRON 0.1mg; SODIUM 62mg; CALC 8mg

Quick Piccalilli

Hands-on time: 15 min.   Total time: 15 min.

Drain 1 (16-ounce) jar California hot mix (cauliflower, jalapeño peppers, carrot, celery, red bell pepper, and pickles), reserving 3 tablespoons pickling liquid. Combine reserved pickling liquid, 1½ teaspoons Dijon mustard, and ¼ teaspoon ground turmeric in a large bowl, stirring with a whisk. Add drained hot mix, 1 cup chopped onion, 1 cup chopped red bell pepper, 1 tablespoon dill pickle relish, and 2 thinly sliced garlic cloves; toss to combine. Cover and chill until ready to serve. Serves 28 (serving size: 1 tablespoon)

CALORIES 4; FAT 0g (sat 0g, mono 0g, poly 0g); PROTEIN 0.1g; CARB 1g; FIBER 0.1g; CHOL 0mg; IRON 0mg; SODIUM 112mg; CALC 1mg

Tarragon Mustard Spread

Hands-on time: 6 min.   Total time: 6 min.

Combine ⅓ cup canola mayonnaise, 2 tablespoons Dijon mustard, 1 tablespoon chopped fresh tarragon, 1 tablespoon honey, 1 teaspoon white wine vinegar, and ¼ teaspoon freshly ground black pepper in a small bowl, stirring with a whisk. Cover and refrigerate until ready to serve. Serves 8 (serving size: 1 tablespoon)

CALORIES 79; FAT 7.3g (sat 0.7g, mono 4g, poly 2g); PROTEIN 0g; CARB 3g; FIBER 0g; CHOL 3mg; IRON 0mg; SODIUM 157mg; CALC 2mg

Creamy Avocado Spread

Hands-on time: 9 min.   Total time: 9 min.

Mash 1 ripe avocado in a small bowl. Stir in ¼ cup light sour cream, 1 tablespoon lemon juice, 2 teaspoons chopped fresh cilantro, ¼ teaspoon salt, and ¼ teaspoon freshly ground black pepper. Serves 13 (serving size: 1 tablespoon)

CALORIES 32; FAT 2.7g (sat 0.7g, mono 1.6g, poly 0.3g); PROTEIN 0.6g; CARB 2g; FIBER 1.1g; CHOL 0mg; IRON 0.1mg; SODIUM 50mg; CALC 2mg

BUILD A HEALTHY SANDWICH

From a Dagwood to a panino, a sandwich can be as healthy as you want it to be. The key: smart portions and choices as you build it layer by layer.

BREADS Great bread utterly transforms a sandwich. But stay right-sized: 1-ounce slices of loaf bread (check the label), 6-inch pita bread, or 2 to 3 ounces of a baguette. Whole grains really do make a difference—more nutrients, more fiber, more flavor, more satisfying.

ENRICHED WHITE 70 calories a slice—no whole grains, little fiber. But sometimes, there's just no substitute.

BAGUETTE White is nice, but multigrain can be delicious; look for whole-grain versions. It's easy to cut it too long—note the proper portion size above.

WHOLE-WHEAT PITA Half a 6-inch pita is the lowest-calorie choice, with just 85.

RYE Most rye breads count as a whole-grain serving, but be aware that two slices are high in sodium (422mg).

100% WHOLE-GRAIN A sandwich made with this bread is your best source of whole-grain nutrition, plus 6g fiber. White whole-wheat counts, too: It's made from an albino wheat.

MEATS & SALADS Many delis pride themselves on towering meat stacks and double scoops of egg salad, taking a simple sandwich into mega-burger calorie territory. Think of these fillings as supporting players while you load on vegetables. Keep portion sizes smart: ½ cup of salads or 2 ounces of deli meats—about two or three thin slices.

EGG SALAD Delicious, but even a half-cup of egg-and-mayo mix can deliver a quarter of your day's 20g sat fat allotment.

LOW-FAT SMOKED HAM Lean (less than a gram of sat fat per serving) but salty—730mg of sodium, 32% of your daily allowance.

BEEF PASTRAMI Delicious, and the lean version is less fatty than you'd think (1.5g sat fat), but a high-sodium choice.

LOWER-SODIUM TURKEY Not only lean, but also delivers about half the sodium of smoked ham.

LOWER-SODIUM ROAST BEEF Has the same fat profile as turkey but is much lower in sodium (just 81mg) and tasty, too.

CHEESES

CHEESES Cheese is delicious, and calcium is good, but portions are key: Stick to 1-ounce servings (picture four dice lying end to end; that's about an ounce of cheddar). If you're going to melt a firm cheese, grate it—it will go farther.

CHEDDAR 200mg calcium per ounce is a fifth of your daily need. But 6g sat fat is more than 25% of your daily allowance.

BRIE A gram less sat fat than cheddar. Less calcium, too.

GOAT CHEESE Tasty; not a great calcium choice but lower in calories and sat fat than many other cheeses.

SWISS One of the calcium kings (272mg per ounce) and less sat fat than cheddar. Also the lowest-sodium choice: 74mg.

PART-SKIM MOZZARELLA 3g sat fat per ounce; good for melting.

CONDIMENTS

CONDIMENTS Generally the right approach here is to avoid "slathering." High-quality condiments (there are tons of creative choices on specialty and supermarket shelves these days) deliver big flavor in small squirts or dollops.

CANOLA MAYO Good-fat oil saves a bit of sat fat, but calories are the same as a tablespoon of regular mayo: 110.

TAPENADE Tangy and low in calories, but the briny olives pack in sodium (a tablespoon has 150mg). Just a dab will do you.

PESTO Yum. Olive oil and pine nuts mean lots of good fats, with fewer calories than mayo (78 per tablespoon).

HUMMUS About a quarter of the calories of mayo; sodium is usually low, even in 2 tablespoons. Bonuses: rich flavor, 2g fiber.

MUSTARD More mustard than mayo, please. It's a virtually no-calorie flavor-booster, but a teaspoon has 56mg sodium.

PILE ON THE GOOD STUFF!

PILE ON THE GOOD STUFF! Fresh vegetables and fruits, with their garden flavors, crunch, fiber, and healthy phytonutrients, should be the real foundation of a great sandwich. Get creative with:

- arugula
- tomato slices
- pear slices
- piles of sprouts
- radish slices
- cucumber
- apple and mango
- sweet peppers
- grilled onions

SNACKS & SIDES

TOSS, FRY, STIR, DIP.

(crunch. munch. reach for another.)

These nachos have all the goodies you dream of, with beans, cheese, sour cream, and salsa topping crisp chips. For maximum crunch, use regular multigrain chips; baked chips go soggy quickly. Skip the jalapeños if you're sharing with children.

Loaded Nachos

Hands-on time: 12 min.   Total time: 16 min.

1   cup fat-free refried beans
¼   cup minced fresh cilantro, divided
¼   cup chopped green onions, divided
32   multigrain tortilla chips (about 3 ounces)
1½   cups (6 ounces) shredded Monterey Jack cheese
3   tablespoons light sour cream
32   pickled jalapeño pepper slices (optional)
Fresh salsa

1. Preheat oven to 375°.

2. Combine refried beans, 2 tablespoons cilantro, and 2 tablespoons green onions in a 1-quart saucepan. Cook over low heat 4 minutes or until thoroughly heated, stirring occasionally.

3. Place chips on a large jelly-roll pan. Dollop bean mixture over chips; top with cheese. Bake at 375° for 4 minutes or until cheese melts. Remove from oven. Dollop sour cream over cheese; sprinkle with 2 tablespoons cilantro and 2 tablespoons green onions. Garnish with jalapeño pepper slices, if desired. Serve immediately with salsa. Serves 8 (serving size: 4 nachos)

CALORIES 138; FAT 7.1g (sat 3g, mono 1.7g, poly 1g); PROTEIN 7.5g; CARB 12g; FIBER 2g; CHOL 15mg; IRON 0.8mg; SODIUM 323mg; CALC 175mg

Here's a great game-day party dip: You can make it ahead and reheat it when you're ready to serve. Chipotle chile powder is spicy, so adjust the amount to suit your taste.

Tex-Mex Beef and Bean Dip

Hands-on time: 20 min.   Total time: 20 min.

½ pound ground sirloin
2 tablespoons no-salt-added tomato paste
1 to 2 teaspoons chipotle chile powder
¾ teaspoon ground cumin
1 (15-ounce) can pinto beans, rinsed and drained

1 (14.5-ounce) can diced tomatoes, undrained
¾ cup (3 ounces) crumbled queso fresco
¼ cup thinly sliced green onions
3 ounces baked tortilla chips

1. Cook beef in a large nonstick skillet over medium-high heat until browned, stirring to crumble. Drain well; return beef to pan. Add tomato paste and next 4 ingredients (through diced tomatoes), and bring to a boil. Reduce heat, and simmer 5 minutes or until thick, stirring occasionally.

2. Spoon meat mixture into a serving bowl; top with crumbled cheese and green onions. Serve with tortilla chips. Serves 12 (serving size: ¼ cup dip and 5 chips)

CALORIES 99; FAT 2.5g (sat 1.1g, mono 0.7g, poly 0.1g); PROTEIN 7.3g; CARB 12g; FIBER 1.9g; CHOL 15mg; IRON 1.2mg; SODIUM 216mg; CALC 53mg

Enjoy the flavor of Buffalo wings without hauling out the deep fryer: A slow cooker makes the work easier.

Buffalo-Style Drummettes with Blue Cheese Dip

Hands-on time: 14 min. Total time: 3 hr. 21 min.

Cooking spray
- 3 pounds chicken wing drummettes, skinned (30 drummettes)
- 1/4 teaspoon freshly ground black pepper
- 3/4 cup thick hot sauce
- 2 tablespoons cider vinegar
- 1 teaspoon lower-sodium Worcestershire sauce
- 2 garlic cloves, minced

Blue Cheese Dip
- 30 carrot sticks
- 30 celery sticks

1. Preheat oven to 450°.

2. Line a jelly-roll pan with foil; coat foil with cooking spray. Place chicken on prepared pan; sprinkle with pepper. Lightly coat chicken with cooking spray. Bake, uncovered, at 450° for 7 minutes or until lightly browned.

3. Combine hot sauce and next 3 ingredients (through garlic) in an oval 4-quart electric slow cooker coated with cooking spray.

4. Remove chicken from pan; drain on paper towels. Place chicken in slow cooker, tossing gently to coat with sauce. Cover and cook on HIGH for 3 hours or until chicken is very tender. Serve with Blue Cheese Dip, carrot sticks, and celery sticks. Serves 15 (serving size: 2 drummettes, about 1 tablespoon dip, 2 carrot sticks, and 2 celery sticks)

CALORIES 95; FAT 4.8g (sat 1.7g, mono 1.6g, poly 0.7g); PROTEIN 7.9g; CARB 4g; FIBER 0.5g; CHOL 25mg; IRON 0.4mg; SODIUM 248mg; CALC 42mg

Blue Cheese Dip

Hands-on time: 5 min. Total time: 5 min.

- 1 cup (8 ounces) 1/3-less-fat cream cheese
- 1 cup fat-free sour cream
- 6 tablespoons blue cheese, crumbled and divided
- 1/4 cup canola mayonnaise
- 4 garlic cloves, minced

1. Beat cream cheese in a medium bowl with a mixer at low speed until smooth. Add sour cream, 3 tablespoons blue cheese, mayonnaise, and garlic, beating until smooth.

2. Stir in 3 tablespoons blue cheese. Serves 18 (serving size: about 1 tablespoon)

CALORIES 45; FAT 3.7g (sat 1.4g, mono 1.4g, poly 0.5g); PROTEIN 1.3g; CARB 2g; FIBER 0g; CHOL 8mg; IRON 0mg; SODIUM 74mg; CALC 29mg

Adobo Chips with Warm Goat Cheese and Cilantro Salsa

Hands-on time: 17 min. Total time: 1 hr. 52 min.

Salsa:
- 1 (7-ounce) can chipotle chiles in adobo sauce
- 2 cups chopped fresh cilantro (about 1 bunch)
- 1 cup finely chopped tomatillos (about 4 medium)
- ¼ cup minced red onion
- ¼ cup fresh lime juice

Chips:
- 2½ teaspoons fresh lime juice
- 1 teaspoon canola oil
- ½ teaspoon paprika
- ¼ teaspoon ground cumin
- 8 (6-inch) white corn tortillas

Cheese:
- ½ cup (4 ounces) block-style fat-free cream cheese, softened
- ¼ cup (2 ounces) goat cheese

1. To prepare salsa, remove 2 chipotle chiles from can; finely chop to measure 2 teaspoons. Remove 1 teaspoon adobo sauce from can, and set aside for chips (reserve remaining chipotle chiles and adobo sauce for another use). Combine chiles, cilantro, tomatillos, onion, and ¼ cup lime juice in a medium bowl; cover and chill 1 hour.

2. Preheat oven to 375°.

3. To prepare chips, combine 2½ teaspoons lime juice, canola oil, reserved 1 teaspoon adobo sauce, paprika, and cumin in a small bowl, stirring with a whisk. Brush 1 tortilla with about ¼ teaspoon juice mixture, spreading to edge. Top with another tortilla; repeat procedure with juice mixture. Repeat procedure 6 more times (you will have 1 stack of 8 tortillas). Using a sharp knife, cut tortilla stack into 6 wedges. Place wedges in a single layer on baking sheets. Bake at 375° for 15 minutes; turn wedges. Bake an additional 10 minutes.

4. Reduce oven temperature to 350°.

5. To prepare cheese, combine cream cheese and goat cheese in a small bowl; stir until blended. Spread cheese mixture in a shallow 6-ounce ramekin or glass or ceramic baking dish; cover with foil. Bake at 350° for 10 minutes or just until warm. Serves 8 (serving size: 6 chips, 1½ tablespoons cheese mixture, and about ¼ cup salsa)

CALORIES 95; FAT 3.3g (sat 1.2g, mono 0.9g, poly 0.6g); PROTEIN 4.9g; CARB 13g; FIBER 1.8g; CHOL 4mg; IRON 0.5mg; SODIUM 131mg; CALC 60mg

If you can't find baby artichoke hearts, use quartered artichoke hearts and chop them. Serve this warm dip with your favorite multigrain crackers.

Artichoke, Spinach, and White Bean Dip

Hands-on time: 15 min.   Total time: 35 min.

¼ cup (1 ounce) grated fresh pecorino Romano cheese

¼ cup canola mayonnaise

1 teaspoon fresh lemon juice

¼ teaspoon salt

¼ teaspoon freshly ground black pepper

⅛ teaspoon ground red pepper

2 garlic cloves, minced

1 (15-ounce) can organic white beans, rinsed and drained

1 (14-ounce) can baby artichoke hearts, drained and quartered

1 (9-ounce) package frozen chopped spinach, thawed, drained, and squeezed dry

Cooking spray

½ cup (2 ounces) shredded part-skim mozzarella cheese

1. Preheat oven to 350°.

2. Place first 8 ingredients (through white beans) in a food processor, and process until smooth. Spoon into a medium bowl. Stir in artichokes and spinach. Spoon mixture into a 1-quart glass or ceramic baking dish coated with cooking spray. Sprinkle with mozzarella. Bake at 350° for 20 minutes or until bubbly and brown. Serves 12 (serving size: ¼ cup)

CALORIES 87; FAT 5.4g (sat 1.4g, mono 2.3g, poly 1g); PROTEIN 3.7g; CARB 4.9g; FIBER 1g; CHOL 6mg; IRON 0.7mg; SODIUM 232mg; CALC 91mg

Serve this quick after-school snack to your kids as an alternative to traditional fried cheesesticks.

Baked Mozzarella Bites

Hands-on time: 15 min.   Total time: 18 min.

1/3   cup panko (Japanese breadcrumbs)
3   (1-ounce) sticks part-skim mozzarella string cheese

3   tablespoons egg substitute
Cooking spray
1/4   cup lower-sodium marinara sauce

1. Preheat oven to 425°.

2. Heat a medium skillet over medium heat. Add panko to pan, and cook 2 minutes or until toasted, stirring frequently. Remove from heat, and place panko in a shallow dish.

3. Cut mozzarella sticks into 1-inch pieces. Working with 1 piece at a time, dip cheese in egg substitute; dredge in panko. Place cheese on a baking sheet coated with cooking spray. Bake at 425° for 3 minutes or until cheese is softened and thoroughly heated.

4. Pour marinara sauce into a microwave-safe bowl. Microwave at HIGH 1 minute or until thoroughly heated, stirring after 30 seconds. Serve with mozzarella pieces. Serves 4 (serving size: 3 mozzarella bites and 1 tablespoon sauce)

CALORIES 91; FAT 5.1g (sat 2.8g, mono 1.3g, poly 0.3g); PROTEIN 7.2g; CARB 6.7g; FIBER 0.1g; CHOL 12mg; IRON 0.3mg; SODIUM 162mg; CALC 162mg

For the best crunch, coat the onion rings with breadcrumbs in batches—working in smaller amounts will keep the crumbs dry.

Barbecue-Flavored Onion Rings

Hands-on time: 10 min.   Total time: 29 min.

3 tablespoons all-purpose flour
1 tablespoon sugar
1 teaspoon chili powder
1 teaspoon ground cumin
½ teaspoon paprika
¼ teaspoon salt
¼ teaspoon ground allspice

2 large eggs
1 pound Vidalia or other sweet onions, cut into ¼-inch-thick slices and separated into rings (about 2 medium onions)
1½ cups dry breadcrumbs, divided
Cooking spray

1. Preheat oven to 450°.

2. Combine first 7 ingredients in a large bowl, stirring with a whisk. Add eggs; beat with a whisk until blended. Dip onion rings in egg mixture, briefly draining off excess. Place half of onion rings in a large zip-top plastic bag; add ¾ cup breadcrumbs to bag. Seal bag, and shake to coat onion rings. Arrange coated onion rings on a baking sheet coated with cooking spray. Repeat procedure with remaining onion rings and ¾ cup breadcrumbs; arrange onion rings on second baking sheet coated with cooking spray. Lightly coat onion rings with cooking spray.

3. Bake at 450° for 10 minutes. Turn onion rings over; lightly coat with cooking spray, and bake 9 minutes or until browned and crisp. Serve immediately. Serves 6 (serving size: ½ cup)

CALORIES 187; FAT 3.4g (sat 0.9g, mono 0.9g, poly 0.8g); PROTEIN 7g; CARB 32g; FIBER 2.8g; CHOL 71mg; IRON 2.1mg; SODIUM 335mg; CALC 80mg

Bacon, bourbon, and maple syrup make this American classic special. Check your beans 10 to 15 minutes ahead of time to make sure they're not drying out.

Bourbon Baked Beans

Hands-on time: 23 min.   Total time: 11 hr. 31 min.

1 pound dried navy beans (about 2½ cups)	¼ cup Dijon mustard
3 applewood-smoked bacon slices	1½ teaspoons Worcestershire sauce
1 cup finely chopped onion	¼ teaspoon freshly ground black pepper
5 cups water, divided	1 tablespoon cider vinegar
½ cup maple syrup, divided	1 teaspoon salt
¼ cup plus 2 tablespoons bourbon, divided	

1. Sort and wash beans; place in a large Dutch oven. Cover with water to 2 inches above beans; cover and let stand 8 hours or overnight. Drain beans. Wipe pan dry with a paper towel.

2. Preheat oven to 350°.

3. Heat pan over medium-high heat. Add bacon to pan, and cook 4 minutes or until crisp. Remove from pan, reserving 1½ tablespoons drippings in pan; crumble bacon. Add onion to drippings in pan; cook 5 minutes or until onion begins to brown, stirring frequently. Add beans, bacon, 4 cups water, ¼ cup maple syrup, ¼ cup bourbon, and next 3 ingredients (through pepper) to pan. Bring to a boil; cover and bake at 350° for 2 hours.

4. Stir in 1 cup water, ¼ cup maple syrup, and 2 tablespoons bourbon. Cover and bake 1 hour or until beans are tender and liquid is almost absorbed. Stir in vinegar and salt. Serves 13 (serving size: ½ cup)

CALORIES 199; FAT 3.1g (sat 1.1g, mono 0.7g, poly 0.5g); PROTEIN 7.8g; CARB 31.8g, FIBER 5.6g; CHOL 4mg; IRON 2.1mg; SODIUM 307mg; CALC 66mg

Bear-Flavored Beans? **THE ORIGINAL NATIVE AMERICAN RECIPE FOR BAKED BEANS** combined the beans with maple sugar and bear fat. The recipe was adapted by early American settlers, who replaced the maple sugar with molasses and the bear fat with pork fat.

Bread-and-Butter Pickles

Hands-on time: 16 min. Total time: 26 hr. 46 min.

5½   cups thinly sliced pickling cucumbers
       (about 1½ pounds)
1½   tablespoons kosher salt
   1   cup thinly sliced onion
   1   cup granulated sugar
   1   cup white vinegar
 ½   cup cider vinegar
 ¼   cup packed brown sugar
1½   teaspoons mustard seeds
 ½   teaspoon celery seeds
 ⅛   teaspoon ground turmeric

1. Combine cucumbers and salt in a large bowl; cover and chill 1½ hours. Drain; rinse cucumbers under cold water. Drain; return cucumbers to bowl. Add onion to bowl.

2. Combine granulated sugar and next 6 ingredients (through turmeric) in a medium saucepan; bring to a simmer over medium heat, stirring until sugars dissolve. Pour hot vinegar mixture over cucumber mixture; let stand at room temperature 1 hour. Cover and refrigerate 24 hours. Store in an airtight container in refrigerator up to 2 weeks. Serves 16 (serving size: about ¼ cup drained pickles)

CALORIES 18; FAT 0.1g (sat 0g, mono 0g, poly 0g); PROTEIN 0.4g; CARB 4.4g; FIBER 0.5g; CHOL 0mg; IRON 0.1mg; SODIUM 168mg; CALC 8mg

This easy slaw is just the side to serve with hamburgers, fish sandwiches, hot dogs, or pulled barbecue.

Cabbage Slaw

Hands-on time: 16 min. Total time: 16 min.

   4   cups shredded cabbage
1½   cups thinly sliced radishes
 ½   cup diagonally cut green onions
   3   tablespoons olive oil
   2   tablespoons fresh lemon juice
 ⅓   cup chopped fresh mint
 ½   teaspoon salt
 ¼   teaspoon ground red pepper

1. Combine first 5 ingredients; toss. Sprinkle with mint, salt, and pepper. Serves 6 (serving size: ½ cup)

CALORIES 81; FAT 6.9g (sat 1g, mono 4.9g, poly 0.8g); PROTEIN 1g; CARB 5g; FIBER 2g; CHOL 0mg; IRON 0.6mg; SODIUM 218mg; CALC 36mg

> **Happy (Pickled) New Year:**
> **MT. OLIVE PICKLES HOSTS THE ANNUAL NEW YEAR'S EVE PICKLE DROP** in Mount Olive, North Carolina. A three-foot lighted pickle descends the company's 45-foot flagpole, and there are plenty of pickles to snack on.

Bread-and-Butter Pickles

Cabbage Slaw

Chipotle Black Bean Dip with Corn Chips

Hands-on time: 25 min. Total time: 47 min.

  6   (6-inch) corn tortillas
Cooking spray
 1/8 teaspoon salt
  1   teaspoon olive oil
  1   cup chopped onion
  1   teaspoon cumin seeds
  1   garlic clove, minced
 1/4 teaspoon dried oregano
  1   (15-ounce) can black beans, undrained
 1/4 cup (1 ounce) shredded part-skim
      mozzarella cheese
  2   tablespoons crumbled queso fresco
 1/3 cup canned no-salt-added diced tomatoes,
      undrained
  1   chipotle chile, canned in adobo sauce
  2   tablespoons chopped fresh cilantro

1. Preheat oven to 400°. Cut each tortilla into 6 wedges. Arrange in a single layer on a baking sheet coated with cooking spray. Sprinkle with salt. Bake at 400° for 10 minutes or until golden brown and crisp.

2. Heat oil in a saucepan over medium heat. Add onion; cook 8 minutes or until tender. Add cumin and garlic; cook 1 minute. Add oregano and beans; bring to a boil. Mash with a potato masher. Reduce heat; simmer 10 minutes or until thick, stirring occasionally.

3. Spoon bean mixture into a 3-cup gratin dish coated with cooking spray. Top with cheeses. Bake at 400° for 12 minutes or until hot and bubbly.

4. Combine tomatoes and chile in a mini food processor; process until smooth. Spoon tomato mixture over bean mixture. Sprinkle with cilantro. Serves 6 (serving size: about 1/4 cup dip and 6 tortilla chips)

CALORIES 142; FAT 3.5g (sat 1g, mono 1.1g, poly 0.5g); PROTEIN 6.6g; CARB 27.7g; FIBER 6g; CHOL 4mg; IRON 1.6mg; SODIUM 502mg; CALC 128mg

Creamy Potato Salad

Hands-on time: 16 min. Total time: 39 min.

 1 1/2 pounds baking potatoes, peeled
  1/3 cup canola mayonnaise
   1   tablespoon white vinegar
   2   teaspoons spicy brown mustard
  1/4 teaspoon salt
  1/4 teaspoon freshly ground black pepper
  1/2 cup chopped green onions (4 onions)
  1/4 cup sweet or dill pickle relish
   2   hard-cooked large eggs, finely shredded
  1/8 teaspoon freshly ground black pepper (optional)
Chopped fresh parsley (optional)

1. Place potatoes in water to cover. Bring to a boil; cook 16 to 18 minutes or until tender. Drain; cool 15 minutes. Cut into cubes.

2. Combine mayonnaise and next 4 ingredients in a large bowl. Add potato, onions, relish, and eggs; toss to coat. Serve immediately, or cover and chill. Sprinkle with 1/8 teaspoon pepper and parsley, if desired, just before serving. Serves 8 (serving size: 1/2 cup)

CALORIES 173; FAT 8.8g (sat 1.1g, mono 4.5g, poly 2.2g); PROTEIN 3.1g; CARB 20.3g; FIBER 1.9g; CHOL 56mg; IRON 0.6mg; SODIUM 236mg; CALC 19mg

Chipotle Black Bean Dip with Corn Chips

Creamy Potato Salad

Parmesan-Coated Potato Wedges

Garlic Fries

Tossing the fries in a small amount of butter makes them unbelievably rich.

Garlic Fries

Hands-on time: 17 min. Total time: 1 hr. 7 min.

4 teaspoons vegetable oil
¾ teaspoon salt
3 pounds peeled baking potatoes, cut into ¼-inch-thick strips
Cooking spray
2 tablespoons butter
8 garlic cloves, minced (about 5 teaspoons)
2 tablespoons finely chopped fresh parsley
2 tablespoons grated fresh Parmesan cheese

1. Preheat oven to 400°.

2. Combine first 3 ingredients in a large zip-top plastic bag, tossing to coat.

3. Arrange potatoes in a single layer on a baking sheet coated with cooking spray. Bake at 400° for 50 minutes or until potatoes are tender and golden brown, turning after 20 minutes.

4. Place butter and garlic in a large nonstick skillet; cook over low heat 2 minutes, stirring constantly. Add potatoes, parsley, and cheese to pan; toss to coat. Serve immediately. Serves 6

CALORIES 286; FAT 7.7g (sat 3.2g, mono 1.8g, poly 2.3g); PROTEIN 5.4g; CARB 50g; FIBER 3.5g; CHOL 12mg; IRON 1mg; SODIUM 360mg; CALC 40mg

Parmesan-Coated Potato Wedges

Hands-on time: 20 min. Total time: 50 min.

¾ teaspoon kosher salt
1.5 ounces all-purpose flour (about ⅓ cup)
3 large egg whites
1 tablespoon water
¾ cup (3 ounces) grated fresh Parmigiano-Reggiano cheese
½ cup panko (Japanese breadcrumbs), finely crushed
2 (8-ounce) baking potatoes, each cut lengthwise into 8 wedges
2 (8-ounce) sweet potatoes, each cut lengthwise into 8 wedges

1. Preheat oven to 425°.

2. Combine salt and flour in a shallow dish. Combine egg whites and 1 tablespoon water in a shallow dish, stirring with a whisk. Combine cheese and panko in another shallow dish.

3. Dredge potato wedges in flour mixture. Dip in egg white mixture; dredge in cheese mixture. Divide potato wedges between 2 baking sheets lined with parchment paper. Bake at 425° for 30 minutes or until golden, rotating pans after 20 minutes. Serves 8 (serving size: 4 wedges)

CALORIES 165; FAT 2.4g (sat 1.3g, mono 0.6g, poly 0.1g); PROTEIN 7.4g; CARB 28.5g; FIBER 2.7g; CHOL 7mg; IRON 1.2mg; SODIUM 360mg; CALC 109mg

This easy, five-ingredient grilled corn gets its flavor from jalapeño peppers that are roasted, chopped, and stirred into honey butter.

Grilled Corn on the Cob with Roasted Jalapeño Butter

Hands-on time: 26 min.   Total time: 31 min.

1 jalapeño pepper
Cooking spray
7 teaspoons unsalted butter, softened
1 teaspoon grated lime rind

2 teaspoons honey
¼ teaspoon salt
6 ears shucked corn

1. Preheat grill to medium-high heat.

2. Place jalapeño on grill rack coated with cooking spray; cover and grill 10 minutes or until blackened and charred, turning occasionally.

3. Place jalapeño in a small paper bag, and fold to close tightly. Let stand 5 minutes. Peel and discard skins; cut jalapeño in half lengthwise. Discard stem, seeds, and membranes. Finely chop jalapeño. Combine jalapeño, butter, lime rind, honey, and salt in a small bowl; stir well.

4. Place corn on grill rack. Cover and grill 10 minutes or until lightly charred, turning occasionally. Place corn on serving plate; brush with jalapeño butter. Serves 6 (serving size: 1 ear corn)

CALORIES 124; FAT 5.5g (sat 3g, mono 1.5g, poly 0.7g); PROTEIN 3g; CARB 19.2g; FIBER 2.5g; CHOL 12mg; IRON 0.5mg; SODIUM 113mg; CALC 4mg

If you're making these poppers for a party, you can stuff the peppers, cover, and chill. Then grill just before your guests arrive.

Grilled Stuffed Jalapeños

Hands-on time: 29 min.   Total time: 38 min.

2 center-cut bacon slices, cooked and crumbled
½ cup (4 ounces) cream cheese, softened
½ cup (4 ounces) fat-free cream cheese, softened
¼ cup (1 ounce) shredded extra-sharp cheddar cheese
¼ cup minced green onions
1 teaspoon fresh lime juice
¼ teaspoon kosher salt
1 small garlic clove, minced
14 jalapeño peppers, halved lengthwise and seeded
Cooking spray
2 tablespoons chopped fresh cilantro
2 tablespoons chopped seeded tomato

1. Preheat grill to medium-high heat.

2. Combine bacon, cheeses, and next 4 ingredients (through garlic), stirring to combine. Divide cheese mixture among pepper halves. Place peppers on grill rack coated with cooking spray. Cover and grill 8 minutes or until bottoms of peppers are charred and cheese mixture is lightly browned. Place on a serving platter. Sprinkle with cilantro and tomato. Serves 14 (serving size: 2 pepper halves)

CALORIES 56; FAT 4.1g (sat 2.2g, mono 1.1g, poly 0.2g); PROTEIN 2.9g; CARB 2.1g; FIBER 0.5g; CHOL 13mg; IRON 0.2mg; SODIUM 157mg; CALC 55mg

Macaroni Salad

Heirloom Tomato,
Watermelon, and
Peach Salad

Heirloom Tomato, Watermelon, and Peach Salad

Hands-on time: 11 min.   Total time: 2 hr. 11 min.

    2   tablespoons fresh lime juice
  1½   tablespoons extra-virgin olive oil
    1   tablespoon honey
    1   tablespoon white rum
   ¼   teaspoon salt
   ⅛   teaspoon ground red pepper
    3   cups cubed seedless watermelon
  1½   cups sliced peaches
   ½   cup vertically sliced red onion
   ¼   cup torn fresh mint leaves
    2   tablespoons thinly sliced fresh basil
    1   pound heirloom beefsteak tomatoes, cut
         into 1-inch chunks
   ⅓   cup (about 1½ ounces) crumbled goat cheese

1. Combine first 6 ingredients in a large bowl, stirring with a whisk. Add watermelon and next 5 ingredients (through tomatoes); toss gently. Cover and refrigerate 2 hours or until thoroughly chilled. Sprinkle with goat cheese just before serving. Serves 8 (serving size: about ¾ cup)

CALORIES 90; FAT 3.8g (sat 1.1g, mono 2.3g, poly 0.4g); PROTEIN 2g; CARB 12.5g; FIBER 1.5g; CHOL 2mg; IRON 0.5mg; SODIUM 95mg; CALC 22mg

Cut back on the black pepper for a more kid-friendly version of a cookout staple.

Macaroni Salad

Hands-on time: 8 min.   Total time: 14 min.

    1   cup (4 ounces) uncooked elbow macaroni
   ½   cup canola mayonnaise
    1   tablespoon cider vinegar
  1½   teaspoons sugar
   ¾   teaspoon dry mustard
   ½   teaspoon freshly ground black pepper
   ¼   teaspoon salt
   ⅓   cup thinly sliced celery
   ⅓   cup finely chopped red bell pepper
   ¼   cup finely chopped red onion
   ¼   cup grated carrot
    1   tablespoon chopped fresh chives

1. Cook pasta according to package directions, omitting salt and fat; drain.

2. Combine mayonnaise and next 5 ingredients (through salt), stirring with a whisk. Stir in cooked pasta, celery, and remaining ingredients. Cover and store in refrigerator up to 3 days. Serves 6 (serving size: ½ cup)

CALORIES 217; FAT 15.3g (sat 1.4g, mono 8.1g, poly 4.3g); PROTEIN 2.9g; CARB 17g; FIBER 1.3g; CHOL 7mg; IRON 0.8mg; SODIUM 242mg; CALC 13mg

Marinated Heirloom Tomatoes with Mustard and Dill

Hands-on time: 8 min. Total time: 23 min.

1 tablespoon chopped fresh dill
2 tablespoons Dijon mustard
2 teaspoons grated lemon rind
1 teaspoon fresh lemon juice
¼ teaspoon salt
⅛ teaspoon freshly ground black pepper
2 pounds large heirloom tomatoes, cut into
   ¼-inch-thick slices

1. Combine first 6 ingredients in a large bowl. Add tomato slices, tossing gently to coat. Let stand 15 minutes. Serves 6 (serving size: about 5 ounces)

CALORIES 39; FAT 1g (sat 0.1g, mono 0.2g, poly 0.3g); PROTEIN 1.6g; CARB 7.7g; FIBER 1.8g; CHOL 0mg; IRON 0.8mg; SODIUM 238mg; CALC 16mg

Veggies bathed in balsamic vinegar are as irresistible as pickles.

Marinated Asparagus-and-Carrot Salad

Hands-on time: 21 min.   Total time: 4 hr. 21 min.

1	pound asparagus
1/2	cup balsamic vinegar
1/4	cup olive oil
1	tablespoon chopped fresh parsley
1/2	teaspoon salt
1/2	teaspoon freshly ground black pepper
1	garlic clove, minced
4	cups julienne-cut carrot

1. Snap off tough ends of asparagus. Cut into 2-inch pieces. Cook asparagus in boiling water to cover 3 minutes. Drain, and plunge asparagus into ice water; drain. Place vinegar and next 5 ingredients (through garlic) in a large heavy-duty zip-top plastic bag. Seal bag and shake to blend. Add asparagus to bag; seal bag and shake to coat. Chill 3 hours.

2. Add carrot to bag; seal bag and shake to coat. Chill 1 hour. Serves 6 (serving size: 1 cup)

CALORIES 148; FAT 9.3g (sat 1.3g, mono 6.6g, poly 1.1g); PROTEIN 2.6g; CARB 15g; FIBER 3.9g; CHOL 0mg; IRON 2.1mg; SODIUM 260mg; CALC 53mg

Presidential Side: **THOMAS JEFFERSON INTRODUCED AMERICANS TO FRENCH FRIES** in 1801 when he hired a French chef at the White House, who prepared "potatoes fried in the French manner."

Parmesan-Crusted Zucchini Fries

Sweet Potato Shoestring Fries

Parmesan-Crusted Zucchini Fries

Hands-on time: 13 min.   Total time: 33 min.

⅓ cup (about 1½ ounces) finely shredded fresh Parmesan cheese
⅓ cup panko (Japanese breadcrumbs)
½ teaspoon garlic powder
½ teaspoon dried basil
⅛ teaspoon ground red pepper
1 large egg, beaten
3 small zucchini (1¼ pounds)
Cooking spray
½ cup tomato-basil pasta sauce

1. Preheat oven to 450°.

2. Combine first 5 ingredients in a small shallow bowl. Place egg in a separate shallow bowl.

3. Trim ends from zucchini; cut each zucchini in half crosswise. Quarter each zucchini half lengthwise to make 24 zucchini sticks. Dip zucchini in egg; dredge in panko mixture, pressing to coat. Place zucchini on a baking sheet coated with cooking spray. Coat tops of zucchini with cooking spray.

4. Bake at 450° for 20 minutes or until golden brown. Serve immediately with pasta sauce. Serves 4 (serving size: 6 zucchini fries and 2 tablespoons sauce)

CALORIES 94; FAT 3.9g (sat 1.6g, mono 1.1g, poly 0.3g); PROTEIN 6.4g; CARB 9.3g; FIBER 1.8g; CHOL 58mg; IRON 0.9mg; SODIUM 251mg; CALC 128mg

A syrup made from orange juice and spices flavors thin-cut sweet potatoes.

Sweet Potato Shoestring Fries

Hands-on time: 18 min.   Total time: 58 min.

3 tablespoons orange juice
2 teaspoons vegetable oil
½ teaspoon ground ginger
¼ teaspoon salt
⅛ teaspoon ground red pepper
2 large sweet potatoes, peeled and cut into ⅛-inch thick strips (about 1½ pounds)
Cooking spray

1. Preheat oven to 400°.

2. Combine first 5 ingredients in a small saucepan; bring to a boil. Reduce heat; simmer 2 minutes or until slightly thick. Remove from heat; let cool.

3. Combine juice mixture and potatoes in a large bowl; toss well. Remove potatoes from bowl; discard juice mixture. Arrange potato strips in a single layer on a baking sheet coated with cooking spray. Bake at 400° for 30 minutes or until edges are crisp. Serves 4

CALORIES 194; FAT 1.8g (sat 0.3g, mono 0.4g, poly 0.8g); PROTEIN 2.9g; CARB 42.1g; FIBER 5.1g; CHOL 0mg; IRON 1mg; SODIUM 169mg; CALC 38mg

Use Russet or Idaho baking potatoes for these chips.

Sour Cream and Onion Potato Chips

Hands-on time: 34 min.   Total time: 34 min.

1   large baking potato, unpeeled, cut into
    1/8-inch-thick slices
Cooking spray
1 1/2   teaspoons dry ranch dressing mix

1. Arrange one-third of potato slices on a large microwave-safe plate. Coat tops of potato with cooking spray, and sprinkle with one-third of dressing mix.

2. Microwave, uncovered, at HIGH 4 minutes. Turn potato slices over. Microwave at HIGH 3 to 4 minutes or until dried, crisp, and beginning to brown.

3. Remove from plate; cool completely on wire racks. Repeat procedure with remaining potato slices and dressing mix. Serves 6 (serving size: about 10 chips)

CALORIES 52; FAT 0.2g (sat 0g, mono 0.1g, poly 0g); PROTEIN 1.3g; CARB 11.6g; FIBER 0.8g; CHOL 0mg; IRON 0.5mg; SODIUM 71mg; CALC 8mg

To get perfectly thin slices, use a mandoline or the thin slicing blade of a food processor.

BBQ Potato Chips

Hands-on time: 34 min.   Total time: 34 min.

1   large baking potato, unpeeled, cut into
    1/8-inch-thick slices
Cooking spray
2   teaspoons sweet and applewood-smoked
    grilling rub

1. Arrange one-third of potato slices on a large microwave-safe plate. Coat tops of potato with cooking spray, and sprinkle with one-third of rub.

2. Microwave, uncovered, at HIGH 4 minutes. Turn potato slices over. Microwave at HIGH 4 minutes or until dried, crisp, and just beginning to brown.

3. Remove from plate; cool completely on wire racks. Repeat procedure with remaining potato slices and rub. Serves 6 (serving size: about 10 chips)

CALORIES 47; FAT 0.2g (sat 0g, mono 0g, poly 0g); PROTEIN 0.8g; CARB 10.5g; FIBER 1.5g; CHOL 0mg; IRON 0.3mg; SODIUM 86mg; CALC 15mg

Creamy Ranch-Style Dip

Hands-on time: 20 min. Total time: 20 min.

½ cup (4 ounces) ⅓-less-fat cream cheese, softened
3 tablespoons nonfat buttermilk
2 tablespoons chopped fresh flat-leaf parsley
1 teaspoon chopped fresh dill
½ teaspoon minced fresh garlic
¼ teaspoon onion powder
¼ teaspoon salt
¼ teaspoon freshly ground black pepper

1. Combine cream cheese and buttermilk in a small bowl, stirring with a whisk until blended. Stir in remaining ingredients. Serves 6 (serving size: about 2 tablespoons)

CALORIES 52; FAT 4.3g (sat 2.4g, mono 1.1g, poly 0.2g); PROTEIN 2.1g; CARB 1.4g; FIBER 0.1g; CHOL 14mg; IRON 0.1mg; SODIUM 170mg; CALC 34mg

Forget the boxed mixes and chilled store-bought versions: This warm onion dip is on a deliciously different level. Serve it with hearty crackers or slices of French bread.

Warm Caramelized Onion Dip

Hands-on time: 42 min. Total time: 42 min.

- 2 teaspoons olive oil
- 4 cups chopped onion (about 2 large onions)
- 3/4 teaspoon chopped fresh thyme
- 1/2 cup light sour cream
- 1/3 cup (about 1 1/2 ounces) grated Parmigiano-Reggiano cheese

- 1/3 cup (3 ounces) 1/3-less-fat cream cheese
- 1/3 cup reduced-fat mayonnaise
- 1/4 teaspoon salt
- 1/4 teaspoon freshly ground black pepper
- 1/4 teaspoon hot pepper sauce
- 1/4 teaspoon Worcestershire sauce

1. Heat a large nonstick skillet over medium-high heat. Add oil; swirl to coat. Add chopped onion and thyme to pan; sauté 10 minutes or until golden brown. Reduce heat to low; cook 20 minutes or until onions are deep golden brown, stirring occasionally. Remove onion mixture from heat. Add sour cream and remaining ingredients, stirring until blended and cheese melts. Serves 12 (serving size: 3 tablespoons)

CALORIES 81; FAT 4.9g (sat 2.3g, mono 1.2g, poly 0.6g); PROTEIN 3.1g; CARB 7.7g; FIBER 0.9g; CHOL 12mg; IRON 0mg; SODIUM 206mg; CALC 58mg

SWEETS

BAKE, SCOOP, CRUMBLE, SPOON.

(try to leave a little
for someone else's sweet tooth.)

You can use either Dutch process or regular unsweetened cocoa in this pudding. Dutch process cocoa is darker and has a more mellow flavor.

Bittersweet Chocolate Pudding

Hands-on time: 18 min.   Total time: 18 min.

1 cup Dutch process or unsweetened cocoa
3 tablespoons cornstarch
¼ teaspoon salt
3½ cups fat-free milk, divided
1 cup sugar

1 large egg, lightly beaten
1 large egg yolk, lightly beaten
2 ounces bittersweet chocolate, coarsely chopped
1 tablespoon vanilla extract

1. Combine first 3 ingredients in a medium bowl, stirring with a whisk. Gradually add 1 cup milk, stirring with a whisk until blended.

2. Cook 2½ cups milk in a large heavy saucepan over medium-high heat to 180° or until tiny bubbles form around edge (do not boil). Remove from heat; add sugar, stirring with a whisk until sugar dissolves. Gradually add hot milk mixture to cocoa mixture, stirring with a whisk until blended. Return milk mixture to pan; bring to a boil over medium heat. Cook, stirring constantly, 2 minutes or until thick. Remove from heat.

3. Combine egg and egg yolk in a medium bowl; stir with a whisk until blended. Gradually add milk mixture to egg mixture, stirring constantly with a whisk. Return milk mixture to pan. Cook, stirring constantly, over medium heat 2 minutes or until thick and bubbly. Remove from heat. Add chocolate and vanilla, stirring until chocolate melts. Pour into a bowl; cover surface of pudding with plastic wrap. Cool slightly to serve warm, or refrigerate until thoroughly chilled. Serves 8 (serving size: ½ cup)

CALORIES 241; FAT 5.3g (sat 2g, mono 1.9g, poly 0.3g); PROTEIN 7.3g; CARB 43g; FIBER 2.5g; CHOL 55mg; IRON 1.9mg; SODIUM 129mg; CALC 141mg

This light shake is satisfyingly thick. Decrease the amount of malted milk powder if you'd like less malt flavor.

Chocolate Malt Shake

Hands-on time: 5 min.   Total time: 5 min.

2   cups chocolate low-fat ice cream
¼   cup 2% reduced-fat milk
3   tablespoons malted milk powder
2   tablespoons fat-free double chocolate
     sundae syrup

1. Place all ingredients in a blender; process until smooth. Pour into 3 glasses. Serves 3 (serving size: ⅔ cup)

CALORIES 229; FAT 3.3g (sat 2g, mono 0.2g, poly 0g); PROTEIN 4.7g; CARB 47g; FIBER 0.3g; CHOL 8mg; IRON 2.3mg; SODIUM 128mg; CALC 183mg

Soda Shop Lingo: **IN THE '50S, TO ORDER A CHOCOLATE MALT,** you'd ask the soda jerk to "burn one." Want it made with vanilla ice cream? That's a "black and white."

Put the ice cream in the blender last to easily make a smooth shake.

Peach Melba Milk Shake

Hands-on time: 10 min.   Total time: 10 min.

1½ cups 2% reduced-fat milk
 2 cups chopped peeled peaches
1½ cups fresh raspberries
1½ teaspoons fresh lemon juice
 2 tablespoons powdered sugar
 3 cups vanilla low-fat ice cream
14 fresh raspberries (optional)
 7 fresh peach slices (optional)
 7 (6-inch) wooden skewers (optional)

1. Place first 6 ingredients in a blender in the order given; process until smooth. Pour evenly into 7 glasses. If desired, alternately thread 2 raspberries and 1 peach slice on each of 7 wooden skewers, placing 1 skewer in each glass as a garnish. Serves 7 (serving size: ¾ cup)

CALORIES 203; FAT 7.3g (sat 4.5g, mono 1.9g, poly 0.5g); PROTEIN 5.9g; CARB 28g; FIBER 2.4g; CHOL 38mg; IRON 0.6mg; SODIUM 73mg; CALC 199mg

Pull out the big ice-cream freezer for this dessert. The recipe makes 2 quarts, plenty for a crowd yearning for a bowl of homemade ice cream.

Blueberry Cheesecake Ice Cream

Hands-on time: 34 min.   Total time: 2 hr. 36 min.

2 cups granulated sugar
¾ cup ⅓-less-fat cream cheese (6 ounces), softened
4 large egg yolks
3 cups 2% reduced-fat milk

1 cup half-and-half
3 cups fresh blueberries, coarsely chopped
¼ cup powdered sugar
¼ cup water

1. Combine first 3 ingredients in a large bowl; beat with a mixer at high speed until smooth. Combine milk and half-and-half in a medium, heavy saucepan; bring to a boil. Remove from heat. Gradually add half of hot milk mixture to cheese mixture, stirring constantly with a whisk. Return milk mixture to pan. Cook over medium-low heat 5 minutes or until a thermometer registers 160°, stirring constantly. Place pan in an ice-filled bowl. Cool completely, stirring occasionally.

2. Combine blueberries, powdered sugar, and ¼ cup water in a small saucepan; bring to a boil. Reduce heat; simmer 10 minutes or until mixture thickens slightly, stirring frequently. Remove from heat; cool completely.

3. Stir blueberry mixture into milk mixture. Pour mixture into the freezer can of an ice-cream freezer; freeze according to manufacturer's instructions. Spoon ice cream into a freezer-safe container; cover and freeze 1 hour or until firm. Serves 12 (serving size: about ⅔ cup)

CALORIES 268; FAT 7.8g (sat 4g, mono 2.3g, poly 0.5g); PROTEIN 5.4g; CARB 46g; FIBER 0.9g; CHOL 90mg; IRON 0.3mg; SODIUM 100mg; CALC 49mg

Bugged Ice Cream: DURING THE 2011 CICADA INVASION, a shop called Sparky's Homemade Ice Cream in Columbia, Missouri, sold out of their newest flavor within hours. The name of the swarm-inspired sensation? Brown Sugar Cicada.

Use peaches that aren't overripe so they'll hold their shape when cooked. To prevent spills, place the baking dish on a foil-lined baking sheet before putting it in the oven.

Blueberry-Peach Cobbler

Hands-on time: 31 min.   Total time: 1 hr. 31 min.

5 pounds peaches, peeled, pitted, and sliced	1 teaspoon baking powder
2 tablespoons fresh lemon juice	1/2 cup butter, softened
1 cup granulated sugar, divided	2 large eggs
3/8 teaspoon salt, divided	1 teaspoon vanilla extract
6.75 ounces (about 1 1/2 cups) plus 2 tablespoons all-purpose flour, divided	3/4 cup buttermilk
Cooking spray	2 cups fresh blueberries
	2 tablespoons turbinado sugar

1. Preheat oven to 375°.

2. Place peaches in a large bowl. Drizzle with juice; toss. Add ¾ cup granulated sugar, ⅛ teaspoon salt, and 2 tablespoons flour to peach mixture; toss to combine. Arrange peach mixture evenly in a 13 x 9–inch glass or ceramic baking dish coated with cooking spray.

3. Weigh or lightly spoon 6.75 ounces flour (about 1½ cups) into dry measuring cups; level with a knife. Combine 6.75 ounces flour, ¼ teaspoon salt, and baking powder in a bowl, stirring well with a whisk. Place ¼ cup granulated sugar and butter in a medium bowl, and beat with a mixer at medium speed until light and fluffy (about 2 minutes). Add eggs, 1 at a time, beating well after each addition. Stir in vanilla. Add flour mixture and buttermilk alternately to butter mixture, beginning and ending with flour mixture, beating just until combined. Stir in blueberries.

4. Spread batter evenly over peach mixture; sprinkle with turbinado sugar. Place baking dish on a foil-lined baking sheet. Bake at 375° for 1 hour or until topping is golden and filling is bubbly. Serves 12 (serving size: about ¾ cup)

CALORIES 300; FAT 9.6g (sat 5g, mono 2.4g, poly 0.7g); PROTEIN 5.1g; CARB 52g; FIBER 3.5g; CHOL 58mg; IRON 1.5mg; SODIUM 189mg; CALC 51mg

The layer of sauce in the middle of the pudding is the secret to the velvety-rich interior. It's a decadent pairing, but if you want to gild the lily, add a small dollop of whipped cream.

Bread Pudding with Salted Caramel Sauce

Hands-on time: 25 min.   Total time: 1 hr. 50 min.

Bread pudding:
- 5 cups (½-inch) cubed French bread (about 8 ounces)
- 1 cup evaporated fat-free milk
- ¾ cup 1% low-fat milk
- ⅓ cup granulated sugar
- 2 tablespoons bourbon
- 1 tablespoon vanilla extract
- 1 teaspoon ground cinnamon
- ¼ teaspoon kosher salt
- 2 large eggs

Sauce:
- ¾ cup packed brown sugar
- 3 tablespoons bourbon
- 1 tablespoon unsalted butter
- 6 tablespoons half-and-half, divided
- 1 teaspoon vanilla extract
- ⅛ teaspoon kosher salt
- Cooking spray
- Whipped cream (optional)

1. Preheat oven to 350°.

2. To prepare bread pudding, arrange bread in a single layer on a baking sheet. Bake at 350° for 8 minutes or until lightly toasted.

3. Combine evaporated milk and next 7 ingredients (through eggs) in a large bowl; stir with a whisk. Add bread cubes. Let stand 20 minutes, occasionally pressing on bread to soak up milk.

4. To prepare sauce, combine brown sugar, 3 tablespoons bourbon, and butter in a small saucepan over medium-high heat; bring to a boil. Simmer 2 minutes or until sugar dissolves, stirring frequently. Stir in 5 tablespoons half-and-half; simmer 10 minutes or until reduced to about 1 cup. Remove pan from heat. Stir in 1 tablespoon half-and-half, 1 teaspoon vanilla, and ⅛ teaspoon salt. Keep warm.

5. Spoon half of bread mixture into a 9 x 5–inch loaf pan coated with cooking spray. Drizzle 3 tablespoons sauce over bread mixture. Spoon remaining half of bread mixture over sauce. Bake at 350° for 45 minutes or until a knife inserted in center comes out clean. Serve warm sauce with bread pudding. Top with whipped cream, if desired. Serves 8 (serving size: 1 slice bread pudding and about 1½ tablespoons sauce)

CALORIES 300; FAT 4.8g (sat 2g, mono 1.4g, poly 0.5g); PROTEIN 8.5g; CARB 51g; FIBER 0.9g; CHOL 63mg; IRON 1.6mg; SODIUM 349mg; CALC 172mg

To pick a flavorful pineapple, choose a fruit that feels heavy for its size. Give the stem end a whiff—it should have a sweet aroma.

Broiled Pineapple with Bourbon Caramel Sauce over Vanilla Ice Cream

Hands-on time: 14 min.   Total time: 36 min.

½ cup granulated sugar
3 tablespoons plus 2 teaspoons bourbon, divided
3 tablespoons water
1 teaspoon fresh lemon juice
¼ cup heavy whipping cream

1 teaspoon vanilla extract
1 pineapple, peeled and cored
Cooking spray
3 tablespoons brown sugar
2 cups vanilla fat-free ice cream
¼ cup flaked sweetened coconut, toasted

1. Combine granulated sugar, 3 tablespoons bourbon, 3 tablespoons water, and juice in a medium saucepan over medium-high heat; cook 2 minutes or until sugar dissolves, stirring constantly. Bring to a boil; reduce heat to medium, and cook, without stirring, 10 minutes or until golden. Remove from heat. Carefully add cream, stirring constantly (mixture will bubble vigorously). Cool slightly. Stir in 2 teaspoons bourbon and vanilla.

2. Preheat broiler.

3. Cut pineapple crosswise into 12 rings; cut each ring in half. Arrange pineapple on a foil-lined broiler pan coated with cooking spray; sprinkle evenly with brown sugar. Broil 5 inches from heat 12 minutes or until golden brown.

4. Scoop ⅓ cup ice cream into each of 6 bowls. Arrange 4 pineapple slices in each bowl; top each serving with 2½ tablespoons bourbon caramel sauce. Sprinkle each serving with 2 teaspoons coconut; serve immediately. Serves 6 (serving size: 1 sundae)

CALORIES 309; FAT 5.3g (sat 3.5g, mono 1.2g, poly 0.2g); PROTEIN 3.1g; CARB 61g; FIBER 2.3g; CHOL 14mg; IRON 0.6mg; SODIUM 48mg; CALC 86mg

The browned butter and whole-wheat flour add a nutty, rich component to everyone's favorite cookie.

Browned Butter Chocolate Chip Cookies

Hands-on time: 17 min.   Total time: 32 min.

6 tablespoons unsalted butter	¾ cup packed brown sugar
2 tablespoons canola oil	⅔ cup granulated sugar
5.6 ounces all-purpose flour (about 1¼ cups)	½ teaspoon vanilla extract
3.3 ounces whole-wheat flour (about ¾ cup)	2 large eggs, lightly beaten
1 teaspoon baking powder	½ cup semisweet chocolate chips
½ teaspoon kosher salt	⅓ cup dark chocolate chips

1. Preheat oven to 375°.

2. Heat butter in a small saucepan over medium heat; cook 5 minutes or until browned. Remove from heat; add oil. Set aside to cool.

3. Weigh or lightly spoon flours into dry measuring cups; level with a knife. Combine flours, baking powder, and salt; stir with a whisk. Place butter mixture and sugars in a large bowl; beat with a mixer at medium speed until combined. Add vanilla and eggs; beat until combined. Add flour mixture, beating at low speed just until combined. Stir in chocolate chips.

4. Drop by level tablespoonfuls 2 inches apart onto baking sheets lined with parchment paper. Bake at 375° for 12 minutes or until bottoms of cookies just begin to brown. Cool slightly. Serves 40 (serving size: 1 cookie)

CALORIES 95; FAT 4g (sat 2g, mono 1.4g, poly 0.4g); PROTEIN 1.2g; CARB 15g, FIBER 0.6g; CHOL 15mg; IRON 0.5mg; SODIUM 40mg; CALC 13mg

Chocoholic Nation: **EACH AMERICAN CONSUMES** an average of 5 pounds of chocolate per year.

The flour-and-oats mixture serves as both a solid base for the soft butterscotch chip layer and a crumbly, streusel-like topping.

Butterscotch Bars

Hands-on time: 12 min.   Total time: 67 min.

1	cup packed brown sugar
5	tablespoons butter, melted
1	teaspoon vanilla extract
1	large egg, lightly beaten
9	ounces all-purpose flour (about 2 cups)
2½	cups quick-cooking oats
½	teaspoon salt

½	teaspoon baking soda
	Cooking spray
1¼	cups butterscotch morsels (about 8 ounces)
¾	cup fat-free sweetened condensed milk
⅛	teaspoon salt
½	cup finely chopped walnuts, toasted

1. Preheat oven to 350°.

2. Combine sugar and butter in a large bowl. Stir in vanilla and egg. Weigh or lightly spoon flour into dry measuring cups; level with a knife. Combine flour, oats, ½ teaspoon salt, and baking soda in a bowl. Add oat mixture to sugar mixture; stir with a fork until combined (mixture will be crumbly). Place 3 cups oat mixture in the bottom of a 13 x 9–inch metal baking pan coated with cooking spray; press into bottom of pan. Set aside.

3. Place butterscotch morsels, sweetened condensed milk, and ⅛ teaspoon salt in a microwave-safe bowl; microwave at HIGH 1 minute or until butterscotch morsels melt, stirring every 20 seconds. Stir in walnuts. Scrape mixture into pan, spreading evenly over crust. Sprinkle evenly with remaining oat mixture, gently pressing into butterscotch mixture. Bake at 350° for 30 minutes or until topping is golden brown. Place pan on a wire rack; run a knife around outside edge. Cool completely. Serves 36 (serving size: 1 bar)

CALORIES 148; FAT 5.1g (sat 3g, mono 0.9g, poly 1.1g); PROTEIN 2.6g; CARB 23g; FIBER 0.8g; CHOL 11mg; IRON 0.8mg; SODIUM 87mg; CALC 31mg

Fresh tart cherries can be hard to find. If you do, use 3 pounds, omit the dried fruit, and skip step 1 of the recipe. Serve warm with a small scoop of vanilla frozen yogurt for a creamy-crunchy dessert.

Cherry-Almond Crisp

Hands-on time: 30 min.   Total time: 1 hr. 50 min.

1	cup dried tart cherries	3.4	ounces all-purpose flour (about ¾ cup)
1	cup boiling water	¾	cup old-fashioned rolled oats
2	pounds sweet cherries, pitted	½	cup packed brown sugar
⅔	cup granulated sugar	¼	cup sliced almonds
3	tablespoons all-purpose flour	½	teaspoon salt
1	teaspoon vanilla extract	5	tablespoons unsalted butter, melted
¼	teaspoon ground cinnamon	¼	teaspoon almond extract

Cooking spray

1. Combine dried cherries and 1 cup boiling water in a small bowl; cover and let stand 30 minutes.

2. Preheat oven to 375°.

3. Combine dried cherries with soaking liquid, sweet cherries, and next 4 ingredients (through cinnamon) in a large bowl; stir well. Let stand 15 minutes.

4. Pour cherry mixture into a 13 x 9–inch glass or ceramic baking dish coated with cooking spray. Bake at 375° for 40 minutes or until thick and bubbly.

5. While cherry mixture bakes, weigh or lightly spoon 3.4 ounces flour into a dry measuring cup; level with a knife. Combine 3.4 ounces flour, oats, brown sugar, almonds, and salt in a medium bowl, and stir well. Combine butter and almond extract in a small bowl, and drizzle over oat mixture, stirring until moist clumps form.

6. Remove cherry mixture from oven, and sprinkle evenly with streusel topping. Bake an additional 20 minutes or until streusel is golden brown. Let stand 5 minutes; serve warm. Serves 12 (serving size: about ⅔ cup)

CALORIES 277; FAT 7g (sat 3g, mono 2.2g, poly 0.8g); PROTEIN 3.3g; CARB 52g; FIBER 5.5g; CHOL 13mg; IRON 1.5mg; SODIUM 103mg; CALC 36mg

Chocolate Buttermilk Cake

Hands-on time: 15 min.   Total time: 1 hr. 57 min.

Cake:

Cooking spray

9	ounces all-purpose flour (about 2 cups)
¾	cup unsweetened cocoa
1½	teaspoons baking soda
½	teaspoon salt
1⅔	cups nonfat buttermilk
2	teaspoons vanilla extract
1¾	cups granulated sugar
½	cup butter, softened
¾	cup egg substitute

Chocolate frosting:

½	cup tub-style light cream cheese, softened
3	tablespoons fat-free milk
3	ounces semisweet chocolate, melted
3	cups powdered sugar
¼	cup unsweetened cocoa
1	teaspoon vanilla extract

1. Preheat oven to 350°.

2. To prepare cake, coat bottoms of 2 (8-inch) round cake pans with cooking spray. Line pans with wax paper; coat wax paper with cooking spray.

3. Weigh or lightly spoon flour into dry measuring cups; level with a knife. Combine flour, ¾ cup cocoa, baking soda, and salt in a medium bowl, stirring with a whisk until blended. Combine buttermilk and 2 teaspoons vanilla in a 2-cup glass measure. Place granulated sugar and butter in a large bowl; beat with a mixer at medium speed until well blended (about 5 minutes). Gradually add egg substitute; beat well. Add flour mixture and buttermilk mixture alternately to sugar mixture, beginning and ending with flour mixture.

4. Pour batter evenly into prepared pans. Bake at 350° for 38 minutes or until cake springs back when touched lightly in center. Invert cakes onto wire racks, and cool completely.

5. To prepare chocolate frosting, place cream cheese and milk in a medium bowl; beat with a mixer at low speed until smooth. Beat at high speed until creamy. Add melted chocolate; beat well. Combine powdered sugar and ¼ cup cocoa; gradually add sugar mixture to cheese mixture, beating at low speed until blended. Add 1 teaspoon vanilla; beat well 1 minute or until very creamy.

6. Remove wax paper from cake. Place 1 cake layer on a plate; spread with ½ cup frosting. Top with second cake layer; spread remaining frosting over top and sides of cake. Serves 18 (serving size: 1 piece)

CALORIES 314; FAT 8.4g (sat 5g, mono 2.3g, poly 0.4g); PROTEIN 5.1g; CARB 58g; FIBER 2.3g; CHOL 17mg; IRON 1.7mg; SODIUM 284mg; CALC 56mg

If you've ever bitten into an ice-cream sandwich only to feel cheated of cookie, these little rounds deliver what you've been missing.

Chocolate Cookie Ice-Cream Sandwiches

Hands-on time: 35 min.   Total time: 3 hr. 45 min.

4.5 ounces all-purpose flour (about 1 cup)
¼ teaspoon baking soda
⅛ teaspoon salt
½ cup packed dark brown sugar
¼ cup butter, softened

½ cup granulated sugar
⅓ cup unsweetened cocoa
2 large egg whites
Cooking spray
2¼ cups cookies-and-cream light ice cream

1. Preheat oven to 350°.

2. Weigh or lightly spoon flour into a dry measuring cup; level with a knife. Combine flour, baking soda, and salt in a medium bowl, stirring with a whisk.

3. Place brown sugar and butter in a medium bowl. Beat with a mixer at medium speed until creamy; gradually add granulated sugar, beating well. Add cocoa and egg whites, beating well. Gradually add flour mixture, beating until blended.

4. Drop by rounded teaspoonfuls 1½ inches apart onto baking sheets coated with cooking spray.

5. Bake at 350° for 10 minutes or just until edges are set. Cool on pans 2 minutes; remove from pans. Cool completely on wire racks.

6. Spread about 2 tablespoons ice cream onto flat side of 18 cookies; top each with another cookie, pressing gently to form a sandwich. Freeze until firm, about 2 hours. Serves 18 (serving size: 1 sandwich)

CALORIES 124; FAT 3.3g (sat 2g, mono 0.8g, poly 0.2g); PROTEIN 2.1g; CARB 22g; FIBER 0.5g; CHOL 8mg; IRON 0.6mg; SODIUM 70mg; CALC 21mg

Sweet Beginnings: **FIRST SOLD IN 1912,** OREO cookies originally came in two flavors: lemon meringue and cream. More than 7.5 billion of the sandwich cookies are eaten around the world every year.

Because this dessert needs time to chill, it is a terrific make-ahead option.

Chocolate-Hazelnut Mousse

Hands-on time: 16 min.   Total time: 3 hr. 31 min.

¼ cup sugar
¼ cup unsweetened cocoa
2½ tablespoons cornstarch
¼ teaspoon salt
2 large eggs
2 cups 2% reduced-fat milk
¼ cup Frangelico (hazelnut-flavored liqueur)

½ teaspoon vanilla extract
3 ounces bittersweet chocolate, chopped
2 cups frozen fat-free whipped topping, thawed
Whipped topping (optional)
2 tablespoons chopped hazelnuts, toasted

1. Combine first 5 ingredients (through eggs) in a medium bowl, stirring well with a whisk.

2. Heat milk over medium-high heat in a small heavy saucepan to 180° or until tiny bubbles form around edge (do not boil). Gradually add hot milk to sugar mixture, stirring constantly with a whisk. Place milk mixture in pan, and cook over medium heat until very thick and bubbly (about 5 minutes), stirring constantly.

3. Spoon mixture into a medium bowl, and add liqueur, vanilla, and chocolate, stirring until chocolate melts. Place bowl in a large ice-filled bowl for 15 minutes or until mixture is cool, stirring occasionally.

4. Remove bowl from ice. Gently fold in ⅔ cup fat-free whipped topping. Fold in ⅓ cup fat-free whipped topping. Cover and chill at least 3 hours. Top with whipped topping, if desired. Sprinkle with hazelnuts. Serves 6 (serving size: about ⅔ cup mousse and 1 teaspoon hazelnuts)

CALORIES 278; FAT 9.2g (sat 4g, mono 3.5g, poly 0.5g); PROTEIN 6.9g; CARB 39g; FIBER 2.2g; CHOL 77mg; IRON 1mg; SODIUM 177mg; CALC 115mg

Prepare the sauce several days ahead, chill, and reheat just before serving.

Chocolate-Orange Sauce Sundaes

Hands-on time: 15 min.   Total time: 15 min.

1½   cups 2% reduced-fat milk
¼   cup half-and-half
1   tablespoon butter
8   ounces bittersweet chocolate, chopped
2   teaspoons grated orange rind
1½   tablespoons fresh orange juice
1   teaspoon Grand Marnier (orange-flavored liqueur)
12   cups vanilla fat-free frozen yogurt
Orange rind strips (optional)

1. Heat milk and half-and-half in a heavy saucepan over medium-high heat to 180° or until tiny bubbles form around edge (do not boil). Remove from heat; add butter and chocolate, stirring until smooth. Stir in rind, juice, and liqueur. Serve sauce over frozen yogurt. Garnish with orange rind strips, if desired. Serves 16 (serving size: ¾ cup frozen yogurt and 2½ tablespoons sauce)

CALORIES 245; FAT 7.7g (sat 4g, mono 2.5g, poly 0.2g); PROTEIN 7.9g; CARB 40g; FIBER 1g; CHOL 5mg; IRON 1.1mg; SODIUM 138mg; CALC 183mg

Mocha Banana Split

Hands-on time: 8 min.   Total time: 8 min.

1   tablespoon whipping cream
½   teaspoon instant espresso granules
1   medium banana, peeled and cut in half crosswise
½   cup coffee low-fat ice cream
½   cup chocolate low-fat ice cream
4   teaspoons chocolate syrup
4   teaspoons chopped walnuts, toasted
4   teaspoons chocolate-covered espresso beans, chopped
2   cherries

1. Place whipping cream and espresso granules in a bowl; stir with a whisk until soft peaks form.

2. Cut each banana half in half lengthwise. Place 2 banana quarters in each of 2 bowls. Top each serving with ¼ cup coffee ice cream and ¼ cup chocolate ice cream.

3. Drizzle each serving with 2 teaspoons chocolate syrup, and top with half of whipped cream mixture. Sprinkle each serving with 2 teaspoons walnuts and 2 teaspoons espresso beans, and top with 1 cherry. Serves 2 (serving size: 1 banana split)

CALORIES 292; FAT 11g (sat 5g, mono 2.5g, poly 2.2g); PROTEIN 4.6g; CARB 46g; FIBER 2.7g; CHOL 26mg; IRON 0.8mg; SODIUM 25mg; CALC 71mg

Mocha Banana Split

Chocolate-Orange Sauce Sundaes

Chocolate Pudding Pops

Hands-on time: 15 min.   Total time: 4 hr. 15 min.

2½ cups 2% reduced-fat milk
½ cup sugar
½ cup unsweetened cocoa
1 tablespoon cornstarch
Dash of salt
1 large egg yolk
1 teaspoon vanilla extract
2 ounces bittersweet chocolate, finely chopped

1. Combine first 6 ingredients in a medium sauce-pan over medium-high heat, stirring well with a whisk. Cook 8 minutes or until thick and bubbly, stirring constantly.

2. Remove pan from heat. Add vanilla and choco-late, stirring until smooth. Transfer mixture to a bowl; place bowl in an ice-filled bowl. Cover surface of pudding directly with plastic wrap; cool completely.

3. Spoon chocolate mixture evenly into 6 (4-ounce) ice-pop molds. Top with lid; insert craft sticks. Freeze 4 hours or until thoroughly frozen. Serves 6 (serving size: 1 pop)

CALORIES 196; FAT 7.8g (sat 4g, mono 1.2g, poly 0.2g); PROTEIN 5.9g; CARB 32g; FIBER 3.1g; CHOL 43mg; IRON 1.4mg; SODIUM 69mg; CALC 132mg

Cool Invention: **A YOUNG BOY CREATED ICE POPS BY ACCIDENT.** In 1905, 11-year-old Frank Epperson in San Francisco left a soft drink with a stirring stick in it on the porch overnight. He patented his "frozen ice on a stick" in 1923.

Orange Cream Pops

Hands-on time: 28 min.   Total time: 5 hr. 43 min.

4½ cups vanilla light ice cream, slightly
   softened and divided
¼ cup thawed orange juice concentrate,
   undiluted
1 tablespoon grated orange rind
1 drop orange food coloring
1 drop yellow food coloring
¼ cup whipping cream
1 teaspoon vanilla extract

1. Combine 3¼ cups ice cream, orange juice concentrate, and next 3 ingredients (through yellow food coloring) in a large bowl, stirring until colors blend. Beat whipping cream with a mixer at high speed until soft peaks form; fold in vanilla. Fold whipped cream mixture into 1¼ cups vanilla ice cream.

2. Divide half of orange-flavored ice cream among 20 (2-ounce) ice-pop molds. Top with lid. Freeze 30 minutes or until set. Uncover and top each serving with vanilla ice cream mixture; top with lid. Insert a craft stick into center of each mold; freeze 45 minutes or until set. Uncover and top each serving with remaining orange-flavored ice cream. Freeze at least 4 hours or until thoroughly frozen. Serves 20 (serving size: 1 pop)

CALORIES 73; FAT 2.7g (sat 1.6g, mono 0.7g, poly 0.1g); PROTEIN 1.7g; CARB 10g; FIBER 0.2g; CHOL 13mg; IRON 0.1mg; SODIUM 25mg; CALC 57mg

Chocolate Turtle Brownie Sundaes

Hands-on time: 18 min.   Total time: 1 hr. 18 min.

Fudge Sauce
Cooking spray
3 tablespoons butter
1 ounce unsweetened chocolate
1 large egg
1 large egg white
2 tablespoons water
1 teaspoon vanilla extract
3 ounces all-purpose flour (about 2/3 cup)
1 cup sugar
1/3 cup unsweetened cocoa
1/2 teaspoon baking powder
1 tablespoon fat-free milk
10 small soft caramel candies
2 tablespoons coarsely chopped pecans
4 cups vanilla low-fat frozen yogurt

1. Prepare Fudge Sauce.

2. Preheat oven to 350°.

3. Coat bottom of an 8-inch square metal baking pan with cooking spray. Combine butter and chocolate in a large microwave-safe bowl. Microwave at HIGH 1 minute; stir until melted. Add egg and egg white, stirring with a whisk. Stir in 2 tablespoons water and vanilla. Weigh or lightly spoon flour into dry measuring cups; level with a knife. Combine flour, sugar, cocoa, and baking powder; stir into chocolate mixture. Spread half of batter in bottom of prepared pan.

4. Combine milk and candies in a microwave-safe bowl. Microwave at HIGH 1½ minutes; stir until melted. Drizzle caramel over batter in pan; sprinkle with pecans. Drop remaining batter by tablespoonfuls over pecans. Bake at 350° for 35 minutes or until a wooden pick inserted in center comes out almost clean. Cool on a wire rack. Cut into 16 squares.

5. Top each brownie with ¼ cup frozen yogurt and 2 tablespoons Fudge Sauce. Serves 16 (serving size: 1 sundae)

CALORIES 292; FAT 9g (sat 5g, mono 2.6g, poly 0.7g); PROTEIN 4.4g; CARB 52g; FIBER 0.4g; CHOL 27mg; IRON 1.4mg; SODIUM 99mg; CALC 63mg

Fudge Sauce

Hands-on time: 16 min.   Total time: 16 min.

2 tablespoons butter
2 ounces unsweetened chocolate, chopped
1/2 cup sugar
6 tablespoons unsweetened cocoa
1 cup dark corn syrup
1/2 cup fat-free milk
2 teaspoons vanilla extract

1. Combine butter and chocolate in a saucepan; cook over low heat until chocolate melts, stirring occasionally.

2. Combine sugar and cocoa in a bowl; add corn syrup and milk, stirring with a whisk until blended. Add cocoa mixture to saucepan. Bring to a boil over medium heat; cook 1 minute, stirring constantly. Remove from heat; stir in vanilla. Serves 16 (serving size: 2 tablespoons)

CALORIES 125; FAT 3.6g (sat 2g, mono 1g, poly 0.1g); PROTEIN 1.3g; CARB 24g; FIBER 0.1g; CHOL 4mg; IRON 0.6mg; SODIUM 45mg; CALC 17mg

Large chocolate chunks create big, luxurious pockets of melty chocolate in the brownies, but you can always substitute chocolate chips.

Classic Fudge-Walnut Brownies

Hands-on time: 15 min.   Total time: 45 min.

3.4 ounces all-purpose flour (about ¾ cup)
1 cup granulated sugar
¾ cup unsweetened cocoa
½ cup packed brown sugar
½ teaspoon baking powder
¼ teaspoon salt
1 cup bittersweet chocolate chunks, divided

⅓ cup fat-free milk
6 tablespoons butter, melted
1 teaspoon vanilla extract
2 large eggs, lightly beaten
½ cup chopped walnuts, divided
Cooking spray

1. Preheat oven to 350°.

2. Weigh or lightly spoon flour into dry measuring cups; level with a knife. Combine flour and next 5 ingredients (through salt) in a large bowl. Combine ½ cup chocolate chunks and milk in a microwave-safe bowl; microwave at HIGH 1 minute, stirring after 30 seconds. Stir in butter, vanilla, and eggs. Add milk mixture, ½ cup chocolate chunks, and ¼ cup nuts to flour mixture; stir to combine.

3. Pour batter into a 9-inch square metal baking pan coated with cooking spray; sprinkle with ¼ cup nuts. Bake at 350° for 19 minutes or until a wooden pick inserted in center comes out with moist crumbs clinging. Cool in pan on a wire rack. Cut into 20 bars. Serves 20 (serving size: 1 brownie)

CALORIES 186; FAT 9.1g (sat 4g, mono 2.2g, poly 1.7g); PROTEIN 2.8g; CARB 25g; FIBER 1.4g; CHOL 30mg; IRON 0.9mg; SODIUM 74mg; CALC 23mg

Peanuts and Popcorn Brownie Sundaes

Hands-on time: 15 min. Total time: 58 min.

½   cup sugar
2   tablespoons butter, softened
1   teaspoon vanilla extract
1   large egg
¼   cup semisweet chocolate chips
¼   cup fat-free milk
1   ounce all-purpose flour (about ¼ cup)

½   cup unsweetened cocoa
¼   teaspoon salt
Cooking spray
2¼ cups vanilla reduced-fat ice cream
1   cup fat-free caramel sundae syrup
1   cup caramel-coated peanuts-and-popcorn mix, coarsely chopped

1. Preheat oven to 375°.

2. Place first 3 ingredients in a large bowl; beat with a mixer at medium speed until well blended (about 2 minutes). Add egg; beat 2 minutes or until pale. Place chocolate chips in a small microwave-safe bowl, and microwave at HIGH in 20-second intervals until completely melted, stirring after each interval. Add chocolate to sugar mixture; beat until combined. Stir in milk.

3. Lightly spoon flour into a dry measuring cup; level with a knife. Combine flour, cocoa, and salt; add to sugar mixture, stirring just until blended.

4. Scrape batter into an 8-inch square glass or ceramic baking dish coated with cooking spray. Bake at 375° for 18 minutes or until completely set. Cool to room temperature in pan on a wire rack. Cut brownies into 9 squares.

5. Place 1 brownie on each of 9 plates; top each brownie with ¼ cup ice cream and about 1½ tablespoons caramel syrup. Sprinkle chopped peanuts-and-popcorn mix evenly over sundaes. Serve immediately. Serves 9 (serving size: 1 sundae)

CALORIES 318; FAT 6.8g (sat 4g, mono 1.7g, poly 0.3g); PROTEIN 5.6g; CARB 57g; FIBER 2.1g; CHOL 33mg; IRON 1.1mg; SODIUM 215mg; CALC 88mg

Peanuts, Popcorn, and Brownies: **BROWNIES AND CRACKER JACK BOTH DEBUTED AT THE 1893** World's Columbian Exposition in Chicago. Chefs at the city's still-operating Palmer House Hotel created the brownie.

Use a 2-quart ice-cream freezer if you have one; if you're using a 1½-quart tabletop model, it'll be pretty full.

Double Chocolate Ice Cream

Hands-on time: 35 min.   Total time: 2 hr. 5 min.

1⅓ cups sugar
⅓ cup unsweetened cocoa
2½ cups 2% reduced-fat milk, divided

3 large egg yolks
⅓ cup heavy whipping cream
2½ ounces bittersweet chocolate, chopped

1. Combine sugar and cocoa in a medium, heavy saucepan over medium-low heat. Add ½ cup milk and egg yolks, stirring well. Stir in 2 cups milk. Cook 12 minutes or until a thermometer registers 160°, stirring constantly. Remove from heat.

2. Place cream in a medium-sized microwave-safe bowl; microwave at HIGH 1½ minutes or until cream boils. Add chocolate to cream; stir until smooth. Add cream mixture to pan; stir until smooth. Place pan in a large ice-filled bowl. Cool completely, stirring occasionally.

3. Pour mixture into the freezer can of an ice-cream freezer; freeze according to manufacturer's instructions. Spoon ice cream into a freezer-safe container; cover and freeze 1 hour or until firm. Serves 10 (serving size: about ½ cup)

CALORIES 226; FAT 8.9g (sat 5g, mono 1.5g, poly 0.3g); PROTEIN 4g; CARB 36g; FIBER 1g; CHOL 79mg; IRON 0.7mg; SODIUM 37mg; CALC 75mg

With their combo of shortbread-like crust, creamy cheesecake, and fresh summer cherry goodness, these bars will make you the hit of the picnic.

Fresh Cherry Cheesecake Bars

Hands-on time: 20 min.   Total time: 4 hr. 5 min.

4.5 ounces all-purpose flour (about 1 cup)	1 tablespoon water
3 tablespoons powdered sugar	2 teaspoons fresh lemon juice
⅛ teaspoon salt	½ teaspoon cornstarch
5 tablespoons chilled butter, cut into small pieces	¾ cup ⅓-less-fat cream cheese (6 ounces)
3½ teaspoons ice water	⅓ cup plain fat-free Greek yogurt
1¼ cups chopped pitted cherries	⅓ cup granulated sugar
1 tablespoon granulated sugar	½ teaspoon vanilla extract
	1 large egg

1. Preheat oven to 350°.

2. Line an 8-inch square glass or ceramic baking dish with parchment paper. Weigh or lightly spoon flour into a dry measuring cup; level with a knife. Place flour, powdered sugar, and salt in a food processor; pulse 2 times to combine. Add chilled butter, and drizzle with 3½ teaspoons ice water. Pulse 10 times or until mixture resembles coarse meal. Pour mixture into prepared baking dish (mixture will be crumbly). Press mixture into bottom of dish. Bake at 350° for 23 minutes or until lightly browned. Cool completely. Reduce oven temperature to 325°.

3. Place cherries, 1 tablespoon granulated sugar, and 1 tablespoon water in a small saucepan. Bring to a boil. Reduce heat, and simmer 5 minutes or until cherries are tender. Combine lemon juice and cornstarch in a small bowl, stirring with a whisk. Stir cornstarch mixture into cherry mixture; cook 1 minute or until thick. Cool mixture slightly. Spoon cherry mixture into food processor, and process until smooth. Spoon pureed mixture into a bowl, and set aside.

4. Wipe food processor clean. Place cream cheese and next 4 ingredients (through egg) in food processor; process until smooth. Spoon cream cheese mixture over cooled crust; spread evenly. Dollop cherry mixture over cream cheese mixture, and swirl together with a knife. Bake at 325° for 36 minutes or until set. Cool on a wire rack. Cover and chill at least 3 hours. Serves 15 (serving size: 1 bar)

CALORIES 136; FAT 6.9g (sat 4g, mono 1.8g, poly 0.3g); PROTEIN 2.9g; CARB 16g; FIBER 0.5g; CHOL 33mg; IRON 0.5mg; SODIUM 92mg; CALC 23mg

These bar cookies are also known as seven-layer bars. Dress them up by replacing the flaked sweetened coconut with toasted shaved fresh coconut.

Hello Dolly Bars

Hands-on time: 10 min.   Total time: 60 min.

1½ cups graham cracker crumbs (about
      9 cookie sheets)
  2 tablespoons butter, melted
  1 tablespoon water
 ⅓ cup semisweet chocolate chips

 ⅓ cup butterscotch morsels
 ⅔ cup flaked sweetened coconut
 ¼ cup chopped pecans, toasted
  1 (15-ounce) can fat-free sweetened
      condensed milk

1. Preheat oven to 350°.

2. Line bottom and sides of a 9-inch square metal baking pan with parchment paper; cut off excess parchment paper around top edge of pan.

3. Place crumbs in a medium bowl. Drizzle with butter and 1 tablespoon water; toss with a fork until moist. Gently pat mixture into an even layer in pan (do not press firmly). Sprinkle chips and morsels over crumb mixture. Top evenly with coconut and pecans. Drizzle milk evenly over top. Bake at 350° for 25 minutes or until lightly browned and bubbly around edges. Cool completely on a wire rack. Serves 24 (serving size: 1 bar)

CALORIES 123; FAT 4.4g (sat 2g, mono 1.3g, poly 0.6g); PROTEIN 2.1g; CARB 19g; FIBER 0.5g; CHOL 5mg; IRON 0.3mg; SODIUM 64mg; CALC 50mg

Dress up scoops of tangy buttermilk ice cream with in-season berries, sliced stone fruit, or lemon rind strips. Waffle bowls make a fun way to serve dessert, too.

Lemon-Buttermilk Ice Cream

Hands-on time: 9 min.   Total time: 1 hr. 39 min.

1½ cups sugar
  1 cup fresh lemon juice (about 10 lemons)
  2 cups half-and-half

  2 cups whole milk
  2 cups nonfat buttermilk

1. Combine sugar and juice in a large bowl, stirring with a whisk until sugar dissolves. Add half-and-half, whole milk, and buttermilk.

2. Pour mixture into the freezer can of an ice-cream freezer; freeze according to manufacturer's instructions. Spoon ice cream into a freezer-safe container. Cover and freeze 1 hour or until firm. Serves 18 (serving size: ½ cup)

CALORIES 130; FAT 3.6g (sat 2g, mono 1.2g, poly 0g); PROTEIN 2.8g; CARB 21g; FIBER 0.1g; CHOL 18mg; IRON 0mg; SODIUM 54mg; CALC 93mg

Presidential Sweets: **THOMAS JEFFERSON WROTE THE FIRST AMERICAN RECIPE FOR ICE CREAM IN THE 1780s.** The handwritten recipe, which has a recipe on the back for Savoy cookies to accompany the ice cream, is on display at the Library of Congress.

This lightened classic is sweet-tart perfection and a delicious ending to any meal. Brush the edges of the crust with egg wash for nice browning.

Lemon Cream Pie

Hands-on time: 40 min. Total time: 3 hr. 51 min.

½ (14.1-ounce) package refrigerated pie dough
Cooking spray
½ cup sugar
1 tablespoon grated lemon rind, divided
¼ cup fresh lemon juice (about 2 lemons)
3 tablespoons cornstarch
¼ teaspoon salt

2 large eggs
1½ cups fat-free milk
¼ cup ⅓-less-fat cream cheese (2 ounces), softened
2 tablespoons butter, softened
1½ cups frozen fat-free whipped topping, thawed

1. Roll dough into a 12-inch circle; fit into a 9-inch pie plate coated with cooking spray. Fold edges under, and flute. Bake piecrust according to package directions. Cool completely on a wire rack.

2. Combine sugar, 2½ teaspoons rind, and next 4 ingredients (through eggs) in a large bowl, stirring well. Combine milk and cheese in a medium, heavy saucepan over medium-high heat; cook until mixture reaches 180° or until tiny bubbles form around edge (do not boil). Gradually add hot milk mixture to sugar mixture, stirring constantly with a whisk. Return milk mixture to pan, and cook over medium heat 10 minutes or until thick and bubbly, stirring constantly. Remove from heat; stir in butter.

3. Place pan in a large ice-filled bowl for 10 minutes or until mixture cools to room temperature, stirring occasionally. Spoon filling into prepared crust, and cover surface of filling with plastic wrap. Chill 3 hours or until set, and remove plastic wrap. Spread whipped topping evenly over chilled pie, and sprinkle with ½ teaspoon lemon rind. Serves 8 (serving size: 1 slice)

CALORIES 264; FAT 11.9g (sat 6g, mono 3.4g, poly 1.9g); PROTEIN 4.6g; CARB 35g; FIBER 0.1g; CHOL 61mg; IRON 0.3mg; SODIUM 296mg; CALC 72mg

Maragarita Ice-Cream Sandwiches

Caramelized Banana Sundae

Margarita Ice-Cream Sandwiches

Hands-on time: 27 min. Total time: 8 hr.

½ cup unsalted butter, softened
1 cup granulated sugar
1 large egg
5 teaspoons grated lime rind, divided
2 tablespoons fresh lime juice
11.25 ounces all-purpose flour (about 2½ cups)
1½ teaspoons baking powder
⅛ teaspoon table salt
1 teaspoon turbinado sugar
½ teaspoon coarse sea salt
2 cups vanilla reduced-fat ice cream, softened
2 cups lime sherbet, softened

1. Place butter and granulated sugar in a large bowl; beat with a mixer at medium speed 5 minutes or until light and fluffy. Add egg, 1 tablespoon rind, and juice; beat 2 minutes or until well combined.

2. Weigh or lightly spoon flour into dry measuring cups; level with a knife. Combine flour, baking powder, and ⅛ teaspoon table salt; stir with a whisk. Add flour mixture to butter mixture; beat just until combined.

3. Divide dough into 2 equal portions. Shape each portion into a 6-inch log. Wrap logs individually in plastic wrap; chill 3 hours or until firm.

4. Preheat oven to 350°.

5. Cut each log into 16 (about ⅓-inch-thick) slices; place 1 inch apart on baking sheets lined with parchment paper. Sprinkle with 2 teaspoons rind, turbinado sugar, and sea salt. Bake at 350° for 10 minutes or until edges are lightly browned. Cool 2 minutes on pans on a wire rack. Remove from pans; cool completely on wire rack.

6. Place ice cream and sherbet in a bowl; fold together. Scoop ¼ cup ice-cream mixture onto bottom of 1 cookie; top with 1 cookie. Wrap each sandwich in plastic wrap; freeze 4 hours or until firm. Serves 16 (serving size: 1 sandwich)

CALORIES 231; FAT 7.1g (sat 4g, mono 1.7g, poly 0.4g); PROTEIN 3.4g; CARB 39g; FIBER 1.1g; CHOL 28mg; IRON 1.1mg; SODIUM 138mg; CALC 74mg

Caramelized Banana Sundaes

Hands-on time: 7 min. Total time: 7 min.

1 tablespoon butter
1 tablespoon brown sugar
2 tablespoons dark rum
½ teaspoon ground cinnamon
¾ cup thinly sliced banana (about 1 medium)
2 cups vanilla low-fat ice cream
4 teaspoons sliced almonds, toasted

1. Melt butter in a nonstick skillet over medium heat. Add sugar, rum, and cinnamon; stir. Add banana; cook 1½ minutes. Remove from heat.

2. Spoon ½ cup ice cream into each of 4 bowls. Top each serving with about 2 tablespoons banana mixture and 1 teaspoon almonds. Serves 4 (serving size: 1 sundae)

CALORIES 210; FAT 7.6g (sat 4g, mono 2.3g, poly 0.5g); PROTEIN 4.4g; CARB 30g; FIBER 1.4g; CHOL 28mg; IRON 0.4mg; SODIUM 78mg; CALC 136mg

Blondies generally have the same dense texture as brownies, but without chocolate or cocoa in the base batter.

Peanut Butter Cup Blondies

Hands-on time: 20 min.   Total time: 2 hr.

5.6 ounces all-purpose flour (about 1¼ cups)
1 cup granulated sugar
½ teaspoon baking powder
¼ teaspoon salt
⅓ cup creamy peanut butter
¼ cup butter, melted and cooled slightly
2 tablespoons 2% reduced-fat milk

1 teaspoon vanilla extract
2 large eggs, lightly beaten
¼ cup semisweet chocolate chips
Cooking spray
4 (0.75-ounce) peanut butter cups, coarsely chopped

1. Preheat oven to 350°.

2. Weigh or lightly spoon flour into dry measuring cups; level with a knife. Combine flour and next 3 ingredients (through salt), stirring well with a whisk. Combine peanut butter and next 4 ingredients (through eggs), stirring well. Add peanut butter mixture to flour mixture; stir until combined. Stir in chocolate chips.

3. Scrape batter into a 9-inch square metal baking pan lightly coated with cooking spray; arrange peanut butter cups over batter. Bake at 350° for 19 minutes or until a wooden pick inserted in center comes out with moist crumbs clinging. Cool in pan on a wire rack. Cut into 20 bars. Serves 20 (serving size: 1 blondie)

CALORIES 153; FAT 7g (sat 3g, mono 2g, poly 0.8g); PROTEIN 3.2g; CARB 21g; FIBER 0.7g; CHOL 28mg; IRON 0.7mg; SODIUM 98mg; CALC 17mg

You won't have to fuss with candy thermometers for this double-layer fudge. Sweetened condensed milk and a microwave make the method foolproof.

Peanut Butter and Dark Chocolate Fudge

Hands-on time: 9 min.   Total time: 2 hr. 11 min.

1   (14-ounce) can fat-free sweetened
     condensed milk, divided
3/4 cup semisweet chocolate chips
2   tablespoons unsweetened dark cocoa
1/4 teaspoon instant coffee granules

1   teaspoon vanilla extract, divided
3/4 cup peanut butter chips
1   tablespoon peanut butter
1/4 cup salted, dry-roasted peanuts, coarsely
     chopped

1. Line an 8-inch square glass or ceramic baking dish with wax paper. Place 9 tablespoons milk in a microwave-safe bowl. Add chocolate chips, cocoa, and coffee granules. Microwave at HIGH 1 minute or until melted. Stir in ½ teaspoon vanilla. Spread into prepared pan.

2. Combine remaining milk, peanut butter chips, and peanut butter in a microwave-safe bowl. Microwave at HIGH 1 minute or until melted. Stir in ½ teaspoon vanilla. Spread evenly over chocolate layer, and sprinkle with peanuts. Cover and chill 2 hours. Cut into 25 squares. Serves 25 (serving size: 1 square)

CALORIES 123; FAT 4.7g (sat 3g, mono 0.7g, poly 0.1g); PROTEIN 3.5g; CARB 17g; FIBER 0.6g; CHOL 2mg; IRON 0.3mg; SODIUM 47mg; CALC 43mg

Stuck? **ARACHIBUTYROPHOBIA** is the fear of peanut butter sticking to the roof of one's mouth.

Red Velvet Cupcakes

Hands-on time: 1 hr.   Total time: 2 hr. 33 min.

Cupcakes:

8 ounces cake flour (about 2 cups)
½ teaspoon salt
½ teaspoon baking soda
½ teaspoon baking powder
¼ cup unsweetened cocoa
1¼ cups granulated sugar
½ cup butter, softened
2 large egg yolks
1 teaspoon vanilla extract
1 cup whole buttermilk
1 (1-ounce) bottle red food coloring
3 large egg whites
¼ teaspoon cream of tartar
Baking spray with flour

Frosting:

3 tablespoons butter
1 (8-ounce) block ⅓-less-fat cream cheese
2 cups powdered sugar
¼ teaspoon vanilla extract
⅛ teaspoon salt
Red food color paste (optional)

1. Preheat oven to 350°.

2. To prepare cake, weigh or lightly spoon flour into dry measuring cups; level with a knife. Combine flour, ½ teaspoon salt, baking soda, baking powder, and cocoa. Place 1¼ cups granulated sugar and ½ cup butter in a large bowl; beat with a mixer at high speed until well blended. Add egg yolks, 1 at a time, beating well after each addition. Stir in 1 teaspoon vanilla. Reduce mixer speed to low. Add flour mixture and buttermilk alternately to butter mixture, beginning and ending with flour mixture, and beat just until combined. Stir in red food coloring. Using clean, dry beaters, beat 3 egg whites and cream of tartar at high speed until stiff peaks form. Fold one-third of egg whites into batter. Gently fold in remaining egg whites.

3. Place 24 paper muffin cup liners in muffin cups; coat liners with baking spray. Spoon batter into cups. Bake at 350° for 23 minutes or until a wooden pick inserted in centers comes out with moist crumbs clinging. Cool in pans 10 minutes. Remove from pans; cool completely on wire racks.

4. To prepare frosting, place 3 tablespoons butter and cream cheese in a large bowl, and beat with a mixer at medium-high speed until smooth.

5. Add powdered sugar, ¼ teaspoon vanilla, and ⅛ teaspoon salt; beat until smooth. Add food color paste, if desired; stir.

6. Place frosting in a zip-top plastic bag; seal. Snip a ¼-inch hole in 1 corner of bag. Pipe frosting on top of cupcakes. Serves 24 (serving size: 1 cupcake)

CALORIES 200; FAT 8.2g (sat 5g, mono 2.1g, poly 0.4g); PROTEIN 2.7g; CARB 30g; FIBER 0.5g; CHOL 40mg; IRON 0.9mg; SODIUM 191mg; CALC 18mg

Many folks say banana pudding is best the next day, after the cookies have softened and the flavors have mingled overnight.

Roasted Banana Pudding

Hands-on time: 36 min.   Total time: 2 hr. 26 min.

5 ripe unpeeled medium bananas (about 2 pounds)
2 cups 2% reduced-fat milk
⅔ cup sugar, divided
2 tablespoons cornstarch
¼ teaspoon salt

2 large eggs
1 tablespoon butter
2 teaspoons vanilla extract
1 (12-ounce) container frozen fat-free whipped topping, thawed and divided
45 vanilla wafers, divided

1. Preheat oven to 350°.

2. Place bananas on a jelly-roll pan lined with parchment paper. Bake at 350° for 20 minutes. Remove 3 bananas; cool completely. Peel and cut into ½-inch-thick slices; set aside. Bake remaining 2 bananas at 350° an additional 20 minutes. Carefully peel the 2 bananas and place in a small bowl; mash with a fork until smooth.

3. Combine milk and ⅓ cup sugar in a saucepan over medium-high heat. Bring to a simmer (do not boil).

4. Combine ⅓ cup sugar, cornstarch, salt, and eggs in a medium bowl; stir well with a whisk. Gradually add hot milk mixture to sugar mixture, stirring constantly with a whisk. Return milk mixture to pan. Cook over medium heat until thick and bubbly (about 3 minutes), stirring constantly. Remove from heat. Add mashed bananas, butter, and vanilla, stirring until butter melts. Place pan in a large ice-filled bowl for 15 minutes or until mixture comes to room temperature, stirring occasionally. Fold half of whipped topping into pudding.

5. Spread 1 cup custard evenly over the bottom of an 11 x 7–inch glass or ceramic baking dish. Top with 20 vanilla wafers and half of reserved banana slices. Spoon half of remaining custard over banana. Repeat procedure with 20 wafers, remaining banana slices, and remaining custard. Spread remaining half of whipped topping evenly over top. Crush 5 wafers; sprinkle over top. Refrigerate 1 hour or until chilled. Serves 10 (serving size: about ⅔ cup)

CALORIES 295; FAT 5.6g (sat 2g, mono 1.7g, poly 0.2g); PROTEIN 3.9g; CARB 57g; FIBER 2g; CHOL 46mg; IRON 1mg; SODIUM 165mg; CALC 73mg

There is very little flour in these cookies, which allows the flavor of the peanut butter to shine through. Definitely stick with creamy peanut butter for best results.

Peanut Butter–Toffee Chunk Cookies

Hands-on time: 15 min.   Total time: 1 hr. 16 min.

2.25 ounces all-purpose flour (about ½ cup)
1   cup granulated sugar
1   cup packed brown sugar
1¾ cups creamy peanut butter

1   teaspoon vanilla extract
2   large eggs
4   (1.4-ounce) chocolate-covered toffee candy
     bar, coarsely crushed

1. Preheat oven to 350°.

2. Line 3 baking sheets with parchment paper.

3. Weigh or lightly spoon flour into a dry measuring cup; level with a knife. Combine flour and next 5 ingredients (through eggs) in a large bowl. Beat with a mixer at medium speed until smooth. Stir in candy. Shape dough into 54 (¾-inch) balls. Place balls 2 inches apart on prepared pans, flattening slightly with fingers.

4. Bake at 350° for 12 minutes or until edges are browned. Cool cookies on pans 2 minutes. Transfer cookies to wire racks; cool completely. Serves 54 (serving size: 1 cookie)

CALORIES 102; FAT 5.3g (sat 1g, mono 2.3g, poly 1.3g); PROTEIN 2.5g; CARB 12g; FIBER 0.6g; CHOL 9mg; IRON 0.3mg; SODIUM 52mg; CALC 5mg

Nuts for Peanut Butter: **AMERICANS EAT MORE THAN 700 MILLION POUNDS** of peanut butter a year—enough to cover the floor of the Grand Canyon.

5 GREAT DESSERT SAUCES

Drizzle these on top of sliced fruit, use them to inspire a sundae, spoon over cake, layer with yogurt—the possibilities for these all-purpose sweet sauces are limitless.

Ginger-Bourbon Sauce

Hands-on time: 10 min.   Total time: 25 min.

¼   cup whipping cream
1   (1-inch) piece peeled fresh ginger, thinly sliced
½   cup sugar
2   tablespoons water
2   tablespoons bourbon

1. Place whipping cream and ginger in a small saucepan over medium-low heat. Bring to a simmer. Remove from heat, and let stand 15 minutes. Remove and discard ginger.

2. Place sugar and 2 tablespoons water in a small heavy saucepan. Bring to a boil over high heat (do not stir). Reduce heat to medium-high, and cook 5 minutes or until mixture is golden. Remove from heat. Carefully add ginger-infused cream (caramelized sugar will harden and stick to spoon), stirring until sugar melts. Stir in bourbon. Sauce thickens upon standing. Serves 4 (serving size: 2 tablespoons)

CALORIES 164; FAT 5g (sat 3g, mono 1.3g, poly 0.1g); PROTEIN 0g; CARB 26g; FIBER 0g; CHOL 20mg; IRON 0mg; SODIUM 0mg; CALC 0mg

Brandied Cherry Sauce

Hands-on time: 10 min.   Total time: 30 min.

¼   cup sugar
2   teaspoons cornstarch
⅓   cup unsweetened grape juice
3   tablespoons kirsch or other brandy
2½   cups frozen pitted dark sweet cherries, thawed
½   cup dried tart cherries

1. Combine sugar and cornstarch in a medium saucepan, stirring with a whisk. Add juice and brandy, stirring with a whisk until blended. Stir in cherries. Bring to a boil over medium-high heat; cook 2 to 3 minutes or until thick, stirring constantly. Cool to room temperature. Cover and store in refrigerator. Serves 8 (serving size: 2 tablespoons)

CALORIES 100; FAT 0g (sat 0g, mono 0g, poly 0g); PROTEIN 0.5g; CARB 22g; FIBER 3g; CHOL 0mg; IRON 0.4mg; SODIUM 1mg; CALC 5mg

Malted Chocolate–Peanut Butter Sauce

Hands-on time: 13 min.   Total time: 13 min.

¼   cup chocolate malted milk powder
1   (14-ounce) can fat-free sweetened condensed milk
1   ounce unsweetened chocolate, chopped
2   tablespoons peanut butter
1   teaspoon vanilla extract

1. Place first 3 ingredients in a medium saucepan. Cook, stirring constantly, over medium-low heat 6 minutes or until smooth. Remove from heat. Stir in peanut butter and vanilla. Serve warm. Refrigerate in an airtight container. Serves 12 (serving size: 2 tablespoons)

CALORIES 152; FAT 3.2g (sat 1g, mono 1.2g, poly 0.5g); PROTEIN 4.5g; CARB 27g; FIBER 0.6g; CHOL 6mg; IRON 0.5mg; SODIUM 75mg; CALC 108mg

Mixed Berry Coulis

Hands-on time: 18 min.   Total time: 2 hr. 18 min.

1   cup sliced strawberries
1   cup blueberries
1   cup fresh raspberries
⅓   cup sugar
1   tablespoon fresh lemon juice
1   tablespoon Chambord (raspberry-flavored liqueur)

1. Combine first 5 ingredients in a medium saucepan. Cook over medium heat 5 minutes or until berries soften and sugar dissolves, stirring occasionally.

2. Place berry mixture in a blender. Remove center piece of blender lid (to allow steam to escape); secure blender lid on blender. Place a clean towel over opening in blender lid (to avoid splatters). Blend until smooth.

3. Pour pureed mixture through a cheesecloth-lined sieve. Drain well, pressing fruit mixture with the back of a spoon to remove as much liquid as possible. Discard solids. Stir in liqueur. Cover and chill 2 hours. Serves 24 (serving size: 1 tablespoon)

CALORIES 43; FAT 0.2g (sat 0g, mono 0g, poly 0.1g); PROTEIN 0.3g; CARB 10g; FIBER 1.2g; CHOL 0mg; IRON 0.2mg; SODIUM 0mg; CALC 6mg

Serve this over cake, bread pudding, or fruit. Omit the rum for a family-friendly custard sauce.

Vanilla-Rum Custard Sauce

Hands-on time: 10 min. Total time: 40 min.

2   cups 2% reduced-fat milk
1   vanilla bean, split lengthwise
½   cup sugar
1   tablespoon cornstarch
⅛   teaspoon salt
2   large egg yolks, lightly beaten
2   tablespoons dark rum
1   teaspoon butter

1. Place milk and vanilla bean in a large heavy saucepan. Heat to 180° or until tiny bubbles form around edge of pan, stirring frequently (do not boil). Remove from heat. Let stand 30 minutes.

2. Remove vanilla bean from pan. Scrape seeds from vanilla bean; stir seeds into milk mixture, reserving bean for another use. Combine sugar, cornstarch, and salt, stirring with a whisk. Add to milk mixture, stirring with a whisk.

3. Add egg yolks to milk mixture, stirring constantly with a whisk. Bring to a boil, and cook, stirring constantly, 1 minute or until slightly thick and mixture coats the back of a spoon. Remove from heat; add rum and butter, stirring until butter melts. Serve warm, or cover and chill. Serves 17 (serving size: 2 tablespoons)

CALORIES 51; FAT 1.3g (sat 0.7g, mono 0.5g, poly 0.1g); PROTEIN 1.3g; CARB 8g; FIBER 0g; CHOL 28mg; IRON 0.1mg; SODIUM 32mg; CALC 36mg

LOW-CALORIE FRO-YO TOPPINGS

Frozen yogurt is lighter than ice cream and makes for a tangy treat. These topping portions will keep a small cup under 300 calories.

70 Calories
¼ cup blueberries +
1½ tablespoons
sliced almonds

50 Calories
2 tablespoons pineapple +
1 tablespoon
flaked coconut +
2 tablespoons mango

85 Calories
¼ cup banana slices (6)
+ 1½ teaspoons walnuts
+ 1½ teaspoons semisweet
chocolate chips

125 Calories
1 tablespoon white
chocolate chips +
2 tablespoons crumbled
animal crackers

160 Calories
1½ teaspoons
crushed toffee +
2 tablespoons
hot fudge sauce

Nutritional Analysis

How to Use It and Why

Glance at the end of any *Cooking Light* recipe, and you'll see how committed we are to helping you make the best of today's light cooking. With chefs, registered dietitians, home economists, and a computer system that analyzes every ingredient we use, *Cooking Light* gives you authoritative dietary detail like no other magazine. We go to such lengths so you can see how our recipes fit into your healthful eating plan. If you're trying to lose weight, the calorie and fat figures will probably help most. But if you're keeping a close eye on the sodium, cholesterol, and saturated fat in your diet, we provide those numbers, too. And because many women don't get enough iron or calcium, we can help there, as well. Finally, there's a fiber analysis for those of us who don't get enough roughage.

Here's a helpful guide to put our nutritional analysis numbers into perspective. Remember, one size doesn't fit all, so take your lifestyle, age, and circumstances into consideration when determining your nutrition needs. For example, pregnant or breast-feeding women need more protein, calories, and calcium. And women older than 50 need 1,200mg of calcium daily, 200mg more than the amount recommended for younger women.

In Our Nutritional Analysis, We Use These Abbreviations

sat	saturated fat	CARB	carbohydrates	g	gram
mono	monounsaturated fat	CHOL	cholesterol	mg	milligram
poly	polyunsaturated fat	CALC	calcium		

Daily Nutrition Guide

	Women ages 25 to 50	Women over 50	Men ages 24 to 50	Men over 50
Calories	2,000	2,000 or less	2,700	2,500
Protein	50g	50g or less	63g	60g
Fat	65g or less	65g or less	88g or less	83g or less
Saturated Fat	20g or less	20g or less	27g or less	25g or less
Carbohydrates	304g	304g	410g	375g
Fiber	25g to 35g	25g to 35g	25g to 35g	25g to 35g
Cholesterol	300mg or less	300mg or less	300mg or less	300mg or less
Iron	18mg	8mg	8mg	8mg
Sodium	2,300mg or less	1,500mg or less	2,300mg or less	1,500mg or less
Calcium	1,000mg	1,200mg	1,000mg	1,000mg

The nutritional values used in our calculations either come from The Food Processor, Version 10.4 (ESHA Research), or are provided by food manufacturers.

Metric Equivalents

The information in the following charts is provided to help cooks outside the United States successfully use the recipes in this book. All equivalents are approximate.

Cooking/Oven Temperatures

	Fahrenheit	Celsius	Gas Mark
Freeze Water	32° F	0° C	
Room Temp.	68° F	20° C	
Boil Water	212° F	100° C	
Bake	325° F	160° C	3
	350° F	180° C	4
	375° F	190° C	5
	400° F	200° C	6
	425° F	220° C	7
	450° F	230° C	8
Broil			Grill

Liquid Ingredients by Volume

$1/4$ tsp	=					1	ml
$1/2$ tsp	=					2	ml
1 tsp	=					5	ml
3 tsp	=	1 Tbsp	=	$1/2$ fl oz	=	15	ml
2 Tbsp	=	$1/8$ cup	=	1 fl oz	=	30	ml
4 Tbsp	=	$1/4$ cup	=	2 fl oz	=	60	ml
$5 1/3$ Tbsp	=	$1/3$ cup	=	3 fl oz	=	80	ml
8 Tbsp	=	$1/2$ cup	=	4 fl oz	=	120	ml
$10 2/3$ Tbsp	=	$2/3$ cup	=	5 fl oz	=	160	ml
12 Tbsp	=	$3/4$ cup	=	6 fl oz	=	180	ml
16 Tbsp	=	1 cup	=	8 fl oz	=	240	ml
1 pt	=	2 cups	=	16 fl oz	=	480	ml
1 qt	=	4 cups	=	32 fl oz	=	960	ml
				33 fl oz	=	1000 ml	= 1 l

Dry Ingredients by Weight

(To convert ounces to grams, multiply the number of ounces by 30.)

1 oz	=	$1/16$ lb	=	30	g
4 oz	=	$1/4$ lb	=	120	g
8 oz	=	$1/2$ lb	=	240	g
12 oz	=	$3/4$ lb	=	360	g
16 oz	=	1 lb	=	480	g

Length

(To convert inches to centimeters, multiply the number of inches by 2.5.)

1 in	=					2.5	cm	
6 in	=	$1/2$ ft			=	15	cm	
12 in	=	1 ft			=	30	cm	
36 in	=	3 ft	=	1 yd	=	90	cm	
40 in	=					100 cm	=	1 m

Equivalents for Different Types of Ingredients

Standard Cup	Fine Powder (ex. flour)	Grain (ex. rice)	Granular (ex. sugar)	Liquid Solids (ex. butter)	Liquid (ex. milk)
1	140 g	150 g	190 g	200 g	240 ml
$3/4$	105 g	113 g	143 g	150 g	180 ml
$2/3$	93 g	100 g	125 g	133 g	160 ml
$1/2$	70 g	75 g	95 g	100 g	120 ml
$1/3$	47 g	50 g	63 g	67 g	80 ml
$1/4$	35 g	38 g	48 g	50 g	60 ml
$1/8$	18 g	19 g	24 g	25 g	30 ml

Index

Apricot and Prosciutto Thin-Crust
    Pizza, 11
Artichoke and Arugula Pizza with
    Prosciutto, 12
Artichoke, Spinach, and White Bean
    Dip, 237

Arugula
    Pesto, Red Pepper, Arugula, and
      Pistachio, 72
    Pizza, Bacon, Tomato, and
      Arugula, 16
    Pizza with Prosciutto, Artichoke
      and Arugula, 12
    Sandwiches
      Bacon and Egg Sandwiches
        with Caramelized Onions
        and Arugula, 153
      Heirloom Tomato,
        Arugula, and Bacon
        Sandwiches, 161
      Open-Faced Sandwiches with
        Ricotta, Arugula, and Fried
        Egg, 214

Asparagus
    Eggs Benedict Waffle
      Sandwiches, 158
    Pizza with Asparagus and
      Caramelized Onion,
      Grilled, 52
    Salad, Marinated Asparagus-and-
      Carrot, 257
Avocado Spread, Creamy, 223

Bacon
    Pizza
      Bacon, Onion, and Mushroom
      Pizza, 15

      Bacon, Tomato, and Arugula
      Pizza, 16
      Beef and Bacon Pizza, 8
      Cobb Salad Pizza, 35
    Sandwiches
      Bacon and Egg Sandwiches
        with Caramelized Onions
        and Arugula, 153
      Heirloom Tomato, Arugula, and
        Bacon Sandwiches, 161
      Open-Faced Chicken Club
        Sandwiches, 179
      Open-Faced Pimiento Cheese
        BLTs, 164

Bananas
    Banana Split, Mocha, 290
    Pudding, Roasted Banana, 319
    Sundaes, Caramelized Banana, 311

Bars. *See also* **Sweets, Bars**

Beans
    Baked Beans, Bourbon, 242
    Burgers
      Black Bean Burgers,
        Homemade Quick, 125
      Vegetable Burgers, 129
      White Bean and Sage Pita
        Burgers, 131
    Dips
      Artichoke, Spinach, and White
        Bean Dip, 237
      Beef and Bean Dip, Tex-Mex, 231
      Chipotle Black Bean Dip with
        Corn Chips, 246
    Falafel Pocket Sandwiches,
      Mini, 213
    Nachos, Loaded, 229
    Nuevo Cubano, 163

Beef
    Burgers
      Brisket Burgers, Simple, Perfect
        Fresh-Ground, 94
      California Burgers, Out-n-In, 91
      Caramelized Onion–and–Blue
        Cheese Mini Burgers, 78
      Cast-Iron Burgers, 81
      Cheeseburgers with
        Caramelized Shallots,
        Cheddar, 82
      Garlic-Thyme Burgers with
        Grilled Tomato, 85
      Meatball Burgers, Italian, 87
      Mushroom Burgers with Fried
        Egg and Truffle Oil, 88
      Pesto Sliders, 92
      Poblano Burgers with
        Pickled Red Onions and
        Chipotle Cream,
        Spicy, 100
      Salsa Burgers, Southwest, 99
      Steak Burgers, Smothered, 96
    Dip, Tex-Mex Beef and Bean, 231
    Pizza, Beef and Bacon, 8
    Sandwiches
      Cheesesteaks, Philly, 144
      Mushroom and Provolone Patty
        Melts, 142
      Reuben Sandwiches, 147
      Sloppy Joe Sliders, 148
      Steak Baguettes with Pesto
        Mayo, 151
Beet Pizza, Roasted, 59
Bell Peppers
    Pesto, Red Pepper, Arugula, and
      Pistachio, 72

Pickled Peppers, Sweet and
  Spicy, 137
Pizza Supreme, 38
Berries
  Cobbler, Blueberry-Peach, 272
  Coulis, Mixed Berry, 323
  Ice Cream, Blueberry
    Cheesecake, 271
  Milk Shake, Peach Melba, 269
Breads. See also **Pizza Dough**
  Bread Pudding with Salted
    Caramel Sauce, 275
  for burgers, eight good, 134
  for pizza crust, seven good, 70
  for sandwiches, six good, 220
  French Toast Peanut Butter and
    Jelly Sandwiches, 202
  Waffle Sandwiches, Eggs
    Benedict, 158
Broccoli rabe, in Manchego and
  Chorizo Pizza, 19
Burgers, 76–139
  Bean
    Black Bean Burgers,
      Homemade Quick, 125
    Vegetable Burgers, 129
    White Bean and Sage Pita
      Burgers, 131
  Beef
    Brisket Burgers, Simple, Perfect
      Fresh-Ground, 94
    California Burgers, Out-n-In, 91
    Caramelized Onion–and–Blue
      Cheese Mini Burgers, 78
    Cast-Iron Burgers, 81
    Cheeseburgers with
      Caramelized Shallots,
      Cheddar, 82
    Garlic-Thyme Burgers with
      Grilled Tomato, 85

Meatball Burgers, Italian, 87
Mushroom Burgers with Fried
  Egg and Truffle Oil, 88
Pesto Sliders, 92
Poblano Burgers with Pickled
  Red Onions and Chipotle
  Cream, Spicy, 100
Salsa Burgers, Southwest, 99
Steak Burgers, Smothered, 96
breads for, eight good, 134
cheeses for, six good, 135
Chicken Burgers, 106
Chicken Parmesan Burgers, 109
healthy burgers, secrets to a tasty,
  juicy, 132
Lamb and Turkey Pita Burgers, 105
Lamb Burgers with Indian
  Spices and Yogurt-Mint
  Sauce, 102
Meatball Burgers, Italian, 87
100-calorie burger combos, 138
Portobello Cheeseburgers, 126
Salmon Burgers, 121
Salmon Burgers with Pickled
  Cucumber, Hoisin-
  Glazed, 119
Tofu Burgers, Grilled Lemon-
  Basil, 122
toppings for, six good, 136
Tuna Burgers, Asian, 116
Turkey
  Lamb and Turkey Pita
    Burgers, 105
  Meatball Burgers, Italian, 87
  Turkey Burgers, Southwest, 113
  Turkey Burgers with Goat
    Cheese Spread,
    Grilled, 110
  Turkey Burgers with Roasted
    Eggplant, 114

Cabbage Slaw, 244
Cake. See also **Sweets**
Carrot Salad, Marinated Asparagus-
  and-, 257
Catfish Sandwiches, Oven-Fried, 186
Cheese
  Bars, Fresh Cherry
    Cheesecake, 303
  for burgers
    Blue Cheese Mini Burgers,
      Caramelized Onion-and-, 78
    Goat Cheese Spread, Grilled
      Turkey Burgers with, 110
    Parmesan Burgers, Chicken, 109
    six good, 135
  Chips with Warm Goat Cheese
    and Cilantro Salsa,
    Adobo, 235
  Dip, Blue Cheese, 232
  Ice Cream, Blueberry
    Cheesecake, 271
  Mozzarella Bites, Baked, 238
  for pizza
    BBQ Chicken and Blue
      Cheese Pizza, 29
    eight good, 71
    Four-Cheese Pizza, 48
    Manchego and Chorizo
      Pizza, 19
    Margherita Pizza, 56
    Peach and Gorgonzola
      Chicken Pizza, 36
    Roasted Vegetable and Ricotta
      Pizza, 62
    Tomato-Feta Pizza, Fresh, 51
  Potato Wedges, Parmesan-
    Coated, 249
  for sandwiches
    Gruyère and Olive Tapenade
      Sandwiches, Grilled, 207

Mushroom and Provolone Patty Melts, 142
Open-Faced Pimiento Cheese BLTs, 164
Open-Faced Sandwiches with Ricotta, Arugula, and Fried Egg, 214
Panini with Prosciutto and Fresh Mozzarella, Classic Italian, 154
Prosciutto, Fresh Fig, and Manchego Sandwiches, 171
seven good, 221
Summer Tomato, Mozzarella, and Basil Panini with Balsamic Syrup, 216
Tomato and Brie Sandwiches, Grilled, 208
Sauce, Cheesy White, 73
Stuffed Jalapeños, Grilled, 253
Zucchini Fries, Parmesan-Crusted, 259

Cherries
Bars, Fresh Cherry Cheesecake, 303
Crisp, Cherry-Almond, 283
Sauce, Brandied Cherry, 322

Chicken
Burgers, Chicken, 106
Burgers, Chicken Parmesan, 109
Drummettes with Blue Cheese Dip, Buffalo-Style, 232
  Pizza
  BBQ Chicken and Blue Cheese Pizza, 29
  Chicken and Herb White Pizza, 32
  Cobb Salad Pizza, 35
  Peach and Gorgonzola Chicken Pizza, 36

Sandwiches
Barbecue Chicken Sandwiches, 173
Chicken Salad Sandwiches, Herbed, 177
Chicken Sandwiches with Cilantro-Lime Mayo, Spicy, 185
Chicken Souvlaki Pitas with Tahini Sauce, 175
Open-Faced Chicken Club Sandwiches, 179
Peanut-Sauced Chicken Pitas, 180
Sausage-Fennel Subs, 182

Chile Peppers
Burgers with Pickled Red Onions and Chipotle Cream, Spicy Poblano, 100
Butter, Grilled Corn on the Cob with Roasted Jalapeño, 250
Dip with Corn Chips, Chipotle Black Bean, 246
Grilled Stuffed Jalapeños, 253
Mayo, Jalapeño-Cilantro, 136
Relish, Double Pepper-Cucumber, 222

Chips. *See also* **Snacks and Sides, Chips**

Chocolate
Brownies, Classic Fudge-Walnut, 296
Cake, Chocolate Buttermilk, 284
Cookies, Browned Butter Chocolate Chip, 278
Fudge, Peanut Butter and Dark Chocolate, 315
Fudge Sauce, 295
Ice Cream, Double Chocolate, 300

Ice-Cream Sandwiches, Chocolate Cookie, 287
Mousse, Chocolate-Hazelnut, 289
Pops, Chocolate Pudding, 292
Pudding, Bittersweet Chocolate, 266
Sauce, Malted Chocolate–Peanut Butter, 323
Shake, Chocolate Malt, 268
Sundaes
Chocolate-Orange Sauce Sundaes, 290
Chocolate Turtle Brownie Sundaes, 295
Peanuts & Popcorn Brownie Sundaes, 299
Clam Grilled Pizza, Garlicky, 43
Coconut, in Hello Dolly Bars, 305
Coffee, in Mocha Banana Split, 290

Condiments. *See also* **Pesto; Sauces**
Burger Toppings
Chipotle Cream, Spicy Poblano Burgers with Pickled Red Onions and, 100
Goat Cheese Spread, Grilled Turkey Burgers with, 110
Jalapeño-Cilantro Mayo, 136
Pomegranate-Rosemary Ketchup, 136
Quick Pickled Onion Relish, 137
Sambal Ketchup, 137
Sweet and Spicy Pickled Peppers, 137
Tonkatsu Mayo, 136
Pickles, Bread-and-Butter, 244
Salsa, Adobo Chips with Warm Goat Cheese and Cilantro, 235
Sandwich Toppings
Avocado Spread, Creamy, 223

Cilantro-Lime Mayo, Spicy
  Chicken Sandwiches
  with, 185
Double Pepper–Cucumber
  Relish, 222
Mint-Cilantro Spread, 222
Piccalilli, Quick, 223
Tarragon Mustard Spread, 223
Cookies. *See also* **Sweets**
Corn on the Cob with Roasted
  Jalapeño Butter, Grilled, 250
Cucumber Relish, Double
  Pepper–, 222
Cucumbers, in Bread-and-Butter
  Pickles, 244

Desserts. *See also* **Sauces,**
  Dessert; Sweets
Dips. *See also* **Snacks and Sides,**
  Dips
Dough. *See also* **Pizza Dough**

Eggplant, Turkey Burgers with
  Roasted, 114
Eggs
  Burgers with Fried Egg and Truffle
    Oil, Mushroom, 88
  Pizza, Sunny-Side-Up, 65
  Sandwiches
    Bacon and Egg Sandwiches
      with Caramelized Onions
      and Arugula, 153
    Egg Salad Sandwich, 201
    Eggs Benedict Waffle
      Sandwiches, 158
    Open-Faced Sandwiches with
      Ricotta, Arugula, and Fried
      Egg, 214
    Smoked Salmon and Egg
      Sandwich, 193

Fennel Subs, Sausage-, 182
Fig, and Manchego Sandwiches,
  Prosciutto, Fresh, 171
Fish. *See also* **Catfish; Salmon;**
  Tuna
Fries. *See also* **Snacks and Sides,**
  Fries
Fruit. *See also* **specific fruits**

Garlic
  Burgers with Grilled Tomato,
    Garlic-Thyme, 85
  Fries, Garlic, 249
  Pizza, Garlicky Clam Grilled, 43
  Pizza, Roasted Garlic, 61

Ham. *See also* **Prosciutto**
  Dagwood Sandwiches, 157
  Eggs Benedict Waffle
    Sandwiches, 158
  Nuevo Cubano, 163

Ice Cream. *See also* **Sweets, Ice**
  Cream; Sweets, Sundaes

Lamb and Turkey Pita Burgers, 105
Lamb Burgers with Indian Spices and
  Yogurt-Mint Sauce, 102
Lemons
  Ice Cream, Lemon-Buttermilk, 306
  Pie, Lemon Cream, 308
  Tofu Burgers, Grilled Lemon-
    Basil, 122
Lobster Rolls, Picnic-Perfect, 190

Macaroni Salad, 255
Mango, in Nuevo Cubano, 163
Mushrooms
  Burgers with Fried Egg and Truffle
    Oil, Mushroom, 88

Cheeseburgers, Portobello, 126
Patty Melts, Mushroom and
  Provolone, 142
Pizza, Bacon, Onion, and
  Mushroom, 15
Pizza, Double-Mushroom, 46

Nachos, Loaded, 229
Nuts. *See also* **Peanut Butter**
  Brownies, Classic Fudge-
    Walnut, 296
  Crisp, Cherry-Almond, 283
  Mousse, Chocolate-Hazelnut, 289
  Pesto, Red Pepper, Arugula, and
    Pistachio, 72
  Pitas, Peanut-Sauced
    Chicken, 180
  Sundaes, Peanuts & Popcorn
    Brownie, 299

Olive Pizza, Pepperoni, Onion,
  and, 24
Olive Tapenade Sandwiches, Grilled
  Gruyère and, 207
Onions. *See also* **Shallots**
  Burgers with Pickled Red Onions
    and Chipotle Cream, Spicy
    Poblano, 100
  Dip, Warm Caramelized
    Onion, 263
  Mini Burgers, Caramelized
    Onion–and–Blue Cheese, 78
  Pizza
    Bacon, Onion, and Mushroom
      Pizza, 15
    Pepperoni, Onion, and Olive
      Pizza, 24
    Pizza with Asparagus and
      Caramelized Onion,
      Grilled, 52

Relish, Quick Pickled
     Onion, 137
Rings, Barbecue-Flavored
     Onion, 241
Sandwiches with Caramelized
     Onions and Arugula, Bacon
     and Egg, 153
Orange Cream Pops, 293
Orange Sauce Sundaes,
     Chocolate-, 290

Pasta, Macaroni Salad, 255
Peaches
     Cobbler, Blueberry-Peach, 272
     Milk Shake, Peach Melba, 269
     Pizza, Peach and Gorgonzola
          Chicken, 36
     Salad, Heirloom Tomato,
          Watermelon, and Peach, 255
Peanut Butter
     Blondies, Peanut Butter
          Cup, 312
     Cookies, Peanut Butter–Toffee
          Chunk, 321
     Fudge, Peanut Butter and Dark
          Chocolate, 315
     Sandwiches, French Toast Peanut
          Butter and Jelly, 202
     Sauce, Malted Chocolate–Peanut
          Butter, 323
Pear and Prosciutto Pizza, 20
Pesto
     Mayo, Steak Baguettes with
          Pesto, 151
     Red Pepper, Arugula, and
          Pistachio Pesto, 72
     Sliders, Pesto, 92
Pineapple with Bourbon Caramel
     Sauce over Vanilla Ice Cream,
     Broiled, 277

Pizza
Asparagus and Caramelized
     Onion, Grilled Pizza with, 52
Bacon
     Bacon, Onion, and Mushroom
          Pizza, 15
     Bacon, Tomato, and Arugula
          Pizza, 16
     Beef and Bacon Pizza, 8
     Cobb Salad Pizza, 35
Beef and Bacon Pizza, 8
Beet Pizza, Roasted, 59
Cheese Pizza, Four-, 48
cheeses for, eight good, 71
Chicago Deep-Dish Pizza, 30
Chicken
     BBQ Chicken and Blue
          Cheese Pizza, 29
     Chicken and Herb White
          Pizza, 32
     Cobb Salad Pizza, 35
     Peach and Gorgonzola
          Chicken Pizza, 36
Clam Grilled Pizza, Garlicky, 43
Cobb Salad Pizza, 35
crust, secret to a perfectly
     crispy, 69
crusts, seven good, 70
Farmers' Market Pizza, Local, 55
Garlic Pizza, Roasted, 61
Margherita, Pizza, 56
Mushroom Pizza, Double-, 46
Prosciutto
     Apricot and Prosciutto Thin-
          Crust Pizza, 11
     Artichoke and Arugula Pizza
          with Prosciutto, 12
     Pear and Prosciutto Pizza, 20
     Prosciutto Pizza with Tangy
          White Sauce, 27

Salmon Thin-Crust Pizza,
     Smoked, 45
sauces, five good, 72
Sausage
     Chicago Deep-Dish Pizza, 30
     Manchego and Chorizo
          Pizza, 19
     Pepperoni Deep-Dish
          Pizza, 23
     Pepperoni, Onion, and Olive
          Pizza, 24
     Pizza Supreme, 38
     Sausage Pizza, 41
Sunny-Side-Up Pizza, 65
Supreme, Pizza, 38
Tomato–Feta Pizza, Fresh, 51
200-calorie pizza slices, 74
Vegetable and Ricotta Pizza,
     Roasted, 62
Pizza Dough
     Homemade Pizza Dough, 66
     resting, 68
     secret to crispy crust, 69
     Whole-Wheat Pizza Dough, 67
Plum Sandwiches, Open-Faced
     Prosciutto and, 167
Pomegranate-Rosemary
     Ketchup, 136
Pork. *See also* **Bacon; Ham;
          Prosciutto; Sausage**
     Sandwiches with Mustard Sauce,
          Pulled Pork, 168
Potatoes. *See also* **Sweet Potato**
     Chips, BBQ Potato, 260
     Chips, Sour Cream and Onion
          Potato, 260
     Fries, Garlic, 249
     Salad, Creamy Potato, 246
     Wedges, Parmesan-Coated
          Potato, 249

Poultry. *See also* **Chicken; Turkey**
Prosciutto
  Pizza
    Apricot and Prosciutto Thin-
      Crust Pizza, 11
    Artichoke and Arugula Pizza
      with Prosciutto, 12
    Pear and Prosciutto Pizza, 20
    Prosciutto Pizza with Tangy
      White Sauce, 27
  Sandwiches
    Open-Faced Prosciutto and
      Plum Sandwiches, 167
    Panini with Prosciutto and
      Fresh Mozzarella, Classic
      Italian, 154
    Prosciutto, Fresh Fig, and
      Manchego Sandwiches, 171
Pudding. *See also* **Sweets, Pudding**

Salads
  Asparagus-and-Carrot Salad,
    Marinated, 257
  Heirloom Tomatoes with
    Mustard and Dill,
    Marinated, 256
  Heirloom Tomato, Watermelon,
    and Peach Salad, 255
  Macaroni Salad, 255
  Potato Salad, Creamy, 246
  Slaw, Cabbage, 244
Salmon
  Burgers, Salmon, 121
  Burgers with Pickled Cucumber,
    Hoisin-Glazed
    Salmon, 119
  Pizza, Smoked Salmon Thin-
    Crust, 45
  Sandwich, Smoked Salmon and
    Egg, 193

Sandwiches. *See also* **Burgers**
  Bacon
    Bacon and Egg Sandwiches
      with Caramelized Onions
      and Arugula, 153
    Heirloom Tomato, Arugula, and
      Bacon Sandwiches, 161
    Open-Faced Chicken Club
      Sandwiches, 179
    Open-Faced Pimiento Cheese
      BLTs, 164
  Beef
    Cheesesteaks, Philly, 144
    Mushroom and Provolone Patty
      Melts, 142
    Reuben Sandwiches, 147
    Sloppy Joe Sliders, 148
    Steak Baguettes with Pesto
      Mayo, 151
  breads, six good, 220
  Caesar Salad Bagels, 199
  Catfish Sandwiches, Oven-
    Fried, 186
  cheeses, seven good, 221
  Chicken
    Barbecue Chicken
      Sandwiches, 173
    Chicken Salad Sandwiches,
      Herbed, 177
    Chicken Sandwiches with
      Cilantro-Lime Mayo,
      Spicy, 185
    Chicken Souvlaki Pitas with
      Tahini Sauce, 175
    Open-Faced Chicken Club
      Sandwiches, 179
    Peanut-Sauced Chicken
      Pitas, 180
    Sausage-Fennel Subs, 182
  condiments, five good, 222

  Dagwood Sandwiches, 157
  Egg
    Bacon and Egg Sandwiches
      with Caramelized Onions
      and Arugula, 153
    Egg Salad Sandwich, 201
    Eggs Benedict Waffle
      Sandwiches, 158
    Open-Faced Sandwiches with
      Ricotta, Arugula, and Fried
      Egg, 214
    Smoked Salmon and Egg
      Sandwich, 193
  Falafel Pocket Sandwiches,
    Mini, 213
  Farmers' Market Sandwiches,
    Grilled, 204
  Gruyère and Olive Tapenade
    Sandwiches, Grilled, 207
  healthy sandwich, build a, 224
  Lobster Rolls, Picnic-
    Perfect, 190
  Nuevo Cubano, 163
  Peanut Butter and Jelly Sandwiches,
    French Toast, 202
  Pork Sandwiches with Mustard
    Sauce, Pulled, 168
  Prosciutto
    Open-Faced Prosciutto and
      Plum Sandwiches, 167
    Panini with Prosciutto and
      Fresh Mozzarella, Classic
      Italian, 154
    Prosciutto, Fresh Fig, and
      Manchego Sandwiches, 171
  Salmon and Egg Sandwich,
    Smoked, 193
  Sausage-Fennel Subs, 182
  Shrimp Po' Boys, Pan-Seared, 189
  Tofu Banh Mi, Lemongrass, 219

Tomato and Brie Sandwiches, Grilled, 208
Tomato, Mozzarella, and Basil Panini with Balsamic Syrup, Summer, 216
Tuna Melts, 195
Tuna Pan Bagnat, 196
Zucchini Caprese Sandwiches, Grilled, 210

Sauces
  Dessert
    Bourbon Caramel Sauce over Vanilla Ice Cream, Broiled Pineapple with, 277
    Brandied Cherry Sauce, 322
    Chocolate-Orange Sauce Sundaes, 290
    Fudge Sauce, 295
    Ginger-Bourbon Sauce, 322
    Malted Chocolate–Peanut Butter Sauce, 323
    Mixed Berry Coulis, 323
    Salted Caramel Sauce, Bread Pudding with, 275
    Vanilla-Rum Custard Sauce, 324
  Hoisin-Glazed Salmon Burgers with Pickled Cucumber, 119
  Hollandaise (in Eggs Benedict Waffle Sandwiches), 158
  Mustard Sauce, Pulled Pork Sandwiches with, 168
  Peanut-Sauced Chicken Pitas, 180
  Pizza
    Asian BBQ Sauce, 73
    Basic Pizza Sauce, 73
    Cheesy White Sauce, 73
    Red Pepper, Arugula, and Pistachio Pesto, 72
    Sun-Dried Tomato Pizza Sauce, 72

Tangy White Sauce, Prosciutto Pizza with, 27
Tahini Sauce, Chicken Souvlaki Pitas with, 175
Tahini-Yogurt Sauce, 213
Yogurt-Mint Sauce, Lamb Burgers with Indian Spices and, 102

Sausage
  Meatball Burgers, Italian, 87
  Pizza
    Chicago Deep-Dish Pizza, 30
    Manchego and Chorizo Pizza, 19
    Pepperoni Deep-Dish Pizza, 23
    Pepperoni, Onion, and Olive Pizza, 24
    Pizza Supreme, 38
    Sausage Pizza, 41
  Subs, Sausage-Fennel, 182
Shallots, Cheddar Cheeseburgers with Caramelized, 82
Shrimp Po' Boys, Pan-Seared, 189

Snacks and Sides
  Beans, Bourbon Baked, 242
  Chips
    Adobo Chips with Warm Goat Cheese and Cilantro Salsa, 235
    BBQ Potato Chips, 260
    Chipotle Black Bean Dip with Corn Chips, 246
    Nachos, Loaded, 229
    Sour Cream and Onion Potato Chips, 260
  Corn on the Cob with Roasted Jalapeño Butter, Grilled, 250
  Dips
    Artichoke, Spinach, and White Bean Dip, 237
    Beef and Bean Dip, Tex-Mex, 231

Blue Cheese Dip, 232
Caramelized Onion Dip, Warm, 263
Chipotle Black Bean Dip with Corn Chips, 246
Ranch-Style Dip, Creamy, 261
Drummettes with Blue Cheese Dip, Buffalo-Style, 232
  Fries
    Garlic Fries, 249
    Potato Wedges, Parmesan-Coated, 249
    Sweet Potato Shoestring Fries, 259
    Zucchini Fries, Parmesan-Crusted, 259
  Jalapeños, Grilled Stuffed, 253
  Mozzarella Bites, Baked, 238
  Onion Rings, Barbecue-Flavored, 241
  Pickles, Bread-and-Butter, 244
Spinach, and White Bean Dip, Artichoke, 237
Squash. See also **Zucchini**
Sweet Potato Shoestring Fries, 259
Sweets
  Bars
    Butterscotch Bars, 280
    Cherry Cheesecake Bars, Fresh, 303
    Fudge-Walnut Brownies, Classic, 296
    Hello Dolly Bars, 305
    Peanut Butter Cup Blondies, 312
  Cake, Chocolate Buttermilk, 284
  Cobbler, Blueberry-Peach, 272
  Cookies, Browned Butter Chocolate Chip, 278

Cookies, Peanut Butter–Toffee Chunk, 321
Crisp, Cherry-Almond, 283
Cupcakes, Red Velvet, 316
Fudge, Peanut Butter and Dark Chocolate, 315

Ice Cream. *See also* **Sweets, Sundaes**
Blueberry Cheesecake Ice Cream, 271
Chocolate Cookie Ice-Cream Sandwiches, 287
Double Chocolate Ice Cream, 300
Lemon-Buttermilk Ice Cream, 306
Margarita Ice-Cream Sandwiches, 311
Mousse, Chocolate-Hazelnut, 289
Pie, Lemon Cream, 308
Pops, Chocolate Pudding, 292
Pops, Orange Cream, 293

Pudding
Bittersweet Chocolate Pudding, 266
Bread Pudding with Salted Caramel Sauce, 275
Roasted Banana Pudding, 319
Shake, Chocolate Malt, 268
Shake, Peach Melba Milk, 269

Sundaes
Broiled Pineapple with Bourbon Caramel Sauce over Vanilla Ice Cream, 277
Caramelized Banana Sundaes, 311
Chocolate-Orange Sauce Sundaes, 290
Chocolate Turtle Brownie Sundaes, 295

Mocha Banana Split, 290
Peanuts & Popcorn Brownie Sundaes, 299

Toppings
Low-calorie fro-yo toppings, 325

Tofu Banh Mi, Lemongrass, 219
Tofu Burgers, Grilled Lemon-Basil, 122

Tomatoes
Burgers with Grilled Tomato, Garlic-Thyme, 85
Heirloom Tomatoes with Mustard and Dill, Marinated, 256
Pizza, Bacon, Tomato, and Arugula, 16
Pizza, Fresh Tomato–Feta, 51
Pizza Sauce, Basic, 73
Pizza Sauce, Sun-Dried Tomato, 72
Salad, Heirloom Tomato, Watermelon, and Peach, 255

Sandwiches
Heirloom Tomato, Arugula, and Bacon Sandwiches, 161
Open-Faced Pimiento Cheese BLTs, 164
Summer Tomato, Mozzarella, and Basil Panini with Balsamic Syrup, 216
Tomato and Brie Sandwiches, Grilled, 208

Tuna
Burgers, Asian Tuna, 116
Melts, Tuna, 195
Pan Bagnat, Tuna, 196

Turkey
Burgers
Lamb and Turkey Pita Burgers, 105
Meatball Burgers, Italian, 87
Turkey Burgers, Southwest, 113

Turkey Burgers with Goat Cheese Spread, Grilled, 110
Turkey Burgers with Roasted Eggplant, 114–115
Dagwood Sandwiches, 157

Vegetables. *See also* **specific vegetables**
Burgers, Vegetable, 129
Piccalilli, Quick, 223

Pizza
Chicago Deep-Dish Pizza, 30
Farmers' Market Pizza, Local, 55
Pizza Supreme, 38
Roasted Vegetable and Ricotta Pizza, 62
Sandwiches, Grilled Farmers' Market, 204

Watermelon, and Peach Salad, Heirloom Tomato, 255

Yogurt
Frozen
Chocolate-Orange Sauce Sundaes, 290
Low-calorie fro-yo toppings, 325
Sauce, Lamb Burgers with Indian Spices and Yogurt-Mint, 102
Sauce, Tahini-Yogurt, 213

Zucchini Caprese Sandwiches, Grilled, 210
Zucchini Fries, Parmesan-Crusted, 259

ISBN 13: 978-0-8487-3738-2
ISBN 10: 0-8487-3738-5

ISBN 13: 978-0-8487-4275-1
ISBN 10: 0-8487-4275-3

ISBN 13: 978-0-8487-4236-2
ISBN 10: 0-8487-4236-2

Library of Congress Control Number: 2012948713
Printed in the United States of America
First Printing 2013

Oxmoor House

Editorial Director: Leah McLaughlin
Creative Director: Felicity Keane
Brand Manager: Michelle Turner Aycock
Senior Editors: Heather Averett; Andrea C. Kirkland, MS, RD
Managing Editor: Rebecca Benton

Cooking Light Crave!

Editor: Shaun Chavis
Art Director: Claire Cormany
Project Editors: Emily Chappell, Sarah H. Doss
Assistant Designer: Allison Sperando Potter
Director, Test Kitchen: Elizabeth Tyler Austin
Assistant Directors, Test Kitchen: Julie Christopher, Julie Gunter
Recipe Developers and Testers: Wendy Ball, RD; Victoria E. Cox; Tamara Goldis; Stefanie Maloney; Callie Nash; Karen Rankin; Leah Van Deren
Recipe Editor: Alyson Moreland Haynes
Food Stylists: Margaret Monroe Dickey, Catherine Crowell Steele
Photography Director: Jim Bathie
Senior Photographer: Hélène Dujardin
Senior Photo Stylist: Kay E. Clarke
Photo Stylist: Mindi Shapiro Levine
Assistant Photo Stylist: Mary Louise Menendez
Senior Production Manager: Greg A. Amason
Production Managers: Theresa Beste-Farley, Tamara Nall Wilder

Contributors

Project Editor: Katie Strasser
Recipe Developers and Testers: Erica Hopper, Tonya Johnson, Kyra Moncrief, Kathleen Royal Phillips
Photographer: Mary Britton Senseney
Photo Stylists: Katherine Eckert Coyne, Anna Pollock
Food Stylist: Ana Price Kelly, William L. Smith
Nutritional Analyst and Writer: Jessica C. Cox, RD
Nutritional Analyst: Keri Matherne, RD

Copy Editors: Dolores Hydock, Kate Johnson
Proofreaders: Jasmine Hodges, Julie Bosche
Indexer: Nanette Cardon
Interns: Susan Kemp, Sara Lyon, Staley McIlwain, Emily Robinson, Maria Sanders

Time Home Entertainment Inc.

Publisher: Jim Childs
VP, Strategy & Business Development: Steven Sandonato
Executive Director, Marketing Services: Carol Pittard
Executive Director, Retail & Special Sales: Tom Mifsud
Director, Bookazine Development & Marketing: Laura Adam
Executive Publishing Director: Joy Butts
Associate Publishing Director: Megan Pearlman
Finance Director: Glenn Buonocore
Associate General Counsel: Helen Wan

Cooking Light®

Editor: Scott Mowbray
Creative Director: Carla Frank
Executive Managing Editor: Phillip Rhodes
Executive Editor, Food: Ann Taylor Pittman
Special Publications Editor: Mary Simpson Creel, MS, RD
Senior Food Editors: Timothy Q. Cebula, Julianna Grimes
Senior Editor: Cindy Hatcher
Assistant Editor, Nutrition: Sidney Fry, MS, RD
Assistant Editors: Kimberly Holland, Phoebe Wu
Test Kitchen Director: Vanessa T. Pruett
Assistant Test Kitchen Director: Tiffany Vickers Davis
Recipe Testers and Developers: Robin Bashinsky, Adam Hickman, Deb Wise
Art Directors: Fernande Bondarenko, Shawna Kalish
Senior Deputy Art Director: Rachel Cardina Lasserre
Designers: Hagen Stegall, Dréa Zacharenko
Assistant Designer: Nicole Gerrity
Photo Director: Kristen Schaefer
Assistant Photo Editor: Amy Delaune
Senior Photographer: Randy Mayor
Senior Prop Stylist: Cindy Barr
Chief Food Stylist: Kellie Gerber Kelley
Food Styling Assistant: Blakeslee Wright
Production Director: Liz Rhoades
Production Editor: Hazel R. Eddins
Assistant Production Editor: Josh Rutledge
Copy Chief: Maria Parker Hopkins
Assistant Copy Chief: Susan Roberts
Research Editor: Michelle Gibson Daniels
Administrative Coordinator: Carol D. Johnson
CookingLight.com Editor: Allison Long Lowery
Nutrition Editor: Holley Johnson Grainger, MS, RD
Associate Editor/Producer: Mallory Daugherty Brasseale